The Theatre of the Oppressed in Practice Today

RELATED TITLES

Culture, Democracy and the Right to Make Art: The British Community Arts Movement
Edited by Alison Jeffers and Gerri Moriarty
ISBN 9781474258357

Justice Performed: Courtroom TV Shows and the Theaters of Popular Law
Sarah Kozinn
ISBN 9781472532343

Performance and Community
Edited by Caoimhe McAvinchey
ISBN 9781408146422

Phakama: Making Participatory Performance
Caoimhe McAvinchey, Lucy Richardson and Fabio Santos
ISBN 9781350044456

The Art of Rehearsal: Conversations with Contemporary Theatre Makers
Edited by Barbara Simonsen
ISBN 9781474292016

The Theatre of the Oppressed in Practice Today

An Introduction to the Work and Principles of Augusto Boal

Ali Campbell

methuen | drama

LONDON · NEW YORK · OXFORD · NEW DELHI · SYDNEY

METHUEN DRAMA
Bloomsbury Publishing Plc
50 Bedford Square, London, WC1B 3DP, UK
1385 Broadway, New York, NY 10018, USA

BLOOMSBURY, METHUEN DRAMA and the Methuen Drama logo are
trademarks of Bloomsbury Publishing Plc

First published in Great Britain 2019

ISBN: HB: 978-1-350-03142-5
PB: 978-1-350-03141-8
ePDF: 978-1-350-03143-2
eBook: 978-1-350-03140-1

Typeset by Deanta Global Publishing Services, Chennai, India
Printed and bound in Great Britain

To find out more about our authors and books visit www.bloomsbury.com
and sign up for our newsletters.

For Mo

Contents

Illustrations

All photographs by the author unless otherwise credited.

Acknowledgements

As well as the thirty years of companies, collaborators and friends I connect and converse with in this book, there are some who deserve a special mention.

Professors Jane Plastow (Leeds University) and Jen Harvie (Queen Mary, University of London), my ever-patient writing and research mentors respectively.

Dr Caoimhe McAvinchey, who paved the way for this book to happen.

Anna Brewer and Lara Bateman, who have overseen the development process from commissioning to publication.

Talia Rodgers and Pauline Gladstone-Barrett, who first listened to my stories and saw their worth.

Susan Nicholls for her powers of transcription.

Jules Deering and Rupert Dannreuther for wizardry with photographs.

And my heartfelt gratitude to Sue Mayo, Geraldine Ling, Julian Grant, Simon Stewart-Richardson, Rosie Waters, Keith Lawrence, Hari Marini, Suzanne Rider, Nick Milner and Ralph Yarrow.

PART ONE

Principles in Practice

Prologue

Frame Zero
(The National Theatre of Uganda, Kampala, March 1990)

Outside the National Theatre, standing in partial shade at the edge of the square, every day I pass a woman as I go inside.

I'm usually in a hurry. Our AIDS education project has had the resources only to support a group working together for five days, and tomorrow we will be presenting our Forum piece, *Akatale*, to an audience of HIV workers, community nurses, academics, NGO representatives and of course artists working in Development Theatre. I have one day left. Where has the time gone?

The woman is standing near a group of large overflowing bins, infrequently emptied. I think they belong to the theatre but everybody passing seems to chuck stuff in there. Around the bins a group of ghoulish Maribou storks patrol, each as tall as the woman herself, scavenging what even the poorest street people of Kampala have already rejected as inedible or beyond the Ugandan genius for recycling. Maribou storks are the stuff of nightmares: seen from behind they might almost be ancient crones in dusty feathered cloaks, until in passing you see their great beaks sorting through the rotting detritus of downtown Kampala.

The woman is selling plastic bags. Every day she collects them, washes them and flattens them out. Every day she stands in exactly the same spot, not bothering to call out as some of the more enterprising hawkers do but just standing, with a single bag unfolded to show how clean it is and perhaps displaying the logo of some fancy shop nearby. The others are draped across her skinny arm.

The woman's head is neatly wrapped in a rag. She is wearing a clean but threadbare t-shirt (again, with a logo) and a bright wrap around her skinny hips. Her legs are stick thin and her skin is greyish. She looks sick. The products the bags once held are not for her. Her feet are gnarled, in disintegrating flip-flops. I have no idea what age she is but I know from experience that if I guess from how old she looks, I will always be guessing her to be older than she is.

Some days I buy a bag and we smile at each other. Not today. I'm late.

Gandhi urges a simple daily reflection to those of us who need to reset the moral compass on our endeavours. It is very simple.

How – he asks – will my actions today affect the poorest; the least powerful person?

It is over twenty-five years since I created that project in Kampala, but that woman is present to me still. As I write, as I set out what I have learned through my work in the Theatre of the Oppressed over that time, I am resolved to keep her always in my mind.

Present.

Frontispiece Augusto Boal in storytelling mode: Queen Mary, University of London; 1999.

Introduction: About Augusto Boal and the Aims of This Book

Augusto Boal (1931–2009) was one of the most influential theatre directors, activists and theorists of the twentieth and early twenty-first centuries, exploring through a long and prolific career in Brazil and internationally the possibilities of a workable Marxist theatre aesthetic in the Brechtian tradition, by way of the revolutionary theories of his distinguished contemporary Paulo Freire. The result has often been described as a system, open to reinterpretation and adaptation to a wide range of contexts and a bewildering plurality of content.

Herein lies the challenge to the scholar-artist seeking to extrapolate a set of guiding principles from the body of Boal's work, rather than to delineate fixed rules whereby the abundant manifestations of the Theatre of the Oppressed (TotO) might be assessed and its ethos – of empowerment through the enactment of 'rehearsal for the revolution' – interrogated through the ever-shifting prism of the work itself.

Since Boal's death the complex issue of his legacy and its impact has been contested, sometimes acrimoniously, as individuals, groups and companies have sought to maintain a commonality of purpose and a consistency of delivery across their widely differing practices and contexts. Is the Theatre of the Oppressed a system, a movement, a toolbox of techniques or – as Boal often called it – a method? Is it governed by shared beliefs so open to adaptation and multiple interpretation that we are ultimately only bequeathed a relativistic sense of its values, lacking a coherent, core integrity? Or is it possible – as Augusto himself once told me – that there are *laws* operating wherever the Theatre of the Oppressed is authentically practised, that are as subtle yet ultimately as irresistible as those that govern gravity?

There are already many clear and comprehensive accounts of Boal's work itself, from the excellent overview afforded by Frances Babbage to case studies and critiques by James Thompson and Helen Nicholson. Together with this comprehensive body of scholarship we have Boal's own evolving (and sometimes self-contradictory) reflections, most recently in the *Aesthetics of the Oppressed*. But it has long been clear (since Boal began to withdraw from active international participation in training, theoretical dissemination and collective reflection upon his work) that this question of whether there is a clear, identifiable, underlying set of *principles* must be addressed. How does a scholar/artist such as the present writer identify and articulate these principles *in practice,* in such a way as to do justice to the open-endedness and flexibility that gives the techniques such an abundant, generative quality, whilst addressing the need for clarity around legacy, consistency and indeed quality control that has resurfaced regularly since Boal's death?

These are the questions this book will seek to explore. I have had to devise new ways, structures and techniques to bring the story of my own journey in the TotO to an exemplification of that exploration.

In this first section I will introduce one of these bespoke techniques, Frame Throwing, to recreate through thick description, to unpack and to interrogate examples from my own practice of Forum, including my teaching and adaptation of it, with the aim of identifying its underlying principles in practice as they arise. Frame Throwing will reappear throughout the book as a way of anchoring, in the deep ecology of practice, discussions that might otherwise stray into the abstract. As a practitioner I seek to complement existing discourse with living examples, unpacked in such a way as to evidence the key questions around the Theatre of the Oppressed in general and Forum in particular. These detailed recreations of the work are the heart of this book, beginning with that first touchstone project, devised over a three-month residency at Makere University in Kampala, Uganda in 1990, in collaboration with the National Theatre of Uganda and funded by a Winston Churchill Fellowship.

With Boal's encouragement, I had gone to Uganda in January 1990 while my first intensive experience of the TotO techniques and pedagogy was still very fresh. I had been trained in the theory and practice of Forum and Image Theatre only a few months before. Boal's only words on the fifth day of that course in Nottingham had been: 'Don't worry Ali. You are a very good Joker. When you ask people to go over there, they go; to sit, they sit; to make an Image – they do it. So go to Uganda. Tell me what you learn there. Try to film it!'

His words are with me still, as are the vivid moments of truth that the work opened up to me and that I now share for what I hope will be their present helpfulness in illuminating some of the complexities of Boal's work and his sometimes bewildering claims upon it, as we all move forward without him.

I write as a critical friend and with great love.

For the reasons above (some academic, some formal, some personal) my first set of frames in **Chapter One** is therefore an exercise in beginning *in media res,* continuing as I have begun with the deep-drilled example of *Akatale*: an AIDS education project in Kampala, Uganda.

How, in depth and detail, does a Forum Theatre session work?

In the Theatre of the Oppressed we are always at the beginning! And for this reason I defer to **Chapter Two** for a more detailed description and analysis of Boal's pedagogy as I experienced it first hand in 1989, focusing on how storytelling was a key plank of his teaching method, as it is of mine.

How do we learn the most effective ways to create TotO in a training situation … and how not to make it?

Chapter Three is an essay in 'difficultation': one of Augusto's more delightful coinages. I go into the most challenging questions I myself and many colleagues face when it comes to the ways we share our practical experience and thereby our understanding of TotO.

What is the legacy of TotO and how does our diaspora of a movement intend to maintain quality control?

Chapters Four and **Five** will go more fully into my own discoveries in the rolling out, adapting and customization of Forum and Image Theatre. I delve into three seminal iterations of Forum with groups and companies I have worked with internationally: the ATOBA artists' alliance against AIDS in Malawi; GRAEAE Theatre Company (the leading Disabled-led performance organization in the UK); and lastly the children and actors UK-wide with whom I co-devised and toured the primary school Theatre in Education (TIE) project *Poor Ted*, seen by over a quarter of a million children between 1995 and 2005. With these two chapters, this book's key findings and questions culminate in an (incomplete!) audit of TotO's working principles as they have emerged through our practice. We claim neither to be exhaustive, nor prescriptive: only honest and helpful.

Where do we go from here?

My aim as a writer, evidencing key questions about Forum out of a lifetime of practice, is to foreground and to celebrate what can only be learned through the risk, the journey and the imperfect mode of research that is iterative, collaborative practice.

These aren't the sort of questions we can 'answer', but I believe in walking with them, in exploring them and in doing my best to address and to evidence them with hard-won examples of my own work and that of others I have been in direct contact with over my long journey. That directness of contact is offered not only as validating shared, collaborative *experience* but as rendering it – through mindful acts of choice and distillation – as *expertise,* arising from practice with others, risked alongside others, supported by others, debated with others and held as testimony by others. I only find my way in relationship with those others and all of them matter to me. Their voices fill **Parts Two and Three** of this book and its structure mirrors the unfinished conversation of our collaborations together. This book is theirs and belongs to all of us. If I have missed anyone out it is due solely to lack of the genuine collaborative contact that has been necessary for me to work with the voices of others in this way. If my inevitable exclusions offend, I apologize.

Finally, I want to offer this book in a spirit of helpfulness to all the many students, early-career practitioners and everyone over the years who has asked me for more working examples of how Augusto's inspiration has rippled out internationally in such a dizzying array of incarnations. This book is part critique, part memoir and most importantly a quest, through the language of performance practice itself, to identify and extrapolate key, abiding and non-prescriptive principles, as a service to the future of the Theatre of the Oppressed. It is therefore both personal and political. In content and in form I have constantly sought to align the judgements of the head with the assertions of the heart: to bring rigorous structure into reflexive dialogue with the storytelling – the telling of Truth to Power – which Augusto himself brought to the theatre where his politics were enacted. I haven't set out with a pre-decided auto-ethnographic approach in essaying all of this, but in the due crafting of the current work, it has quietly chosen me.

My ultimate and perhaps most cherished aim is to claim a central position for Oracy as a core element of the pedagogy and the dissemination of the Theatre of the Oppressed, as it was at the heart of Boal's own workshops, when he would sit and unfurl one of his incomparable anecdotes. Nobody who heard those stories has ever forgotten them: there is a power in them to be tapped into and it still resides in his personal legacy: a love and a practice of Oracy. There was far more in his making of space for story than just an illustrative relating of the past. Augusto famously used to declare that the past, recreated in the present, transforms the future. I intend to reclaim that storytelling voice, as part of his and of my own pedagogy.

Some context

Augusto Boal was the man who woke me up. From the first time we met (at Nottingham University in 1989) up to his death, we corresponded, worked alongside each other at conferences and symposia, argued and shared ideas. We also disagreed about the dissemination of the techniques of the Theatre of the Oppressed, especially when it came to their adaptation and customization for accessibility and cultural appropriateness.

Throughout the 1980s, first as a member of the legendary Professor Dogg's Troupe under ED Berman and then as the artistic director of BREAKOUT TIE, I had, as a community theatre practitioner, been working in the territory of arts-based activism in mostly urban settings in the UK, often making scratch performances in the space of a single day. Often – if not always – the aim was in some appropriate manner to configure participation into the work, moving along a scale of spectator involvement, from performance **for** the target audience (issue-based 'infomertials' with a message) through performance **with** the audience but always stretching towards – if stopping short of – performance **by** the audience. That final step, that further tip in the actor/spectator power relationship, was often potentially there between us, but we somehow lacked a structure or mechanism to enable it to happen without what we imagined would be anarchy.

The method I was trained in had, therefore, a strong ideological underpinning: we were putting high-quality, newly devised work into spaces that had never seen live performance; we were opening up that performance through innovative, structured participation; and we were reaching huge audiences. But we made the work as professional artists apart, in our studio, and we predetermined its content, its underlying strategy and its intention.

When I first encountered Augusto's work – as the English translation of *Theatre of the Oppressed* found its way into TIE and Young People's Theatre (YPT) companies – there wasn't all that much on the page I didn't already do, or believe in, or agree with. The overarching aim – to rehearse the revolution through a theatre that enacted solidarity – was clearly an extension of Brecht's vision of a theatre that would provoke *action*.

Now I had found in Augusto's writing a system that took that most universal language – performance – and potentially made its use accessible, with increasing autonomy, to the widest possible public: to those who might have wonderful stories to tell and indeed stories *to tell to* Power, but had hitherto been denied the space or the training to enact such a revolutionary vision on the ground, in the community or on the street. Long before I met Augusto I read him and recognized immediately a theatre that myself and others sought, aspired to and passionately believed in. Here, in print, this aspiration was rendered in thrillingly radical, workable terms.

In this book I will track my own journey from the first time I worked with Augusto himself through that period (especially in the 1990s) when European and North American practitioners began to adapt and customize the techniques of the Theatre of the Oppressed in a wide range of educational and community settings, gathering at a series of international festivals to share their work and identify the cultural and political fault lines that inevitably opened up within it.

As a critical friend to Augusto I have only one present aim: to bring the clearest examples of what I have learned *through* the work to the task of evidencing and extrapolating its principles. Boal himself often asserted that theatre is in itself a form of knowledge. Throughout this book I will frame examples of discovery and failure alike so as to show as precisely as I can how the activity of performance-making with others in itself has moved (and still moves) the Theatre of the Oppressed forward as a whole.

I am aiming to recreate as vividly as possible moments of particular significance because they have, over the intervening years, yielded deeper layers of meaning, pertinent to the unfinished business of researching Forum. Those years and this journey have seen me modify, through collaboration, my own practice and to engage with that of others in a wide range of community and development settings. That is how Image and Forum Theatre have been unpicked and developed by the many groups and individuals I have been privileged to work with.

I will give Augusto the last word:

In truth the Theatre of the Oppressed has no end, because everything which happens in it must extend into life. The Theatre of the Oppressed is located precisely on the frontier between fiction and reality – and this border must be crossed. If the show starts in fiction, its objective is to become integrated into reality, into life.[1]

---

[1] *Games for Actors and Non-Actors* (1992).

Chapter 1

What Is Forum and How Does It Work?

[handwritten: Structure]

[handwritten in left margin: Positionality]

Frame One
(Queen Mary, University of London [QMUL]; May 2018)

One of my students drops in during my office hour at Queen Mary, University of London. Her group are making a piece of Forum Theatre and they intend to explore and to deconstruct the role of the Joker in the system of the Theatre of the Oppressed that we call Forum. I've been teaching at QMUL for twenty years and the conversation that follows is the one I've had the most often when exploring with students the wonderful, demanding, bewildering and inspiring techniques imparted to us by my own teacher and mentor, Augusto Boal. In this conversation, I hasten to add, we are both students: the one who 40 years older than the other addressing the opening question from that perspective and from the position of having clocked up rather more flying time in using Forum.

Student Number One, aged twenty-something (S1)
We're stuck.

Student Number Two, aged sixty-something (S2)
OK let's look at that. What do you mean by stuck?

[handwritten: Brecht's dialectics]

S1   We've made a Model and we think it's really good, but every time we try to work out the role of the Joker we get stuck.

S2   Tell me more about the point of stuck-ness.

S1   So the Model is a provocation, right?

S2   Yes. It asks the audience or Spectactors a clear question.

S1   And we made the Model without too much trouble. It's clear who the Antagonist is: they have the most power in the scene and we show them gradually abusing it more and more. There are several places the Spectactors might shout Stop! And then the Joker will accept Interventions from them and we will try one or two of these out.

S2   Remember the pieces need to be quite short.

S1   Yes, we just want to show a couple before interrogating the role of the Joker. That's what the piece is really about. We know the Joker is a role intended to empower the audience but we want to challenge the fact that this role in turn is so powerful that in the wrong hands that power could be abused.

S2   So is the stuck-ness about showing that paradox at the heart of the Joker role? Performing it so that we see first of all what its intention is and then how that might in the wrong hands produce the opposite effect in practice?

S1   YES! I mean how are we to make sense of passages like this? How? Every time we read this and try to discuss ways to show our questioning of the role, we get so stuck! Look:

> 'The character whom the author wishes to link empathetically with the public performs the protagonic function …
>
> If we could separate the *ethos* and the *dianoia* – and we can only do it for didactic purposes – we would say that the Protagonist assumes an ethical behaviour and the "Joker" a dianoethic one …

The "Joker's" is a magical reality; he creates it. If necessary, he invents magic walls, combats, soldiers, armies. All the other characters accept the magic reality created and described by the Joker.'[1]

S2   Right.

S1   But everything you've shown us in practicals has been about how Interventions are a rehearsal for the revolution, not Magic. And the Joker should be as much as possible a conduit and enable a flow of ideas into the space, maximizing the Spectactors' capacity to perform their own best possible solutions. For those to be witnessed and learned from. A rehearsal for real social change. A rehearsal for the revolution!

S2   And this seems to contradict all of that, as it is on the page.

S1   That's why we're stuck!

And so am I. Our practical sessions have been full of enthusiasm: the simplicity of the basic setting up of Forum taking us right into the heart of the practice of it, with an abundance of invention that I have come to expect from students as gifted and as questioning as the one who has visited me. We are in fascinating ethical, aesthetic and political territory before we know it, with Model after Model asking such excellent questions not only of the world but of the stated aims and intentions of Forum itself, not least the claims made of it in passages such as the one quoted above.

And that is where the stuck-ness always happens. It's to do with the claims made of Forum on the printed page. It's about what happens when we theorize in ways that cut us off from the living reality of example and enactment.

---

[1] *Theatre of the Oppressed,* pp 181–2.

When Forum works it is clear to any audience, anywhere, what is going on. The system itself and the way to operate as a Joker only takes a few days to train people up in, especially if they already see themselves as performers and have good group skills when it comes to devising. The young people I am privileged to work with have all of that in spades. Here's how those first few days usually go:

- We play, often sharing a wider set of warm-ups and exercises than those described in *Games for Actors and Non-Actors*, which remains my favourite of Boal's books.

- We work out sequences of games and exercises that take us through a de-mechanization: breaking old habits of performance and perception; opening ourselves up to the possibility and indeed *desirability* of change and surprise in the space. We improvise. We laugh. We build up the capacity for instant invention in one another.

- We begin to use the *prospective techniques* of Image Theatre to identify our shared experience of oppression, often stumbling over new and arresting ways to show one another how power operates in our lives and how its abuse manifests itself in lived reality.

- We offer up personal stories that bring detail to the fleshing out of those examples, maximizing their potential for identification from others.

- We make Models for the Forum.

- We bring the Models to the Forum, taking turns to inhabit the system as trainee Jokers and as Spectactors who get bolder and stronger as they act out possible strategies to overcome oppression.

- The Spectactors are witnessed in their Interventions and more: they see *themselves* in the act of Intervention and know themselves to have the power to transfer their capacity for resistance, transformation and revolution into lived, social reality. This is Paolo Freire's process of Conscientization.

Repaso de la metodología

the embodiment — the personal perspective of the method

Frame Two

I remind my student of how far we have come together and that we have inhabited and enacted out own working definitions of all the key terms needed to talk about Forum. Then it hits me. *Again.*

Praxis → theory → praxis

The key to unlocking the stuck-ness is to look *away* from that printed page and re-source ourselves in the body of work we have already created together. That work too is a reference book, written in our own hands, eyes and memories and walked through by our own performing bodies. It's in a language we all understand – performance – and in our experiments with Forum we have devised a shared lexicon that opens up terms such as Joker in ways that only the experience of working with the role can do. On the page, we can be trapped in paradox. In the Forum, we are free.

I make a list of rehearsal tasks, honouring the fact that the group in question intend to deconstruct and question the Joker role. They are addressing the question asked most often in my thirty years of working with the techniques of the Theatre of the Oppressed: 'What is the role of the Joker?' and their answers will truly be their own.

1 Run the Model.
2 Appoint a Joker.
3 Demonstrate a couple of Interventions.
4 Let the Joker abuse the role, once it is clear how it *should* be done. Let them silence someone, ignore someone, or applaud one Intervention as the 'best' or even do something completely silly: 'Magic'.
5 Have someone new shout STOP!
6 Have them replace the Protagonist.
7 Repeat!
8 *Allow people to make their own minds up.*

I was grateful to my student for visiting me at the very point I was considering my preface to this book. I hope that in my use and framing of stories from my own experience to interrogate the system of Forum Theatre that I do the work a service, especially to a new generation of Jokers. What I share in this spirit arises from a long, rich and varied career where I have been gifted with many insights, all gained in solidarity with others and in a mode of working best summed up as: 'Do first; talk after.' That's why this book is the shape it is and has been created in the way it has.

I love the discussions we have before and after we stand up together to bring our questions to the Forum. But *Forum itself is the discussion* and it never asks one simple question to be 'answered' or poses a straightforward problem to be 'fixed'. The answering is in the making: in the risk and adventure of shouting STOP! and entering the performance space where solutions, not answers, abound.

Do first, talk after

Frame Three
(The National Theatre of Uganda; Kampala; 1990)

I walk past the woman with her plastic bags on sale. I will buy one on the way out if she's still there. I am late. I am busy. I have a head full of questions.

As we have improvised throughout our first couple of days, again and again we have made the Image of a Woman. There is nobody in the room – whether they are an HIV researcher tracking the vectors of transmission, a nurse on the front line or a Theatre for Development (TfD) worker seeing the consequences of AIDs in the wider community – who does not recognize this figure, bearing as she does the full brunt of the consequences of HIV transmission. In many cases and in the absence of scientific data, she also bears the blame, carries the family, brings up the orphaned grandchildren and digs the fields abandoned by those too weak and sick to work. She is always carrying something, this woman, and using Image Theatre we have brought her into the room again and again. Women and men both have taken turns in representing her and more than that: standing in her shoes. We all know the adage that to educate a woman is to educate an entire community. In using Boal's Image Theatre we have honoured this maxim daily.

We aren't working with script. I prefer to wait until the group feel a particular Image has demanded to be woven into what will be the eventual performance, so for the moment we are documenting each of these resonant and recurrent Images on its own A3 sheet. I always urge the group (whether or not the Image makes sense in terms of linear story) to capture those that give us the goose-bumps. Amid much hilarity (a Scottish accent and idiom are well received here!) the first Image has long since been chosen. At the top of the sheet is the title: I AM THE WOMAN. In the centre is a simple matchstick drawing: she is carrying a nameless burden on her head and the detail of her face has been left not empty but open, for identification by anyone in the group. This includes men: we are roughly 50/50 in gender composition and as we work through embodied techniques to animate, unpack and dynamize her story, we have agreed that anyone can step into the woman's shoes, and has to be able to if the group arithmetic requires it. We are aware too that this simple permission around the woman's identity and the actors' capacity is leading us to a place of identification. This, as with all our techniques, is the underlying solidarity that we try to enact (not just espouse) in everyday rehearsal.

At the bottom of the large sheet is a blank space where such dialogue as we might require will be noted if it comes out of our dynamizing improvisations. We aren't after too much of this: we are in a country with many mother-tongues and we need to make a piece of work that can travel and translate readily and easily. Furthermore, the Images that we make (starting with this one) must be legible at a great distance: it is common for an entire community to turn up to a Development Theatre

this is for conoceurs with similar questions on ToTO after years of practice n' application (not beginners).

presentation and as there is a strong and popular practice of this already well established in Uganda, we need to make the aesthetics of *Akatale* legible from a distance without simplification and accessible without generalization. The Woman is universal, but she remains an individual and must stand as one.

She is standing now, in the pose we have agreed, hands raised above her head and carrying a burden you can see is exhausting without its needing to be specifically named as cassava, worry, water or indeed AIDS itself. A nurse from the Health Education sector is holding the Image. She is carrying the burden of meaning. She isn't at all sure what to do with her face so she turns partially away and at that moment the entire group gets the goose-bumps. This is it! The moment of truth. Its going to be something to do with turning away; with wanting to leave the impossible pressures of her situation (however you might read it on any one day). I can hear very busy scribbling in the otherwise silent room. A3 sheets are filling with Images that unfold from this single, generative one.

As Augusto Boal has shown me again and again in my training, its all in the looking. You can't *teach* that looking, exactly: you can only open up the space we call our Theatre so that it becomes more and more possible, urgent – desirable, even – to see what we look at. I remember Augusto asking again and again the question he used most of all, at moments like this: 'What do you see?'

And a story pours out. In ten minutes it's there, although three careful days have gone into the building up of that space and that permission *to see and to tell what you see*, plainly.

- *The Woman has had enough and she is leaving.*
- *What is she leaving?*
- *An abusive husband.*
- *Why is she leaving him now?*
- *She has seen him giving another woman a lot of money. (Nervous laughter. But now we've said it: you can't un-ring a bell!)*

- *What might the consequences be?*
- *She will be abandoning her children.*
- *To what?*
- *Maybe crime.*
- *And maybe AIDS.*

he just explains/ results, we unders/ tand how they come thru that

By the end of the day we have the full Storyboard of *Akatale*: a circular one, centring on the Woman as the beginning, the end and the moral heart of what will be a short piece largely told through dance and mime. We will keep all the other Images that have been generated and arrange them so that they radiate out from and continually return to her burden of choice. We will open up to the audience which of these Images, given the huge uncertainties around HIV transmission (it's 1990, remember) might have something to do with her choice and whether it might lead in some way to her infection and that of her two boys and her daughter (yes: they have also now appeared). The audience will need to name the moments where she might have different choices, despite the apparent impossibility of her situation: avoiding what Boal calls 'magic' solutions but trying nevertheless to open up points where it is possible for the Spectactors to move beyond mere *identification* with her plight to possible moments of *Intervention* where they might realistically shout Stop! and act out other ways for her to go.

But for now, as we put flesh and bones (our own!) onto the story, she is still standing there. Still burdened. Still challenging us to act in solidarity, not merely give to her good advice.

The Storyboarding technique is something I brought to the work from many years' devising with TIE and YPT companies in the UK: a way to democratize what can be fetishized as the role of the writer in 'Western' scripted theatre. Even working with a very enabling dramaturge or facilitator I had often encountered a moment when after an exhilarating series of devising sessions, the control was taken back by the writer or by a director who then had the veto on what 'worked'

Figure 1 Malawi storyboard. Two 'Multipliers' (trainee Jokers) customizing a template for community-led Forum Theatre; Domasi village, Zomba, Malawi.

theatrically and – often unthinkingly – reasserted a form that betrayed its content, especially when the fragility and provisionality of the stories entrusted to us by the groups we worked with didn't allow the luxury of an 'ending' of any sort. If Forum, as I already knew, handed over to the audience the power to enact a range of possible solutions to the questions posed by the performance, then how might we also honour, in form as well as content, the provisionality of these stories in the way we explored them, documented them, unpacked them and stood them up in our theatre?

Image Theatre, with its wonderful generative exercises and its hands-on enactment of 'prospective techniques', was a big section of the Toolbox I had been looking for. Many of these exercises, especially the use of tableaux, were already known to me, but here they were grounded and configured within a clear Marxist aesthetic. The tools of production could be shared transparently before the participating group. The building blocks of story and performance could be fashioned by a whole group, and alongside this excavating and embodiment of meaning, the group's shared capacity to read Images and a collective cognizance of themselves as boosting that capacity, would go hand in hand, eye to eye, Image to Image. The Image Theatre techniques Boal had opened up to us fostered a delight, an agency and an empowerment inherent in their negotiation: their distillation and choosing, their presentation

real creacion colectiva

and their reading. In the abundant and open-ended exercises of Image Theatre I found a collective dramaturgy that I hadn't been able to find on the printed page.

It wasn't a flattening out of multiple and even contradictory possibilities for interpretation. It was the sense that a piece could genuinely be read in more than one way and from more than one point of view and that while the Images were being replayed in the room there was no need for that meaning to be reduced to a single one, however pressing the need to document it appropriately might be.

The Storyboard (from Dogg's Troupe days of scratch devising in parks) saved me and more than that, was something I already knew and brought fully fledged and tested into the room from the first day I worked directly with Boal on Forum. Here was a way that the whole piece of a Forum performance might be devised, keeping it open to interpretation. And embedded in that piece, handing over to the Spectactors the responsibility to intervene, there could be a scene or scenes that posed a very sharp challenge with a clear Protagonist: a Model.

With *Akatale* the politics of bringing Forum to the task of AIDS education whilst observing the imperative to honour (admit, even) the drastic incompleteness of our knowledge about the context of HIV transmission, found its formal solution in the Storyboard. We knew from early research that one vector of HIV transmission had been from the shores of Lake Victoria where women seeking an advantageous place in the highly competitive lakeside market trading with fishermen (this at a time of no refrigeration of the catch) had been known to trade sexual favours in order to jump the queue and save time before heading city-wards to re-sell the fish. Closer to home, as we devised Image by Image scenes where the intersection of economics and patriarchy in urban Kampala could be shown in an open-ended, non-judgemental way, we generated – through Image Theatre techniques often rapidly deployed – a kaleidoscope of 1990s Kampala: the *matatu* (minibus) owners who used their profits to set themselves up as landlords; the powerful position that put these Sugar Mummies and Sugar Daddies in when it came to letting at inflated rents to vulnerable tenants; the profits that enabled them to stand back from the consequences of their activities by relocating to Mombasa and appointing heavies to do their dirty work: all of these were quickly stood up as Images with no rules about whether women played men or vice versa. Only our goose-bumps as we hit upon moments of truth were to be our guide and those Images would each be given a page on the Storyboard. Sequencing came later and given the very incompleteness of what we knew about HIV transmission in Uganda the final, almost circular Storyboard should have come as no surprise: a widening spiral is, after all, what an epidemiologist would recognize as an unchecked vector of transmission.

How to make it into a 'good performance'? Constantin Mpongo, our resident dancer and the artistic director of the Coffee Workers' Dance Company of Bugolobo, put it to us best: 'You need to be as fit as a footballer!'

I handed the Toolbox to him immediately.

As *circularity* emerged ever more clearly as an underpinning principle of this necessarily iterative process, the group continued to show me that although the true Antagonist (or put simply, the Enemy) was the HIV virus itself, there are actions that we can clearly identify through first still Images and then dynamized ones, so as to empower the audience to project, to identify, to name and to *own* patterns of behaviour that increase the risk of HIV infection.

This developed without ever naming any group as more or less at risk and pre-deciding that they are the problem. They are not. There are behaviours around HIV and that is that. This is still the best way to proceed in any form of sex education. We needed all the Images and artistically we wanted to show them all – whilst avoiding chaos – so as to give to villagers upcountry a much-needed experience of art, as a thing in itself. But we also needed to show all of the ways that risk is increased and how they all pass through the body of the Woman. We were not doing an infomercial. There was, at the time of devising *Akatale,* already some very good health education in parts of Uganda, through storytelling and dance, around malaria and family planning. But what we found ourselves doing was increasingly not that. There is absolutely no point in telling penniless village women to use condoms!

So it was that our final Storyboard began and ended with the same Image of a woman: The Woman. And converging on her figure, carrying such burdens of work, responsibility and blame, were all the lines of possible transmission we had identified and embodied through our Image Theatre sessions.

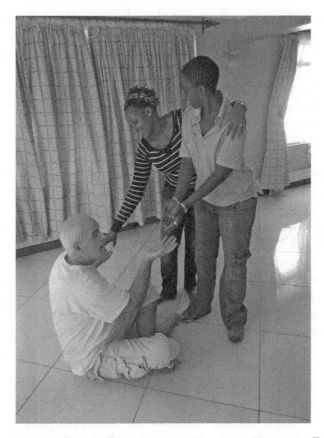

Figure 2 Image Theatre. The author and trainee Jokers in an Image Theatre exercise; Nairobi, Kenya.

Here is the Storyboard of *Akatale* in full:

- The Woman
- The Poor House
- The Children
- *Matate!*
- Sugar Mummies/Sugar Daddies
- The Woman Dreams
- The Woman Considers Her Choices

It was written on large separate sheets that could be arranged in different ways, to varying dramatic effect.

From this structure the full piece unfolded, with minimal dialogue and with a non-naturalistic style, tactically agreed in the workshop, including permission to act across gender. This found its way into electrifying dance sequences in the public performance (*Matate!* and Sugar Mummies/Sugar Daddies).

It doesn't take long now to tell the story of the piece, distilling as it did just enough contextualizing information for the audience of Spectactors to see how much of the action was actually connected in some way to possible HIV transmission and how none of these vectors could simply be dealt with or stopped by mere public information campaigns (theatre included). The form honoured this incompleteness of information and grew directly from the way we had used the Prospective Techniques (Boal's term) to open up the territory of AIDS in Uganda and enact its invisible presence through ordinary bodies and lives, without pointing the finger at any one group, individual or behaviour. As Boal always put it, universal truths about the larger power relationships governing a society are inscribed in the microcosm of even the smallest daily transactions on any street corner, seen correctly.

And seeing correctly, seeing The Woman, was what *Akatale* set out to do.

Frame Three
(The National Theatre; Kampala)

The floor is a good colour.

This isn't a superficial aspect of the context for today's Forum. The National Theatre of Uganda is an imposing building in the centre of Kampala. The last time I was here was with my great friend and colleague the late Prof. Rose Mbowa, who patiently translated for me as we sat through a five-hour adaptation of a famous folk tale. The outlay on a ticket for this show reflected its significance as a day-long social event, with plenty of coming and going throughout several intervals of varying lengths for snacks and to scan the audience for anyone gossip-worthy. Men from my own AIDS Education group were there and I was made to feel incredibly welcome, if slightly exposed, as the only White audience member and surely not someone who would understand Buganda? Rose translated for me and pointed out that the allegory, based on a traditional folk tale about a power struggle among the animals, had once been pointed out to the then President Idi Amin as potentially critical of his regime. As our long day at the theatre drew to a close I reflected on the extent of that theatre's potential power: the inescapable testimony of the row of bullet holes in the wall of the bar where one director had gone over the line and most of all the quiet testimony of Rose herself who had been arrested and tortured during Amin's regime. He had sent the tanks into the campus of Makerere (once the crown jewel of East African universities) and that and the bullet holes pointed me towards one thing: if ever I might doubt the potential threat presented to the Oppressor by artists and intellectuals (we theatre-makers above all) to speak Truth to Power, those bullet holes and Rose's whispered testimony put me right.

But what about our Forum? That day, the audience were dressed to kill and clearly equated getting their money's worth with both the length and the technical showiness of the performance. It was brilliantly lit and choreographed, showing off the resources of the main stage at every opportunity. People applauded settings as the curtain rose and indeed the curtain was used very frequently to elicit just that reaction. There seemed no reason to sit through the whole thing: everyone knew the story anyway and the social side of the event was given far more space than the equivalent West End experience might lend it. I was, rather, reminded of the Crush Bar at the Coliseum where as a community artist on the precarious fringes of the opera world I had once or twice watched the power-brokering that went on between artists, funders, patrons and their minions (all squeezed into twenty minutes) and had reckoned the Borgias would have felt most at home. In London, you can *see* an opera most days, but if you want to get to make one, you need to get into that Crush Bar and *be seen*.

In that main auditorium then, a few days back, the expectation was of a spectacle that delivered – in quantity as well as quality, offstage as much as on – an all-round, full-on, performative, social experience for Kampala society, with an agenda of watching and being watched that reminded me more of my single visit to Ascot than any time I'd spent at the Royal Court.

I told Rose during one interval I didn't think we could ever do *Akatale* on that main stage. She agreed.

(Now, thirty years on, when I think about that floor colour and our choice of the Green Room, I'm thinking about whether the places we present Forum signal expectations before the performance even begins: that script whose language is the door you walk through; the seat you take and whether it seems to be a 'good' one; your sense of whether being close to the action is a privilege or a danger ('will they get me to *do* something?'). Configured in that space are all those things and my choice of a space has to take that script into account.)

So on this day, in 1990, we've chosen more than just a setting in choosing the Green Room: high ceilinged and airy, with a great big fan stirring the morning breeze from open, sliding windows. There is a faint noise of traffic and a scent of the street. A voice is drifting in, which I know is of the woman who sells the plastic bags just one floor below. And this floor: laid with thick, durable carpet tiles in an earthy brick red that is – as it happens – the exact shade of Uganda's fabled, fertile soil when freshly turned.

The floor is a good colour.

We will be sitting on this floor. It hasn't occurred to me (well, not as fully as it might) that the choice of the room and the decision to seat all but disabled audience on the floor would have so much in it, but we learn these things by doing and as we slide open the door onto the corridor and invite them in, my decision unfolds itself fully to me. With it, I see my part in working with the politics of context and of audience expectation: how we must always keep *wide eyes*, even in that pinpoint concentration of the last-minute rehearsals when all we can see is the play.

What the audience see, then, is the brick red ground and so the statement in the brief programme notes – that *Akatale* is intended for village performances outdoors – takes on an embodied reality, in a way more resonant than I had consciously intended at the time. I just always sit a workshop/showcase audience on the floor!

Rose, with her wonky hip (the story of which I now know better than before), takes one of the few chairs, with a rather grand visitor from a well-endowed NGO and a couple of professors from Makerere beside her. The professor who sits on the floor, however, is the one who gets the attention! A development specialist, with an interest in Forum as a potential methodology, she has read the room in an instant and in a way that perhaps those who have brought more fully developed expectations might not. Her students (one or two of them performers today) whisper to each other as she settles down and smiles. It's a huge moment for them and I take it in for what I now see (in the moment of doing) it really is: even if there is only one chair in the classroom, on any one day that chair is usually hers, but not today.

The 'calling' music on the Ugandan Harp which has been playing from the first gathering of the audience outside (who could hear it through the closed curtains) gradually gets louder to show how we would summon a village to the performance. The musician has kept this work up for twenty minutes and indeed we can *see* the work that he is doing and through him his music: he is shining with sweat as the cast (forming an inner circle on the floor now) urge him forward with a stamping rhythm. The lyric, over and over again, is simply an invitation to the market: one that nobody in Sub-Saharan Africa is ever likely to refuse and one that we now extend to include the market of our new idea:

Forum.

I've described the non-linear structure of *Akatale* and how
that has overturned many of the usual audience expectations
around story. Now, in live performance, I can see where the
choices of my collaborators have paid off when it comes to
opening up the task of discernment to our guests, or as today
we will call them: Spectactors. This is no well-told cautionary
tale about family planning or the dangers to infants of malaria.
This is open-ended and bewildering. The dream sequence
where all the possibilities of the Woman's leaving are danced out
to Constantin's choreography is mesmerizing but not in a way
that lulls you. You are, rather, taught from within the movement
sequence how the movement vocabulary he has used is an
invitation to do the work of making meaning for yourself. And that
meaning, complex, repetitive and elusive as it is, includes how
little we know about the transmission of HIV.

The dance of Sugar Daddies and Sugar Mummies pulls
the audience further in. They are transfixed. The whole cast
dance and your eye begins to notice patterns with a growing
confidence that begins aesthetically (I'm getting this! I'm seeing
this!) and, once you have been reassured by subsequent
patternings that your point of view is valid, demands that you
look at what you see.

An example: the Husband, in the moment that the Woman
catches him paying his Mistress, has used the universal mime
for counting out cash, which in 1990s Kampala involves quite a
large pile of invisible notes, thumbed over, punctuated with a lick
of the fingers that seems increasingly loaded with values other
than monetary and risks other than financial.

She sees him. She knows what he is doing. She turns
to leave. He notices her and braces his hands on his hips in
arrogant defiance. The Mistress disappears. The Woman lifts up
the burden of her life to her head, with graceful arms, with a tear
running down her shining face. She is leaving him, finally.

Or is she? The dance begins and as the ever-wider circles
of her predicament are played out as possible consequences,

we see that money-counting gesture again and again. She and her daughter go on the street. The boys become robbers. The Sugar Mummies and Daddies hire their *matatus* (mini-buses); rent their apartments; sponsor their toy-boys and -girls; and always, always they are counting, thumbing away.

The landlord's Rent Man knocks on a woman's door and counts out the money while she looks anxiously on. He hammers on a second door and this time the woman's hands are empty. She pulls him inside, into her equally empty arms. After a time, the drums drumming, the dancers circling, multiplying all the meanings of this one transaction, the Rent Man leaves, adjusting his dress. He pauses. He thumbs out some cash. He gives it to the woman. She smiles. A heart-breaking smile.

By the time the dance is done we have seen the Woman's moment of truth (of leaving?) scaled up and rolled out, through time and consequence and very often to ends where AIDS appears: again, in movement only, in what has become in only ten years a shorthand for the disease. You cough, you stagger, you scratch your legs, you fall over, you close your eyes. Pneumonia, Malnutrition, Kaposi's Sarcoma, Death.

But which of the Woman's possible circling, bewildering paths might lead to this? What has the movement of money, so ubiquitous here, got to do with it? The incompleteness of the piece (the Model) is an essential to Forum, as is the offering of just enough information and context for the Spectactors to be not just enabled but provoked into trying, first from their seats and then in the space itself, to make sense of the quagmire of possibility she is headed towards unless we can help her. Not through advice. Through Intervention.

I shout Stop!
Rose nearly falls off her chair.
This is it.
Time for Forum.
And my first time as a Joker!

The circularity of the piece is a device I have often used to lead an audience back to the original question or problem posed by a performance: quite a standard strategy and aesthetically a good way of subverting the expectation that a story will have a single ending and – by extension – that a problem can be 'fixed' if we follow the linear clues in a story to deduce a 'solution' that has been pre-decided by the actor-teachers and is already waiting for one of us to score top marks by finding it.

The circularity of *Akatale* took this further by offering as a formal challenge the tracing of the HIV virus along its many possible and always invisible routes to the Spectactors. If we had intended to offer a well-produced *infomercial* about using condoms, it's anyone's guess how many typical blokes (here or anywhere in the world) might change their behaviour, tipsy or loved-up on a Saturday night in Camden or Kampala. My guess is not many.

This, with my shouting Stop! was to be the test of whether a Kampala audience, all of them as well-informed as anyone on the planet could be about HIV in 1990, might sit with the incompleteness of information they already possessed, identify the power structures and lines of transaction along which that virus potentially travelled, sort out where the usual gendered expectations around sexual behaviour might realistically be opened up to change and then … try something!

Another gamble was our use of dance to stand back from the gender of the performers and allow a focus purely on behaviour. The dance sequences repeated the money-changing gesture in so many ways that the eye followed them like a detective's, tracking the exchange of money and questioning whether at any one point there was an accompanying behaviour that might denote an exchange of bodily fluids. It's as simple as that. Whether you are a nurse, an HIV worker, a development theatre practitioner or on some intersection of those roles, you would be bringing your existing knowledge as a Spectactor to your interpretation of what was danced before you and what was now being asked of you by the Joker.

Looking back, I see how much work was done towards this by the dance of the Sugar Mummies and Sugar Daddies and how effective that decision was semiotically as well as aesthetically: flowing, open-ended, weaving an elaborate cross-gendered multiplication of possible issues and meanings within one rhythm. Meanings generated through the dance of connectivity itself and provoking a delight in the application of that connectivity to the overall puzzling form of the piece itself. An application that is one first step towards the Intervention that Forum requires.

Frame Four

One thing I note as I start to explain my role as Joker is that nobody has questioned, smirked at or in other ways reacted negatively to the gender fluidity of the dancing. The performers have swapped genders without recourse to stereotyping and, although we did debate this in rehearsal, the artists have 'won': there is for example one very aggressive Sugar Daddy, seen manhandling a Girl into a taxi and out of sight, throwing money at her without even counting it, who has caused palpable anger, not least because this is a real possibility the daughter in the play now faces if the Woman becomes destitute. The fact that the Sugar Daddy has been danced by a woman and the Girl by a man hasn't even been mentioned, but the gesture with the money has been truly shocking as it exposes in a second how little he thinks of her and also – maybe – how casually the virus can be passed to her. Use a condom? Him? Forget it!

As the Joker I explain what we have seen as a Model. I open up to the Spectactors the opportunity and indeed the responsibility to put their knowledge (from whatever personal source) into practice. I will be shortly replaying the key sequence in the Model (the only naturalistic scene and the one in which the Woman turns to leave) and rather than give the Woman advice I am going to ask everyone 'Don't tell me, show me!'

(The performers giggle. The above has long been known as my motto and years later it surely still is.)

Silence. A polite Ugandan silence. The teacher (if that's how I'm being seen right now) has finished and the question has been asked. I know this silence. The only mistake I might now make is to panic and try to fill it. I restate the aim of the Forum and am greeted with eager nods: yes – I've got it – right – no problem.

More silence.

Do we need to see the Model again?

– No.

Would we each welcome a few moments to turn to a partner next to us and discuss the Woman's choices? What we might do in her shoes?

– Yes please.

I'm so glad I learned that technique somewhere. Simple as it might seem, giving people in pairs time to use their voices and air their ideas quietly is a life-saver, especially when the peer group are self-conscious about speaking out in front of one another. I owe awkward London teenagers a great deal, in this moment!

I draw everyone back from what is now a very lively pairs discussion and 'rewind' the Model to the moment that the Woman decides to leave and dreams that dream of multiple consequence. Mary-Jane Msungu, the head of education at the National Theatre, winks at me to encourage me.

Stop!

I've known some pretty stunning moments of Intervention in my time as a Joker (or co-Joker, when resources allow) but this first was the most formative and everything in my subsequent journey with the Theatre of the Oppressed has been shaped by what Sister Agnes now does.

Sister Agnes is a nun, from Karamajo in the North, where it is said the tallest people in the world come from, men and women both. She is tall! So is Mary-Jane and I can attest they are easily my height (6'3") if not taller. As the Sister shouts Stop! she stands up, like a tree, from the seat that someone has given her out of respect for her cloth. She is all in white, with a large wooden crucifix round her neck, on a braided cord. She is smiling a most marvellous, mischievous smile: quite – I think – un-nun-like really. But she hasn't even started.

She strides majestically from the back of the circle whilst the Spectactors unashamedly gawp. I'm clearly not the only person whose expectations are on the way to serious disruption today. She has been very quiet so far and all I've gathered is that she runs a women's project and is determined to open up debate about AIDS/HIV in the very traditional community she serves.

Determined is how she looks as she moves towards me, grinning. She has one snaggle tooth in that dazzling grin. She glides. She swings her arms, like a boxer.

And then, she hesitates. I don't know what to do. She asks a woman seated on the floor in the front row a question. I can't quite make it out. Her English isn't so good so she repeats herself in Karamajon. The woman on the floor unwraps the Kanga from her waist and gives it to Sister Agnes. Slowly, calmly, determinedly, she ties it loosely over her hips, never taking her eyes off me. I realize what she is doing, in that moment. She says: 'Now, I am the Woman.'

You can hear a pin drop as she takes Mary-Jane's place. She lifts that imaginary burden, graceful and strong. She spots the husband as he counts out the money, which like the burden itself has gathered ever-deeper meaning with each repetition. She puts that burden down. She rubs her tired neck; sighs.

Looks at him; *sees him* in truth. Says:

'I know what you are doing!'

'No, no my darling, you see I was owing her money, and I saw her coming, as you can see, so I was just ...'

'What has she done to deserve it?'

(The audience gasp.)

'... you see I was just passing by and I saw her here and so I ...

'Are you completely *** or what?'

To this day, I don't know what Sister Agnes, as the Woman, calls the Husband. (It's in Karamajon.) The screams of hilarity and more than that, delighted disbelief, drown out everything in the Green Room and I have no doubt they would be heard across Karamajo without any difficulty. In hearing that reaction, I am answered by her, and all my doubts are gone. It's not just what she's said, it's that a nun has said it! But my eyes are on the Kanga. She has completely taken on the identity of the Woman. She has simply needed to signify a temporary suspension of her own identity, creating for herself, in her own time, in a space she now commands, the permission to do so. Of herself, she takes that permission up and this includes swearing, turning the air blue in a brief Intervention that will nevertheless be talked about in Kampala as long as Forum is.

'Children!'

The children appear.

'Your father is here. Ask him about your school fees. Ask him about money for your uniform.'

'... yes but my darling ...'

'Answer the children! And children, if you step on his neck, don't kill him, ah?'

The Father mumbles for a bit and slinks off.

'Now, my children, we have heard all this before. He says what he will do but I don't believe him. I will go to the school, and I will explain to them. We will work together and the fees will be paid. Now get washed, get changed and stay here at home while I go, and see what I can do.'

There are people actually lying on the floor, stunned, slapping the ground, hugging one another, applauding her. One chap has lost it completely and is waving his legs in the air like a beetle on its back. The word *impact* doesn't begin to describe it. From identification with the Woman to assuming her identity; from the temptation to give advice to a demonstration of indelible action, Sister Agnes has shown us the power of Forum. She hands back the shawl. She's done and she relinquishes both role and shawl (wiping her hands on its hem) to show that she has done.

I use the words *accept* and *prejudice* here so as to keep a clear focus on the detail of Frame Three as a microcosm of what is possible if an Intervention is given both space and witness.

My audience, comprising AIDS workers, academics, nurses, performers and development theatre activists, had never met and their Constituency had a provisionality that was twofold. Firstly, we were only together for the duration of that one Forum in 1990, and thus we shared with all audiences who witness what can only be seen once, known once or learned once: the seeing, knowing and learning that is the theatre.

But unlike the village audiences whom in all our devising and discussion were at the centre of our thinking and planning, this room and our invitees had only been *constituted* for the purpose of presenting Forum as fully as possible, to the group most likely to be able to take on board the techniques, customize these (and in many cases translate them) into culturally appropriate forms of performance and so to adapt the basic methodology of the Theatre of the Oppressed, whilst taking into account local and social factors such as the role of women in public discourse.

Forum poses questions. Interventions generate responses (but not answers) and enact consequences (not solutions). It's all in the doing: to rehearse that revolution Boal describes as a future we must build and not just wait for.

Frame Five

The group who enter the studio are shy, deferential and cautious. They have heard of the Theatre of the Oppressed but are in some cases doubtful about whether it will 'work' here. One key factor is operating in our favour as we try this single, presentational experiment at the National Theatre: some very powerful players are in the room, from the directors of major dance companies (such as Constantin Mpongo) to the head of education at the National Theatre (Mary-Jane herself) to Prof. Rose Mbowa whose Music, Dance and Drama (MDD) Department at Makerere runs a compulsory module in the use of arts in education that every single new primary school teacher in Uganda will take before graduation. Influential indeed.

On top of this, there is at this historical moment the political will, in the form of very strong support from Janet Museveni (the president's wife) for those practising Development Theatre to tackle some of the most pressing social and educational challenges faced by the country. And standing one step further back than that, there is the admirable fact that the country has openly admitted the scale of the problem with HIV transmission. This alone (in 1990 at least) has already begun to reduce the rates of infection. That brick red ground is fertile.

So outside the door, and now as we enter the space, we are doubly constituted as a group who would not usually meet but have no doubts about the commonality and legitimacy – the potential for maximum impact – of our shared work on this one day. And we are doubly inhibited too! We might have read *Theatre of the Oppressed* and in some cases (usually travelling abroad) may even have seen Forum, which on its own is not that hard to reproduce as a series of participatory actions. But the circle on the floor, replicating what we have agreed would be the usual setting in a village upcountry, under the tree in the centre of the settlement where public discourse usually takes place, is a circle of peers, who potentially inhibit each others' participation as much as they might share an interest in work that is participatory in the field. I don't know for sure, but my position as the visiting White 'expert' (unmet as yet by the guests, if not the company) alongside Mary-Jane, Constantin and Rose as powerful national figures, evokes I know not what expectations and all of this creates a doubleness in the room. And as the Joker, remembering to smile, offering chairs where I can see they are needed, making sure everyone we expected is here before I wink at the musicians to wind up … in that highly performative role, I can feel the shyness of the audience and can only hope that, with a quick joke and the couple of Augusto's warm-ups that can be done sitting down, I can address this inhibitedness and build in reality the can-do platform that many here have read about, but that we now have to make firm enough to stand upon.

All this has shaped the questions we are holding for one another, each of us – whatever our role in the presentation – keeping one detached eye on the Spectactors and the room as a whole for the signs of what needs to be addressed later in translation, customization and adaptation.

Of course the piece worked as theatre: seen on the scratchy VHS footage we managed to shoot (on the only working camera available to us in Kampala in a pre-digital age!) I can still feel the goose-bumps as the story unfolds. One shot shows the extremely diverse and very

Uganda - Kl HIV

specialized circle of individuals assembled becoming that wonderful
entity without which nothing happens and that is so much more than
the sum of its parts: an audience. *(→ so beyond)*

But a Constituency of Spectators? As I have said earlier I look back
today, with gratitude and greater clarity than then, on our use of the
best performative modes we had at our fingertips and to Constantin's
offer to choreograph the bewildering set of possibilities faced by the
Woman. Dancing with these rather than problematizing them, he saw
that we could furnish the Spectator with enough information about
possible vectors for HIV transmission simply by forging a temporary
lexicon of movements (money-thumbing chief among them) that could
be used as a motif linking all of the separate moments and Images we
knew we had to include, to honour our shared expertise but not so
slavishly as to present these as a public infomertial that happened to
use dance for effect but not towards empowerment of an audience with
a view to real change.

I watch the footage today and I can see that questioning, analytical,
active witness in the eyes of the Spectactors. There! The small gesture
between the Husband and the Mistress chimes with those between the
Sugar Mummy and her Toy-boy; the Landlord and the women in the Poor
House. There is a resonance, but not some pre-decided line of causation.
There are clues, but it is we as an audience who are being asked, not to
solve them, but to follow them into social action beyond this Now.

And so not in 'answering' these opening questions but by framing
them in an enquiry structure that still yields insights to me more than
twenty-five years on, I bring the details to an evidencing of this example,
in a spirit of Oracy but also so as to maintain a centrality of performance
practice in the architecture of this discourse as much as I conducted its
participatory traffic on that day, in the Now of *Akatale*.

Frame Six

As Sister Agnes strides forward, tying the Kanga around her
hips, furious intent focused firmly on the actor playing the
husband (Antagonist) I step aside. Somewhere in my body
memory the right thing to do kicks in, as what I think of

Frame = memoir = applied theory
to Boel as precursor of Post-colonial
practices

enacting an *idea with legs* remorselessly approaches: I might not be acting in the Forum but I am freed up by long practice of improvisational techniques to take this all-important step. Sideways, not towards. I yield to the energy of whatever is about to be enacted: neither unduly mediating nor yet abdicating to leave the Spectactor potentially in isolation. All these things I know from the various etiquettes of Improv as developed over many years and in the UK, customized and tested often in the field of TIE and YPT. Its what Michael Jackson called: 'Getting out of the way of the Music.' It's (just as well) my brain has just frozen in the sudden realization that the Intervention might happen in a different language (there are over 30 mother-tongues to choose from in Uganda) and that includes whatever the language of sexual politics might be that underlies all interactions between women and men in a traditional culture.

The one thing that isn't bothering me is the fact that Sister Agnes is a nun. That, she has shown me so clearly, is not who we are about to meet. She knots the Kanga, moves into the space I have freed up for her and makes the Intervention I have described. I don't even have to find a way of stopping her (as I have heard can sometimes be necessary). As she finishes and walks back, wiping her hands on the Kanga as if to wipe herself clear of the identity of the Protagonist, she has signalled that to me very clearly. Or as Augusto used to say of the legendary Woman in Lima: 'Very, very clearly indeed!'

So much is happening in this frame. I am freezing it here, still absorbing its meanings 25 years on and meditating upon it. Recreated in the continuous Now of performance, that is what a moment of Truth can do. It illustrates, yes, but so much more than that: it furthers and continues to augment my understanding, layered with the subsequent years of meaning and enquiry that accrue to it. It remains in the Now, with meaning radiating from it, partly because of the attention I still choose to give it, but more because my whole politics of attention have been permanently shaped by this moment. In these short revisited seconds then, I can see the crucial principle of the ludic at work, without which Forum cannot exist.

Actors and Joker equally have to *play*: to follow the principles of an improvisational culture of performance practice but with one eye (if possible) on the meta-objective of empowering each Intervention.

As Joker I now accept the Intervention and am changed by it, just as the Spectactors are.

Meanwhile, the actor playing the Antagonist – the Husband – is essentially still dancing with me. We have danced in rehearsal, and in particular in Constantin Mpongo's gruelling warm-ups ('Fit as a footballer', indeed!) and on through our shared time of mutual creation. That has been only four days wide, but we have rehearsed this moment well, as indeed any company must invest rehearsal time in preparing for Interventions. The actor playing the Antagonist, after all, must be braced for not just one potential Sister Agnes but many, striding towards him. As I stand aside, Sister Agnes bears down on him, with only seconds left …

I move aside, holding but not abandoning the space and accepting the Intervention, whatever it might be. That is a democratizing action in itself, shifting as it does the Joker's position towards that of Witness, and the principle it embodies, as I will hereafter call it, is that of *acceptance*, with its rich history in improvisational and ludic cultures not just at my fingertips but imprinted in my body memory: I already know how to accept and I bring that embodied knowing to the Forum and how it is facilitated by the role of the Joker.

And as I move, I sense a countermove: the Antagonist's. He is (as I already know) a dancer as well as an AIDS activist and I have learned from him, all over again (literally: re-membered) what the role of women is in all the best Development Theatre practice already flourishing in Uganda. The role of the Woman is central to all Development Theatre and it is his countermove that now opens up the central question in *Akatale.*

This Woman (in Sister Agnes' Intervention) now occupies that centre, but is not trapped there as a victim. She is no longer carrying anything. Her hands and eyes are open. She is facing the character of the Husband and she knows why she is doing so: so as to turn as the Woman *towards* her challenges and her part in them; so as to bring her own witness to the place she has arrived at in the Now of her life; so as to hold and own that place of rock bottom until, against all the odds, it becomes the springboard for an action *towards* him (authored by herself) and not a reaction *against* him (authored by him). These are political dance moves we have been rehearsing, building our collective capacity to enact such pivotal, improvisational moments as this one.

The Antagonist steps aside, as I do, but we both know we aren't getting 'out of her way'. This is Forum. We are *accepting* her Intervention. We are charged with two complementary performative roles: first, to empower her to make her way, and second, not to point it out to her, whatever the best of our (male) intentions.

So when she speaks and she happens to use both Karamajon and English, she and my fellow actor (the Antagonist) have already shown me what my being a Joker requires, in this moment and from here on in, in theory as well as practice.

I stand aside but do not abdicate. I conduct the traffic but do not direct it. I open the space up and witness what then happens, but do not mediate. I model a positive regard for every Intervention, however slight, by active witness and not directive behaviour.

I dance with the performers.

The Antagonist yields, but not too much: he spars with her, as a trainer does with a boxer, to the end that her skills are honed and supported by his own.

In this way, the actor playing the Husband dances with Sister Agnes' Intervention. She is very tall, as I've said: she draws herself up taller as she speaks. She summons the children to hear what she is going to say to him, or better than that, to hear him failing to explain himself to her.

She says:

'Children: your Father is here!'

The audience can hardly contain themselves. It's not so much what she says as the way she commands the very centre of the circle. You can imagine she commands a space like this in the villages where she works as part of the small NGO her order is affiliated to: using her nun's habit to pull focus and respect and then modestly stating her points about girl's education and family planning (albeit from a Catholicized point of view).

But to this task, as the Woman, she brings that performative skill to bear on one moment, one story and one individual, assuming the Woman's identity but deploying the device of substitution so as to maximize in others the possibilities of identification. With the wrapping of the Kanga, she is assuming a mantle: just as in Dorothy Heathcote's methodology of the Mantle of the Expert, a performative action can open a conduit for an improvised expertise, distilled from many lived experiences – by self and others – into an enacted strategy that witnessed, multiplies the possibilities for the audience, not *to do likewise* (Mimesis) but to *experience themselves in action* arising from reservoirs of untapped possibility: Conscientization.

The Husband prattles on about missed matatus; loans to friends; chances of jobs that might or might not happen. She draws herself one inch taller and I swear she looks as tall as the moon.

'… and I will find the money and then I will be able to give you the money …'

'And then?'

That's all she says and – dancer that he is – he performs a truly wonderful mime of being pile-driven like a post, deeper and deeper into lies of his own making. A stump of a man, fast disappearing into the red earth of Uganda (as echoed in the colour of the Green Room carpet at the National Theatre).

He visibly shrinks. But although she is now seemingly twice his height, it isn't this that diminished him, nor is it the phrase '… and then?' which mild as it seems is clearly truly shocking coming from a woman and certainly a nun playing the Woman. This chap I mentioned before (a social worker) in the inner circle of the audience, is actually screaming with laughter, flat on his back, with his legs waving in the air. I have no idea why the phrase is so funny, but the way the Intervention has been accepted – danced with – allows it to work as a sharp needle might lance a boil – a boil of rage.

What the audience have witnessed is intensely political but could only have been enacted through a language of performance. It is the Husband, we clearly see, who is diminished by his own dishonesty. The Woman, bringing her children into the picture, as not only a resource but as human beings who have a right to know what is happening to their education, has not been burdened by having to solve his problems. She faces huge economic challenges and at this moment she has not an exact idea about how she and the children are going to face them. But that is not what the Intervention is about. Sister Agnes knows, having never seen Forum before, how to make this completely, inescapably clear as she commands the space.

The Husband is the problem. He's not being judged as good or bad, but the trap he has sprung for himself through his own actions has snapped shut. She hasn't judged him, hit him or outwitted him, and neither have the children: 'You can step on his neck, but don't kill him.' She has unmasked him as the author of his own and the family's dilemmas. As the Woman, Sister Agnes isn't going to intervene in the many possible scenes she might have, where the Woman has to make all the choices as a result of the Husband's behaviour: how to rescue her daughter; how to rescue her sons from the criminality of street life; how to avoid prostitution as if that were her fate.

She has exposed him and the actor has danced with that exposure, instinctively knowing that this is what the Intervention and the monumental resolve with which she has confronted him are all about: enacted through pure body politics.

He is the problem. The laughing man in the audience knows it too. That's why he's on the floor. Scaled up, writ large, the Intervention, as both enacted and witnessed, has refused the notion of male behaviours as a problem to be carried by victimized women, and relocated it firmly as a set of actions whereby men repeatedly ensnare themselves and their families, to their own diminishment.

As with all pilot projects, or what Augusto called 'Symbolic Forums' at the end of a training, this powerful Intervention only happened once. The value of it today, in recreating and in framing it in the way I have done, is to identify the questions emergent from a single iteration but requiring a taking-forward and a *holding* that has persisted to the very writing of this book, nearly thirty years later. Persisted for a reason.

My initial questions have been replaced, through the activity of creating and modelling Forum with this carefully chosen group, by fresh, emergent ones. They won't be answered, probably ever, and they will be evidenced and explored in places I will never visit, in languages that I don't understand, in settings where cultural mores operate in ways I can't anticipate.

- Have I merely 'inspired' people or have I usefully equipped them?
- Have I genuinely served the work?
- How does an Intervention actually work? To what extent is Forum governed by ludic principles?
- Seen as a kind of improvisational game, how can we set up actors to accept the offers of Spectactors, whilst keeping an eye on the overarching objective of enacting realistic solutions to the challenges posed to them by the Model?
- How do we train a Joker to manage this traffic in the here and now with minimum prejudice?

Frame Seven

It's the next day and Mary-Jane and I have agreed to meet for a debrief. The above questions are with me: after my initial euphoria they became clearer. It worked! Everybody loved it! Sister Agnes rocked!

But I have noticed myself sliding backward into doubt. Where is the route map for what happens next? Can I legislate or plan for the way that participants take up what has been offered, albeit over a fantastically successful five days in terms of the uplift and overall empowerment arising from the experience we have shared? How do I know whether I have adhered sufficiently to Freire's pedagogy and not just given everyone a boost that will gradually fade?

This is what the five-day training I myself have received in Theatre of the Oppressed hasn't addressed. I am in someone else's Constituency and I am unable because of resources to extend my stay, to run an evaluation (for what those are worth) or to track in any other way the *legacy, sustainability* or *impact* of what I have done in the long term.

Mary-Jane is waiting. She gets up from her desk and walks towards me. She is smiling a complex smile. Part of me (the project manager) just wants to celebrate and then go through a list of positives and negatives for my report to the Winston Churchill Fellowship. Part of me (the performer) wants to be told whether it was a memorable event: an occasion of quality. Part of me (the teacher) is truly hungry to discern what techniques have a real chance of taking root, of being adapted into new and flexible Ugandan iterations.

She is welcoming me and I know she can see how much is going on in my head.

'It was a good day,' she says.

'Was it? I mean was it really?' is my rather needy reply.

'And today our work must go on,' she smiles.

I know she is pointing me forwards. I'm really not that important in her scheme of things. It's been a good, intense input to her many strands of programming and activism. That is all and indeed it is enough. Today is another day and as Augusto has always said, the Theatre of the Oppressed is never finished: how could it be? I remember suddenly what day it really is.   ⟵

La the core of the book

'Happy International Women's Day!' I chirp, trying to cheer myself up at all of these daunting thoughts.

She takes a step towards me, still smiling, and looms: the only time she has ever used her height that way and one of the few times I have ever stood in that exact physical relationship to a woman, anywhere.

This is the moment I realize she isn't 6'3". She's 6'4". She places her long, elegant hand ever so gently on my shoulder, with her fingers lightly to my throat. Winks. And says:

'And what about the other 364 days Ali? What about those?'

We have our lunch. We evaluate and separate the knowns from the unknowns in ways I am still doing, even as I unpack those learnings by my retelling, my sifting, thirty years on. Are Forum and Theatre of the Oppressed a Movement or a Method? Does the furtherance of the work depend on a few charismatic teachers (I hesitate to include myself, but we both know what I mean) or can it be taken up by any group with the right guidance, appropriate facilitation and – it has to be said – a pretty rigorous eye on quality control?

I first forged those guiding questions with Mary-Jane in 1990 and they guide me now. They will be held throughout the remaining examples which comprise the first half of this book. Held, rather than answered. Evidenced, rather than proven.

I intend my signature activity of framing, alongside the iteration of emergent research questions, to become a habit, with its own rhythm and a minimum of mediation from myself, allowing the reader to make her own connections between different modes of discourse. This is to keep a balance above all between *asking* and *telling*: I have my own examples, carefully chosen over a long career, to offer in the present enquiry and to place in dialogue with the questions, ideas and concerns of the reader, in the Now. And my overarching aim, restated here, is this: to maximize the potential for the practice and study of the early career practitioner or researcher to bring their own experience into dialogic relation with my own.

In the first part of this book, I tell. In the second, I ask.

Frame Eight

I leave Mary-Jane with her own notebook full: follow-up ideas that would never have come up had I not been challenged by her as rigorously as I have been:

- A girls' group, working separately;
- The possibility of some of the techniques such as Storyboarding (and its commonality, coupled with anonymity) that might be adapted to peer-led sessions run by and for sex workers;
- A university module (practical, not theoretical).

Marvellous stuff. I'm going to take such a good report home!

Something is missing. I stop on the doorstep of the National Theatre. The bag seller lady is gone.

I never see her again.

Chapter 2

Teaching and Training

Back n' forward A little difficult to follow the story behind

I now have to go back a chronological step in this book – to Autumn 1989 – in order subsequently to go forward. *Reculer pour mieux sauter.*

I have begun *in media res*, with the first experience I had in my career as a Joker, of diving into a working environment (in my case, Kampala in 1990) because it is clear to me that a fundamental principle of the pedagogy underpinning the Theatre of the Oppressed is that we ourselves – the trainee Jokers – experience a Conscientization: a waking up to our own powers as facilitators that parallels and mutually ← reinforces that process of empowerment we aspire to bring about in solidarity with the groups we work with. That has been my own lived experience with Forum and that has shaped the way the current study approaches the reality of learning, working with, adapting and being part of the continuing evolution of the Theatre of the Oppressed in practice. I have chosen to begin in the middle of my first truly independent and formative experience of personal practice, honouring Augusto Boal's own adage that the Theatre of the Oppressed will never be 'finished' (how could it be?) but more than that: there is no clear beginning for me either, other than to speak from as detailed and honest a telling of my first fully autonomous experience of working with Boal's Toolbox (as I still prefer to call it) of techniques.

In Uganda, I was invited to a place where there already existed what I have termed a Constituency: the group of artists, educators and HIV workers who had already identified participatory theatre as a powerful tool with which to advance their project of culturally appropriate AIDS Education. The choice had been made to use the National Theatre as a site for the intensive training and the making of *Akatale* – the training's polished, public outcome. The less tangible but more enduring outcome was to be the customized Toolbox of techniques each participant extrapolated from their experience of that devising and testing process, with a view to adaptation and reuse in their own places of work and struggle, long after the life of the project.

For my part, I found the means to go there and the resources to support me for the three months it took to make the work and earn my place in that group as a co-worker, not somebody parachuting in with fancy new ideas but without a connection to the context they were to be tested in. And because I was drawn so warmly in and immediately put to work by a group who knew their own strengths, weaknesses and priorities, I was able to find my own effectiveness as a Joker on the ground and to gain the unique insight that comes only through Praxis: the experiential journey where we are given a space in which not just to do, but to witness ourselves in the act of doing. But how exactly, on any given day, with one singular group, do we find our way to just that technique or precisely this Image: the one that unlocks the potential Model for a Forum that will speak to many? Who is this Joker, so crucial to the efficacy of the system, who can spot the Intervention that will enact an authentic, revolutionary moment: the Intervention that only a live, embodied performance can bring into being? And how do we guide the actors in our work so as to be truthful and at the same time strategically detached, so as to augment the strength and veracity of this Intervention, or that?

Who decides – for example – whether this particular man, however well-intentioned, can substitute for that unique woman, in such a way as to keep universal his Intervention without (as Augusto would say) recourse to 'magic'? How do we train this Joker and these actors?

I *wanted* the books and subsequently their author to answer these perennial questions by providing me with clear rules, but that wasn't what I *needed*. What I needed was to watch Augusto work. The questions above (the overarching questions of this book) I increasingly stumbled across, working from the (relatively) straightforward directions in a dog-eared copy of *Theatre of the Oppressed* in chilly school halls, in parks and in prisons, were to do with what happens *in between one exercise and another*, in the hidden spaces when snap judgements take place in the mind of the Joker (or facilitator) or as the actors take a breath before improvising the next move within the bigger picture. How was this to be theorized and then made both explicit and practicable, so that our Forum wasn't simply formulaic or just (literally) by the book? How might we ensure that these excellent recipes, these power tools, didn't ossify into something doctrinaire and repetitive? Or worse still, an orthodoxy that might then be imposed irrespective of context, appropriateness or consent?

Frame One
(Nottingham; 1989) first contact with Boal

Augusto enters the room with Adrian Jackson (then of London Bubble; now Cardboard Citizens) and silence falls. He looks a bit nervous and I identify with that: I can identify from experience with the rising adrenaline of a Day One as we facilitators suss out the energy and especially the expectations of a group, working out which warm-ups to choose from a scrolling list of many possibilities; noticing the shyest person in the room (a personal benchmark of mine) and working out which form of words to use when we necessarily have to demystify, to unpack, to explain.

His eyes are quite black: keen, mobile and notably penetrating, as their gaze flits here and there. Rarely have I seen someone scanning a room or reading it so swiftly. Even before Augusto speaks I connect with that business of reading. After some quick introductions he sits in what over the years that follow I get to know as his position of *address*: he chooses an ordinary plastic chair with no arms, squares himself to us with body wide and legs apart, arms freed up and ready for the engrossing gestural dance that accompanies many of his explanations, punctuates his stories and catches our many questions like a star fielder. In this way Augusto always opens up the space in front of him for the moulding and manipulation of *telling out a meaning*, alongside the practical exercises he brings into the room as part of the system of Forum. Over five days we will alternate between full immersion in the incomparable exercises of the Theatre of the Oppressed: in Augusto's words relearning in this democratized pedagogical space how *to see what we look at, feel what we touch and listen to what we hear*.

The exercises flow, one into the other, according to this system of de-mechanization that is essential if we are to un-learn how we used to learn: relearning, in a more holistic, embodied way, how to experience ourselves, singly and collectively, in the act of creating new knowledges and bringing that knowledge of ourselves as active learners to the business of not just talking about but acting out alternatives to the many manifestations of oppression we encounter daily. This is how we are to learn the techniques of the Theatre of the Oppressed, before we leave after our five-day intensive and use them in our own working contexts and indeed in our personal lives. We are immersed in a collective act not just of education but of peer empowerment.

Behind Augusto is a wall crammed with promise. Categorized around the five senses and loosely systematized in such a way as to show multiple routes for the group to follow through de-mechanization to the creation of Forum itself, are lists of all the games, exercises and techniques we *might* be going to use over the five-day process. Some are clearly warm-ups, ice-breakers and problem-solving exercises and as my beginners' nerves dissipate – Augusto is the warmest of teachers and we laugh a great deal – I recognize some of them as coming from the improvisational, ludic culture of the work I am already engaged in. Like jokes, like recipes, like family stories even, these games seem to migrate around the world and to belong to no single group or culture: certainly not to a sole author. I can even improve on one or two of the choices he makes (I fondly imagine) as we start to gel as a group, releasing our nerves through laughter, finding out about one another and the many diverse ways twenty individuals bring to a group their personal life experience through the embodiment of that experience in forms that performance can recreate and rendering that individual experience as *expertise,* accessible to others in the shared project of the Theatre of the Oppressed.

We make, in short, a good beginning.

Boal's religion and his disciples
the phrase to the Master

We move through the day in a rhythm, alternating between playing a sequence of exercises and then sitting to discuss what we have learned, often rewarded (but only, I note, *after* we have created meaning ourselves) with an illustration of how and when these sequences have been developed and worked on with other groups worldwide.

And sometimes we get a story. What stories they are!

Squared to us, positioned to address, clearly seeing there is now a moment to extend the meaning in the room, by way of storytelling, to connect with the social reality beyond it, Augusto sweeps back his silvery mane with a much loved – and often imitated – gesture …

And begins.

I am used to hearing the music of Gaelic (the mother tongue I didn't learn at school) underneath the English spoken by older relatives in the Scottish Highlands, which is where my people came from before industrialization. So it is with Augusto's English speaking and the music of Portuguese underneath it, and Carioca Portuguese at that: the lilt and quite unique seductiveness of the language as it is spoken by the population of the *Cidade Maravilhosa*, Rio de Janeiro.

Behind him are the charts of exercises, most as yet un-played. I am yet to realize that many will remain that way: the facilitator part of me can see that there is no way on earth we can cover them all in a mere five days. He ticks the ones we do end up playing as we go along, though. I like that. But for now, who doesn't want a good story? For a second I perceive that within our group there is an impatience among some to get up and *do more*, whilst at the same time and pulling in what increasingly feels like an opposite direction, is the desire among many to be told more stories and given more examples: to have their questions answered by the Master.

The story we are hearing has emerged organically from doing: it is very clearly Augusto's spontaneous response to the vivid Images we have just brought into the room. We have just created a sequence of Image Theatre in careful steps, opening us up emotionally and resulting in groups of us creating one Image per person of Family, through the bodies of the others in our groups, with minimum discussion or direction, but with an exponential increase in the need for listening, intelligent trust and touch. All very un-English (or Scottish, come to that!). We have been quite exposed by this: I'm not sure what all of the silent Images I've just witnessed have meant, but I can see that some people have really risked themselves in their sculpting and the subsequent replay. Some Images have quivered with ambiguity and fragility. The room has now and then been flooded with pain. I haven't been quite so brave myself, but others have been.

Now I am sitting near Augusto's chair on the floor, sensing that we have truly become a group and have travelled a long way over the first half of the first day and especially for a room full of people who are usually, each of us, the ones in charge of whole schools, companies or arts organizations.

Augusto begins to talk about Image Theatre, de-mechanization and the related processes vital for all of us in the Theatre of the Oppressed to understand as it were from both inside and outside: deploying sequences of first games, then exercises, then techniques to generate a potential in the room for the group to understand itself as already possessing the capacity for social transformation, even revolution.

He tells a famous story, much studied and arguably now over-told, about the woman in Lima who strode out to intervene in an early Model of Forum, not *telling* but *showing* the audience and the well-intentioned, urban actors from Boal's troupe exactly what she meant by 'having a clear argument': with a spendthrift husband, breaking a broom over the actor's back in the process.

That is not the story I am going to re-tell here. I don't want to get stuck in the content or even the entertainment value of such a re-telling, seeking as I am to stand back from the first moment I located the core significance of Oracy in Augusto's personal pedagogy.

He has seen all of our family Images and to my amazement, sitting near him as I am, I can see he has been deeply moved.

He is, I realize, unafraid to say that this is so. There are moments in the work and in my present framing and unpacking of it, when the head and the heart are temporarily aligned. This is one of them. I can see that the story he is beginning to tell has not been planned. I know he has been moved to tell it before he reveals that this is indeed so.

He has been watching, over what up to now have been only a few intensives in Europe and the US, how different groups (in communities, not just training intensives like ours) have worked through this technique: a simple negotiation, construction, presentation and now response to Images of the family. The further into the political North he has travelled, the more these Images have struck him with their increasing sense of Brechtian alienation pervading those from prosperous, urban environments most of all.

He tells us some examples. He reminds us of what we have made and universalizes that making without diluting the sense that the knowledge that is earned through the risky process of Image-making cannot be explained reductively away. He shares the observation that – for example – in relatively poor, small Italian towns he has seen many, many Images of large extended families around tables, the authors of the Images always populating them with people eating together, talking together and co-creating a shared life together, through a culture with the preparation and celebration of food at its heart and at its centre the more profound unspoken nurturance of which food is a signifier.

And in the political North? He stops. He asks what I have come, over the ensuing decades, to know as the key phrase in this reflexive mode of Image Theatre, when we sit and consider what we have learned through our co-creation that could never be arrived at in any other way or modality.

'What did you see?'

None of us knows what to say at first.

He carries on with the story, now a vividly contextualized evocation of cultural difference and in no way a mere re-telling on behalf of a group of people not present today.

'What did you see?'

Relationships? Arguments? Watching TV? Love? Children?

All of these have indeed been present and some more than once across the sequence of twenty-odd Images we have made and witnessed this morning.

'What did you see?'

Someone 'gets it' as the story about Italy and more Southern communities gives up its inner meaning.

'None of them are eating together'

'Yes and what else?'

I silence myself. In this moment, among my peers, I know only what was taught and still I haven't unlearned that self-oppressing habit of learning. If you can't work out the right answer, keep silent. Something has literally been staring us all in the face, but I can't quite name it and I can't say I can't!

Augusto finishes the story. And now I see. Its point is simple, but there is no trite moral to the telling. *None of the families are looking at each other.*

It takes me a moment for what has happened in this teaching story to sink in. I've noticed what a keen-sighted person Augusto is, from the odd comment he has made as our Image Theatre has played past him today. He has used that phrase 'What do you see?' many times, merely – or so I thought – as a prompt. But in the Now of storytelling we are being taken below the surface of this seemingly simple unpacking. The whole exercise is about *radical seeing*. Image Theatre is indeed about seeing what we look at. We have to invest in the making before we can learn that seeing that comes not just from empathy but from identification.

In Nottingham, in 1989, our many Images of families do indeed contain so few people looking at each other that now, hearing the question and answer rhythm of Augusto's characteristic guided reflection, we are being led, using the fleshed-out examples of what we ourselves have risked something of personal value to make, towards a truth in the room that could be arrived at in no other way.

The story doesn't have an ending. It connects us, however, in a way that absolutely does not leave us feeling 'We had to be there' or at odds with groups who have arrived at something very different to our own imagining of family. It connects us in a way that can only be arrived at collectively, through the shared risk and emotional adventure of making.

Augusto carries on. He scales up his story to describe a workshop in Sweden where materially there is at this historical moment (1989) the highest standard of living, supported by a well-funded Social Security system and open to the greatest possible number of citizens, in the developed world. And yet the participants in his workshop there, having initially questioned whether they would be able to dredge up enough examples of oppression to work with a system conceived in Brazil under a military junta, have after working for a few hours eventually told him how high the suicide rate is there.

The further north, the fewer Images of family or of simple, daily, nurturing social intimacy and community-making have appeared. And alongside that trend, this Swedish group (many of whom were social workers) pointed out – in their making as much as their discussion – that not all oppressions are visible and explicit in affluent societies.

Augusto finishes the story. He explains that at this point he could see he would have to address the task of adapting both techniques and pedagogy to the more materially prosperous countries in Europe where oppression (one might argue) is more subtle – hidden even – than when it is routinely enforced with guns.

Boal was a real genius at the kind of educative unpacking of embodied material I have described above. Invested and (inevitably) opened up emotionally by what we had made in this and many other sequences of Image Theatre over those five days, we would pause and engage with him in the always imperfect and arguably impossible task of calming the room down: standing back so as to explore that question *What do you see?*; universalizing, from that initial unpacking, the underlying issues connecting personal Images so as to expose the power relationships inscribed there; and, finally, discussing how Images or more fully formed Models might be brought to the Forum in a politically literate session of the Theatre of the Oppressed.

The techniques themselves could extend our discussion by collective, embodied means, not skimming over the difficulty but working through it as a group. But more often than not another question would be asked that took us back into personalized discussion. As a most reflexive and responsive teacher, Augusto rarely cut these discussions short and consequently the day would end with far more exercises un-played than things unsaid.

It was all – it seemed to me – about balance. To be honest, quite a bit of what was playing out as a conflict of aims within sessions was simply about time management, and the need for pretty straightforward self-discipline from participants. And our group became unbalanced more and more often as we approached the public or 'symbolic' Forum that was to mark the end of our process. I don't set this fault line out from a self-righteous distance at the time of writing. Below I will describe how I fell right into it as it gaped very wide indeed and the adrenaline of an approaching public showing lent both heat and pressure to differences that had at first appeared quite slight, or only to concern one or two of us in the group. But right in that gap, in the place of paradox between personal and political, in the very middle of what seem to be the insoluble contradictions and inner tensions within Boal's pedagogy: right there in that uncertainty and difficulty I first experienced in Nottingham were to be found the invaluable, guiding questions that by virtue of their very difficulty I have navigated for almost thirty years. They are the questions that have birthed this writing in both form and content, as I hope to show in the remaining sections of my book.

The tension between the widening divide between practitioners wanting to boost their capacity and those whose agenda was more around self-development was often mirrored by Augusto's self-contradictory response to the room as a whole. Often, he instinctively and quite viscerally responded to questions from his audience in ways that appeared to settle a question verbally whilst exacerbating the underlying pedagogical issue in non-verbal ways: the reality of the relationship between charismatic teacher (seated, talking) and budding discipleship (on the floor, listening passively, ever wanting *more*). Within that self-reinforcing feedback loop the Frequently Asked Questions were as follows, presented here as ***Frame Two***, with my immediate reactions to them on their being asked, in 1989, in italics.

Frame Two

When/how do I myself use that technique we just did?

Augusto has displayed all of the techniques on the wall that *might* be used, creating an expectation that we might also pick up some pointers around autonomous navigation through them, but unintentionally undermining the transparency that produced the display.

Some of us are here to make the most of the training in five days whilst others crave personal development as an end in itself. The simplest warm-ups are applauded. It's therapeutic group-soup. That's what many participants expect (nothing to do with Augusto) and the marketing of the workshops and their pricing has done nothing to disabuse them of these expectations.

What is the role of the Joker?

The discussion that follows only ever builds up the mystique of this central role (which is never delegated over five days) rather than dedicating that time to *rehearsing* it. The Joker role clearly holds all the power: brokering Interventions, selecting Spectactors and controlling momentum. It is a balancing act between editing, improvising and chairing. At its best, it democratizes; at its most problematic, it censors. It needs to be tried out and rehearsed, but repeated discussion paradoxically ensures that this kind of pedagogical space isn't there. People want to contemplate the role but not the risk of inhabiting it.

There is a very important role for Oracy in the work but it needs to be framed and understood as that: complementing experiential learning so as to create a bridge between the studio and the field; the techniques and those they are for but who are not represented. Often we are listening to a story and defaulting into wishing we'd been there or hoping that one day we might do this. We *want* this kind of story, but right now we don't *need* it. It is comforting after a very exposing and revelatory Image exercise to have it grounded, put to bed by a brilliantly told example of how well it worked elsewhere. But often we are left wondering whether it will work when we try it? How exactly did he set it up again? Will we get a chance to find our own words or ways to set things up? What about the other three exercises on the wall that now there isn't time to do because we've been ... hearing a story about the first one?

'What happens if ...' is not a question that can be answered with a story. It is the expression of an anxiety around the facilitation and adaptation of new techniques that are self-evidently very powerful and that need to be rehearsed by people in a safe space, constituted in such a way as to facilitate a supportive training group with the clear aim of empowering as many new facilitators as possible. That's my position, anyway. Because I'm a facilitator!

Looking back now I can see that the problem with Masterclass settings such as Nottingham in 1989 was that this relationship with Augusto the charismatic teacher and the management of time and energy that it required to be enacted wasn't what a lot of people (to my mind) had come for. I can see today that it was what we more grassroots practitioners *needed* but that it wasn't what everyone in the room *wanted*. Here in reality, in practice, is the fault line of TotO as it has panned out in the political North: not in disputing the indisputable, proven efficacy of Forum in the field, but in a fudging around the aims, needs, wants and expectations of those who attend high-end training; can pay for it and are almost inevitably representative of but not *part of* the groups they work with. The platform for the pedagogy wasn't a platform at all. It concealed a shaky

(handwritten margin: first world anxieties)

(handwritten bottom: - Not critical enough about privileges of taking a master-class vs going to practice Toto in Africa - Not a real did. between frames n' analysis.)

compromise between expectations and reality: full of holes that are dangerous because unacknowledged. We repeatedly found ourselves discussing the role of the Joker, but only Augusto was one.

We never became the Joker.

Are we doing Theatre or Therapy?

This question still (again, to me) characterizes those who have a high expectation of a personal development experience, at the hands of the charismatic teacher, enabling them to feel better about the oppressions they experience (or more often, witness) but without running the same risk. A Masterclass seems to afford this space without challenging the accompanying expectation. It is when we enter into practice with the aim (for practitioners) of imparting as many useful techniques in five days as possible that these divergent expectations play out oppositionally, with increasing frustration on both sides.

Why the need for this question? It simply would never be asked by any of the groups we either work with or aspire/ claim to.

But the discussions saw Augusto in his element. The response to repeated questioning is at its best a story and when Augusto told a story he temporarily reconciled the need to be given real examples of practice with the desire to hear more from the Master (rather than try something as one's own master!).

It's a paradox. I am woken up by the teacher/facilitator to my own experience as *expertise* and enabled to put that to the service of a further, transitive learning relationship with the one who is teaching. But for the first time in my own career in the UK, I was among a mixed group of directors, theorists (tape machines abounded) and those who would rather have discussion as an end itself and hear the stories as a way of eliciting original material about the teacher, not the reality of the method. So what seemed increasingly like a hijacking of sessions for personal reasons and an insistence that we

Not relations with texts or interactions of Toto / it dwells in his own universe. It doesn't get into the conversation, is a bubble of a conver-sation.

sit and talk rather than do, I now understand to have been a tension playing out between divergent expectations (on the micro level) that scaled up evidence fundamentally different cultures of teaching and performance (on the macro).

I gradually realized over that five days that it is up to me to take what works and leave the rest.

Frame Three

We have been using Images to de-mechanize our own internalized inability *to see what we look at daily*: the society we are immersed in but are rarely required to critique with a view to its transformation, accustomed as we are to the benefits of the status quo. We have been using Images, as that is the only way we can replace a way of *looking* that has been schooled with a way of seeing that can be owned by us and used by us in the conflicts we as artists and activists are part of in our own lived social reality.

The exercises are on the wall, suggesting how this sequence enacts an ideology. The practice we have done requires an immersion in the techniques of the system (if that's what it is) of the Theatre of the Oppressed including the skills involved in their sequencing, as much as in any one individual exercise or game. I have realized that after that immersive stage of learning and of using these techniques for ourselves, what is missing from that doing and making, what can't been seen on the wall with its promising lists and charts of the 'Arsenal' of techniques, what can't be explained away in discussion (much as we need to talk after such powerful Images have been created among us) is that moment where without dilution or dumbing down we are shown how to scale up, to universalize, to connect this training with the groups we aspire to work for but haven't yet worked with.

Now that scaling up and universalization has been opened up to us by Augusto, partly – but only partly – through Story. To make Models for fresh Forum, we have to bring our own stories into the room. High time, I reckon. I now have to go through what

I so often expect the people I work with to risk when I ask them to tell me their stories. I have to be grounded in what the risk of that feels like.

We are offered a chance to propose topics around personal experience of oppression to move this activity forward and one of us suggests homophobia. That'll do me, as a Gay man. I move towards him and quickly realize that the group forming comprises two Gay and two Straight men.

I'm not at all sure about using a very personal story at this exact point: the part of me that keeps wanting to jot down ideas about how to enable groups to make working Models for the Forum at speed would be happy just to get on with it. But I am equally aware that we have to immerse ourselves in an example of personal oppression in order to be sufficiently invested in the work to find ourselves aligned not just ideologically but emotionally with the work that follows, which I am assuming will involve a critique of the Model itself *as a Model*: a boundaried and safe use of that Model to enable Boal to demonstrate which techniques to apply to it as a Joker in a Forum that we will briefly practice, followed by (my most eager expectation) a chance to become that Joker ourselves, connected to the piece that has emerged from a group with which we have some kind of identification in common. I know from many years of making and touring participatory work that it needs to be rehearsed: not in a fixed way so as to shut down unexpected Interventions (of whatever kind) but in the way that actors prepare for improvisational work, by flexing their rapid response muscles in a safe space, before opening things up to a roomful of strangers.

But I am in a roomful of strangers, here and now, in Nottingham, and I am working on a scene which shows a Gay man being prevented from coming to the funeral of a partner who has died of AIDS.

The story isn't mine, but to any Gay man who has lived through the 1990s it is a very familiar, raw and indeed still untold one. Even before we are called back to run the Models as sketches I feel the lack of boundaries around sharing this as almost vertiginous, and I like to think of myself as a pretty resilient workshop participant. I have no idea how we have ended up with a Straight man playing a Gay one and a Gay man (me) playing the Oppressor. I am unclear as to whether we are going to do the Forum now, for real, with Augusto as the Joker, or whether we will simply show the Model and discuss possible Interventions and maybe ways to tweak it so as to make its essential conflict more clear. We are talking about homophobia, aren't we? At what point exactly will we hear some feedback? If this is purely an internal affair, then I won't have any trouble detaching sufficiently from the highly emotional content of the short scene, so as to be able to jot down ways to create boundaries when – for example – I use the work with large groups of secondary school students. I am looking to develop more confidence around bridging that gap between when young people call out ideas and then actually get up to enact them. Who might actually be exposed, triggered or in other ways be, in fact, Oppressed by this vivid, powerful method of experiential learning?

In short, what are the ground rules here? I catch the eye of the other Gay man in the group and all we have time to do is signal that we'll talk later, once we've worked out where exactly we are in this moment.

And we run the Model. It goes quite well, I think.

STOP!

A woman wants to intervene at the moment that the surviving partner tries to approach the funeral. Her Intervention is simply this: 'How can he inflict yet more shame on that grieving family?'

And the bottom falls out of the day.

I step out of this frame precisely here, because this was the moment where the agendas of different participants in the Nottingham training were exposed as not only divergent in terms of differing life experience that participants brought to the artificial setting of the Masterclass, but furthermore played out as conflict between people who had invested almost oppositional agendas and expectations in their attendance.

There were, at this and many other similar intensive training events, too many chefs. Some of us, because of who we were, the groups we worked with and represented, the expectation of learning new techniques and the intention to reconfigure them with what we already knew, were well aware that to go more deeply into the way that Forum works we would at some point need to make Models or short scenes out of either personal experience or the issues we dealt with back in what I am calling our Constituencies.

Others seemed to be bringing to the training had – as I have said – a far more personalized agenda. It is as if for some the opportunity to open up a personal story was a therapeutic or even a cathartic one and it is plain to see that this can be played out as a conflict of interest.

This is the first real fault line I noticed in the way that Augusto set up the making of Models and although he might have made it much clearer that these would be taken apart in public and used in an openly experimental way, I don't believe any amount of careful setting up would ever have addressed that ever-present pull, in one direction towards the personal and in the other to a more stood-back approach, acting upon material that however emotive was part of a pedagogical exercise pointing beyond the room and requiring participants to maintain their own boundaries.

This present study is no post-mortem. Those who attended that intense and in every way formative five-day workshop will all have their own take on what happened. It is enough to note here that apart from leaving with many new techniques and more than that a galvanizing vision from Boal that configured them in sequences enacting a radical ideology, I also met some of the people who have to this day been key players in the development and adaptation of the 'Arsenal' of techniques of the Theatre of the Oppressed in a wide range of settings and in many evolving applications: Adrian Jackson's award-winning work with Cardboard Citizens and Tim Wheeler's with Mind The Gap among them. Indeed, I would foreground this networking and relationship-building as not a mere by-product of a very intense and often fraught process, but as one of its enduring consequences. The exercise in boosting our capacity to work together and continue that work in new alliances was a priceless legacy from Nottingham for those of us who because of funding structures, areas of expertise, resources and geography were often working alone with only the book to guide us (I had hitherto been working from a single copy of *Theatre of the Oppressed* and that was all I had).

But the ways those fault lines played out as conflict (often very wounding) between otherwise like-minded people also had consequences. It is these I am most committed to addressing in the here and now, as crucial issues underpinning the pedagogical choices that at many points since have sometimes undermined the overarching ethos of solidarity that characterizes our movement, however diverse its participating groups and practitioners may be. I bring to this task examples of how some of our gatherings in Europe exemplified and enacted unresolved paradoxes exposed by the translation of the work from its Brazilian origins and cultural milieu to a grafting onto entirely different constituencies in the political North. I will frame examples of these in the following chapter with this aim solely in mind: to unpack current unresolved questions around the dissemination of the techniques of Forum (in particular) and these are questions that must be explored if we are to continue to maintain a quality of concerted agreement about what the essence of the work is in both pedagogy and practice, as it moves forward and is adapted, hybridized and sometimes even discarded as inappropriate to the emerging contexts in which we find ourselves.

Without Boal.

Chapter 3
How Do We Adapt Forum?

Throughout this book I will endeavour to model in form as well as content the iterative processes whereby I myself, those connected to me through the work and (writ large) the movement of the Theatre of the Oppressed as a whole have developed a fluid, working pedagogy. That pedagogy arises from practice (what in the Academies we term Praxis) and is extrapolated from it. The way we impart experiential techniques must, I believe, be accompanied by an account of how we manage the risk of using them. There can be no final or fixed template for doing Forum and Image Theatre the 'right' way, because we use these techniques not only in collaboration but also in an attempt at solidarity with those we aspire to empower through that collaboration. That means to negotiate, to fail, to chop and to change. The need to refer – for consistency, guidance and quality control – to what I call the recipes for the games, exercises and techniques that are the life of the systems underpinning Forum and Image Theatre (the focus of this book) is a valid and urgent one, but it carries with it a risk. What happens if I am working with, say, a group of young people and using an exercise like the Great Game of Power, which as developed and documented by Boal's collaborators in CTO Paris remains one of my absolute favourites? There it is, in *Games for Actors and Non-Actors* (still my most-often-read, dog-eared of Boal's books) with straightforward steps in print to follow and even photographs showing what happens when a particular group use the recipe to recreate the exercise in their own space and context, with their own bodies, with their own skills and life experiences, to project upon the startling series of skeletal power structures it unfailingly produces.

I set up the exercise (as I still do in my studio at Queen Mary, University of London, with every new group I open up the techniques to) and the group begin to play. The instructions are clear and the outcomes often surprising and abundant. But what happens if today is not the right day and the exercise is – today – not the right one? If the group have already shown me that they are more interested in making and reading Images made from their own bodies and generated through a different exercise such as Hypnosis?

How do I teach, not the techniques but the moment of response in between one technique and the next, where a particular group on one never-to-be-repeated day show the facilitator what further path to take, and why? How do I impart not just the recipes for techniques but the sequencing and responsiveness at the heart of the role of the Joker?

Figure 3 Great game of power. Image Theatre exercise; Jana Sanskriti Theatre Company; Badu, Kolkata, West Bengal.

Frame One
(Kolkata, West Bengal; 2012)

It is a hot night in 2012 on the Maidan, the huge central park in Kolkata where Jana Sanskriti host the more public-facing performances from their biannual Muktadhara Festival. There are groups from all over the world here. It's the biggest draw in town, but then I haven't been to the Durga Puja yet (and that's another story!).

The stage seems far away, across a sea of people. Right now they are watching a short film on a screen above the stage.

Augusto has just addressed the Festival by a film link from Julian. He is dying. He blesses Jana Sanskriti as a group 'who take the Theatre of the Oppressed seriously'. I know I am never going to see him alive again. The film ends. All of us are going to have to find our own way, together, from now on. We are going to have to maintain the Movement (or is it a Method?) and that is going to mean living with all kinds of uncomfortable questions about sustainability, training, governance and … quality control.

How can I still be watching – more than twenty years in – Forum plays that seem to be unthinking photocopies? It might be the setting that seems to shrink the work: not many of even the strongest Forum plays can withstand this kind of exposure to a huge, nearly unworkable audience. To be fair, most of them do work although their theatricality is often aesthetically thin. The best in terms of participation are 'Jokered' by pairs who have worked out ways of making Interventions not just possible but desirable to make, even with mics.

One Forum shines out. Not that it's a competition, but this one is the 'real thing'. And yet, even as the music starts, I'm wondering who I am to decide what 'real thing' means in relation to work from contexts I am ignorant of and countries I've never been to.

A baby girl is being born. The birth is happening maybe 50 yards away from me, in the middle of the Maidan in Kolkata, on a hot night, watched by a thousand people, maybe more.

The stage is lit by a string of bare bulbs. You can hear the generator chuffing away: a counterpoint to the sounds of birth from the stage. The audience immediately in front of me comprises row on row of village women whom I know Jana Sanskriti have bussed in to see this Forum piece by the excellent Mandala Theatre Company from Kathmandu. I can spot Bárbara Santos (whom I've known for twenty years) sitting in among them. I think she's been working with them. The birth scene sends a palpable ripple of reaction moving through them. It's being done as almost-dance, centred on a huge vaginal hoop covered with red fabric, manipulated so as to pulse with big, bold, rhythmic movements: expressionistic but at the same time inescapably visceral in the way the Theatre of the Oppressed can be, at its best. It's one woman's noisy, messy labour, writ large. It's universal without being diluted by the scenographic tactics required to reach the back of a sprawling audience in a busy park. It's one woman's story, but not just any woman. It's truthful without being naturalistic.

In the Maidan, on a hot Kolkata evening, there is a huge vagina, centre stage. An actor squeezes through it. It's all pretty graphic.

Some women laugh (covering their mouths, checking each other out) and some wince. They've all been there, have helped at or seen such births. So far, so good.

One last push and … its a girl. An unwanted girl, in rural Nepal. As the 'baby' is held up, her father looks away.

As the Model unfolds from this attention grabbing opening it is (as always with Forum) the pain of it that does the keenest work of universalizing the issues at play. The birth pangs are one kind of pain, but the rejection of the girl baby by her father is quite another. The mother presents to her husband this beautiful baby – now shrunk from the adult actor who was birthed through the hoop to a more manageable bundle in her arms – and again he turns his head away. She tries again. He won't look. It's only a girl.

The women all around me go very, very quiet.

I start explaining to my co-worker Rose Sharp that a good Forum piece will contextualize this crucial moment without letting us Spectactors off the hook. As indeed it does: we see a backstory in which the Elders (in this case from rural Nepal) pressurize the father; see the conflict this produces in him as a good man who has married for love; see the way that larger social and cultural oppressions are inscribed in the microcosm of this little family and are now being re-enacted and reinforced before the baby girl is even one day old. We are taken through this information with an elegant and economical performance style that is uncompromising in its political clarity without losing the emotional truth that packs such a punch, at night, across a sea of upturned faces, not just eliciting empathy but commanding identification. The women in front of me know what they are looking at. They haven't been drilled in the protocols of indoor scripted performance. They see this scene and they wince. They witness the Elders' pressure on the man; the man's rejection of the baby; the wife's particular pain. And then they talk!

Up comes the Joker, microphone in hand, and the part of me that is the researcher, stood back a little from this huge yet intimate event, checks the fact that the Joker is – has to be, surely? – a woman. I've just got time to explain to Rose that the role of the Joker is to conduct the traffic of Interventions before the Forum proper kicks off, with a queue of women waiting by the steps at the foot of the stage and – again, I note carefully – one or two satellite assistant Jokers moving back through the audience to encourage the less bold, spotting the tentatively half-raised hands of women who maybe have an idea for an Intervention but only half believe they can actually dare to enact it. All are spotted and encouraged. Out they come and join the line of what I've always thought of as *ideas with legs*: possible Interventions in a seemingly impossible situation that could be replicated across most of the planet, one way or another, with the political North no exception.

As each new Intervention is tried, we see raging, pleading, reasoning, begging, fighting … and nothing works. No easy fixes here. The actors reset themselves deftly between Interventions, giving each a balanced platform in terms of time, weight and respect, and they keep on coming. Another point on my inner researcher's list: Mandala Theatre from Kathmandu have trained actors well in the rapid-fire tightrope act that Forum requires of performers, so as to make each new Intervention count but not give way to magic, tokenism or easy fixes. Snap judgements, made as they are in any skilled Improv, afford each new Intervention a performed response that gives it a chance to unfold; to be read; to impact on this huge audience in ways that might affect one woman one way and the woman sitting next to her in quite another, with consequences we will never know and cannot track or measure, but that a well-run Forum must strive to give a platform to: a credence and a life.

When up comes a man!

('Can they do that?' Rose asks. 'Now you're asking,' I reply.)

The Joker in this Forum is clearly happy and confident at tackling head-on the questions around identification/substitution that have exercised the Theatre of the Oppressed from its inception. Surely a man can give advice from his seat, but not truly replace a woman in any meaningful way? Oh the arguments we've had on that score! None to my mind have been – or can be – resolved: they are perennial, circular, iterative. Woe betide the Joker who fudges their decision, in the few seconds they have to decide whether to allow a man to replace a woman, an Able-Bodied (A/B) a Disabled character, or a White a Black one. You might care, you might sympathize, you might empathize, you might even identify … but can you substitute? For my part, I learn something new every time the issue comes up, but another part of me would love, once and for all (if only for that poor Joker's sake), to be able to refer to a straightforward set of Rules. No such set of rules, as far as I know – as this man climbs the stairs – exists.

No question has been asked of TotO more often than 'What is the role of the Joker' in workshop upon workshop, conference upon conference. It seems so clear to me, standing back, that this repetition (there never was a straight 'answer') is because the question itself is the wrong one. There are, surely, if we correctly understand, only learning points, as we put legs on our ideas and take them for a walk, up into the Forum, into the shoes of the Protagonist? It's the framing of that question about the role of the Joker that is misguided. I've only ever heard it at gatherings where discussion or 'Q and A' was the format, and never more so than when the person in the chair was Augusto himself. Who wouldn't want to elicit, even provoke, another of his marvellous stories? Again and again it was asked and although it seemed plain to me (and still does) that the 'answer' was to learn with and through the work, in honest interrelationship with the groups we do it with, those groups were never present at such privileged discussions, at conferences to which they were rarely invited and in workshops they often could not or would not attend.

It was the set-up that militated against the 'answering' of the question about that all-important and oh-so-powerful role. It was the context. A wonderful story, however well-told, can only ever be that: a shining example. At best, we are left wishing we had been there, or could see, speak or act like that. Unless, that is, the story is framed in such a way as to point us towards principles that we ourselves are invited to put into practice beyond the story's ending, through trial and error, back into the social reality of our own context (or what I am calling Constituency). Sometimes I'm not the Joker. In this frame, Sima Ganguly (whom I call 'Didi' or Sister to this day) is the person who shows me how to use the Joker's power.

Frame Two

Up he comes, then: a very beautiful young man (another ripple from the village women ... and me!) who does something so simple it takes my breath away. I can see him still, years later, as he takes the bundle/baby, borrows the original woman's shawl, looks at the actor playing the husband and simply smiles. And what a smile. It lights up the biggest park in Kolkata. The audience are silent, intent.

The 'husband' looks away again. (I admire this actor! He won't make it easy on anyone and he's so skilled in response.) But this time the 'wife' takes his chin in her hand and – so

*gently – turns his head back again, to look at her, at the baby, at
the lives with which his own life has been woven.*

And he turns away. And she makes him look again.

'Look. I am who you love. This child is from that love. Look.'

In rural Nepal, maybe, this is all she has the power to do. Who
knows what the Elders can force upon a family. I have one friend
in Kathmandu who fosters dozens of abandoned girls whose
lives have begun this way. But this is the Intervention that has
sent the most palpable ripple of identification – and more, of
Witness – through the Spectators and out beyond the confines
of the singular event that has precipitated it. The new mother has
so little power that any attempt at what Augusto calls 'magic'
will be a patronizing failure. But all this man, in his Intervention,
is doing is to make her husband not just look at her, but see
her. Might this be a possible action? Might this Intervention shift
the sense of possibility in the audience towards further action,
towards meaningful change, even towards change in men? The
Joker – Sima – is allowing this to happen. To me, as a man,
sitting here, I can see that in that snap decision to allow this
particular Intervention is a moment, caught in microcosm, of
running the same risk: Augusto's definition of solidarity with the
Protagonist, without which the action on this stage would just
be a game. But on another day, in the same setting, with the
same Forum Model posing exactly the same questions (only with
a different audience) the man's Intervention might not be OK.
Indeed it might be worse than no Intervention at all.

How does the Joker decide?

What is there to prevent a group or an individual from cherry-picking
from the key texts of the Theatre of the Oppressed only the gist of
Forum as a game, whereby we use a set of power tools such as that
afforded Spectators to intervene or abuse the gatekeeping role of the
Joker itself, unwittingly reinforcing oppression in the enactment of what
we might believe is Forum, regardless of our good intentions?

Most of the times I have encountered badly made and conducted Forum it has been well-intentioned but poorly delivered and, most of all, ineptly run. The form, perhaps because of the relative simplicity of its basic shape on the page, is open to a kind of unthinking replication and the delivery of what Boal often termed 'good advice': an energizing exercise in trying out putative 'solutions' maybe, but falling short of that definition of solidarity as *running the same risk*, which surely must include an awareness of setting: of an agreed place and context as well as a consensus around content.

What is to stop any old Intervention being made, with none of what Augusto (in that heart-wrenching little film) called 'seriousness'? And without him, without guidelines or principles or quality control or the right kind of training – underpinned by an agreed interpretation of the literature and the ideology – who on earth, in these split seconds of Forum, *decides?*

Frame Three

Two seats along from me is a woman. She is looking at me. She seems quite shy and she keeps covering her mouth with the edge of her sari. I look away, but I know she has been looking at me with a purpose and so I look (shyly) back. She meets my eye and nods with her head towards the action that has just happened on the stage. The young man who has made the Intervention is receiving the biggest applause of the night but that's not what she's directing me to look at. I'm not telepathic, but I know that look. It says: 'Did you see that? Good, wasn't it?' I smile at her. She smiles back (forgetting to cover her mouth) with a great, wide, traditional, betel-stained, village smile. Something, some truth, some spark of possibility has jumped between us. And we will never see each other again.

In this instance (*framed,* to my present purpose) I've seen Forum at its finest: temporarily transcending the usual boundaries of gender and circumstance; enacting solidarity beyond mere sympathy and so well-managed, so skilfully performed.

I'm glad we came to this one!

For me, it is the networking at such events (conferences, Masterclasses, symposia) and the relationships that are forged there that are their enduring legacy of social and creative capital. I use that word **capital** because I am talking about all the ways that TotO at its best enacts a Marxist reclaiming of the means of production, and that stands as much for creative capital as any other kind. In Kolkata I got very little from the discussions about the future of TotO that inevitably were becoming more heated, confusing and subjective. But I did, from moments such as the above, take away some renewed resolves that over the subsequent years of practice have guided me:

- That I need to ensure at every turn going forward that before the choice of Forum is made, wherever I might find myself using it, I must be sure that choice is being made by and within a Constituency of people who have in some way identified themselves as Oppressed;

- That whenever possible I will avoid 'Jokering' on my own and will try to share that role, modelling dialogic collaboration;

- That in training for trainers, when questions about the role of the Joker come up, I will be careful what kind of 'answer' I might give and vigilant that I ought to be using quality time supporting others in their try-outs of the role rather than putting on a display of my own prowess.

Frame Four

We meet Jane Plastow (Professor of Development Theatre at Leeds and a great debunker of Boalian mythologizing) coming back from a British Council hosted seminar with Professor Ralph Yarrow (University of East Anglia) and others, on busy, noisy Chowringee. Bad vibes abound. There has been a polarizing argument triggered by Jane's challenging the notion of a 'classical' linear structure, claimed often by Boal and giving the impression of a TotO lineage direct from Aristotle via Brecht. To me, Forum and Image Theatre are (and remain) a Toolbox that can be customized according to any context, in furtherance of one clear ideology, but that's all the theory I've got to offer, after seeing Mandala. I'm glad I missed the session. One day I'll need to state my own position, but not on a hot night standing on Chowringee. Jane looks shaken. She has felt attacked. She needs a beer and we repair to the Fairlawn Hotel on Sudur St.

Bárbara Santos has very heatedly advanced the vision of the Theatre of the Oppressed as a Movement, as something organic, as a Tree. I'm sure there's a way of reconciling that Image with the need critically to navigate the many inflated claims and expectations of the work, but right now, on the dusty street, all I have is yet more questions and the sense that a seminar isn't where they can ever be fully addressed. That and that my friends are hurting.

In the next chapter I will return to a chronological telling of how my own journey to that seminal meeting at Muktadhara began, and in that telling to frame what I now see as my own emergent position in TotO as a scholar-artist, coming from the work, taking questions out of practice and returning to it, always with fresh questions.

And always that overarching question: are we a Movement, or do we just use a Method?

Chapter 4
Collaboration

Throughout the 1990s I tried many ways of making performance with community groups around the world, from the schools I always work in (primary especially is my true home!) to prisons with Glyndebourne Education, from the work I began with my beloved Lawnmowers in Gateshead to three years' intense and life-changing reworking of the core TotO system with GRAEAE, the UK's longest-standing disabled-led theatre company. My questing took me many times back to sub-Saharan Africa, spurred on by a very personal commitment to using all the Applied Arts and pedagogical strategies I had been so fortunate to acquire in the fight against AIDS.

Here and in Chapter Five, selected with a triangulation between head and heart from those apparently divergent relationships and makings, are formative encounters that (as I have explained in Chapter Three) are offered as reflexive stories, seeking to access to the reader and especially the student or early-career practitioner the principles in practice of TotO as I have understood them, departed from them, lost them and, most of all, been given them back, altered by those who have challenged me about them and remade them in ways I could never have imagined on my own.

Malawi; 1995

Gripped by ancestral spirits

Throughout the 1990s and after a long period of institutional navel-gazing, the British Council, with the most honourable of intentions, piloted a scheme called ACD: Arts and Culture in Development, which sought to replace a postcolonial, 'parachuting' approach to short-term development projects (notably across Africa) with sustainable relationships, negotiated and shaped by the recipients on the ground and supported for sustainability after each intensive training (T4T) or Intervention.

Sustainability, impact, legacy and Intervention were new terms then and each is worth a chapter on its own, especially on the ways they have been appropriated, watered down and now blandly feature in laminated mission statements everywhere. But the whole architecture of the initiative was hugely promising and I had a relationship of great trust with one of the British Council officers responsible for enacting it with integrity, Keith Lawrence, who brought me into well-configured working relationships with many groups and institutions over that formative decade, where I found my own way, through the journeying required by my practice, to a lived and tested understanding of the techniques of the Theatre of the Oppressed.

I can't state too clearly how easy it is simply to demonstrate Forum. I've done that in the National Theatre in Kampala, under a tree in Malawi, on a beach in Tanzania, in an office in Nairobi, in a compound in Ouagadougou, in a school in Cairo, in a village in Eritrea and in a prison in Sudan.

I was halfway through the wonderfully economic Handshake Forum (a silent proto-Model: most useful!), reworking it with the famous Dah women's theatre company, in Belgrade when I was summarily evacuated, mid-workshop, by grim British Council personnel who'd just been alerted that the city was about to be bombed, by America, from the very RAF base at Wittering where I'd been running Image Theatre and music workshops with composer Jonathan Dove only few months before. That was another time the goodbyes were brief. Such are the paradoxes of our work as artists as it places us in the middle of powerlessness and unknowing, often alone, with only some notional inner compass to hand with which to extricate ourselves. You have, indeed, to *be there*.

That silent Handshake Forum, where the simple task presented by the Model is to elicit a Handshake from a figure of power (an Antagonist) who repeatedly refuses it, provokes most effectively as many tactics as possible from the Spectactors, each being free to make an Intervention as Protagonist. I always use it on Day One of any T4T. We have fun. I check I've indicated all the correct terms (as in this paragraph) as having been not only illustrated but enacted. I make sure that everyone knows that this is a skeleton of how Forum will work when they themselves flesh it out from their own lived experience.

There. That's Day One, session one sorted. Then we begin to make work that is specific to the group who have invited me and as this chapter intends to demonstrate, establish a clear sense that the Toolbox I have brought to share is adaptable (up to a point) for cultural appropriateness and flexibility of not just form but content. The main point of the British Council initiative, for example, was to ensure this and that was what took a decade to determine (I won't say 'to get right'). A substantial part of that time was the brokering of appropriate relationships with institutions and NGOs that were capable of maintaining a group of trainee practitioners beyond the necessarily limited time span of the T4T itself, which as I have said is relatively simple – at least in the early stages – to deliver. What that boiled down to (and I haven't seen it bettered) was that an NGO would be identified that was already embedded in work with target groups and was clearly showing a participatory relationship with them rather than a patriarchal (and patronizing) top-down set-up such as exemplified by far too many charities. This host group would have identified artists, social workers, health consultants and others who didn't need to be convinced that a participatory arts approach was the most effective in the Constituencies that they knew far better than we did. They just wanted to get hold of the power tools of Forum, experience them in a safe (and supported) T4T context and then try them out with the groups they already worked with while the facilitator was still about to give them – and enable others to give – constructive feedback. Lastly, the aim of all ACD projects was to create what my research mentor Prof. Jen Harvie has subsequently termed Bespoke Templates that can be left behind in the safe hands of those who have co-created them, through the negotiated and iterative processes described, so as to ensure that sustainability, impact and legacy are things that happen and not just aspirations.

How does that work on the ground? Of many examples I might have chosen the first that has chosen me, as it were, is a month

I spent in Malawi in 1995 as a guest of the British Council in Lillongwe, with a coalition of artists (musicians, dancers, actors and writers) AIDS Educationists and community development workers, under the umbrella and in partnership with ATOBA, an NGO created for the purpose of community-led initiatives to combat AIDS and led by the late Isaac Chirwa, a charismatic and fiercely independent leader and himself a chief, who was at every turn very happy to remind me who was boss. I miss him. He was one of the best and toughest people I ever shared this ever-evolving work with. I offer an account here of what we made and most importantly failed at making, together with that excellent band of artists, many of whom were already stars of radio soap operas (there was no domestic TV and of course no internet) and who received me with generosity, tolerance of my blunderings and subsequently real bravery as we began to face the enormity of the task we had set ourselves – namely, to create together over a month, six AIDS Educational Forum Models, each in a different language (there are over 30 mother tongues in what is known as Malawi) and to be tested *in situ* in three separate geographical locations for suitability, effectiveness and cultural appropriateness.

Frame One
(Lillongwe, Malawi; 1995)

Beginnings are such important times. We've had a press conference at the airport: the radio stars in the ATOBA cohort, whilst eager to get on with trying some of the techniques first hand, are well aware of the attention they can not only command but redirect to the furtherance of the overall project aims. Madonna's time here has yet to come. I'm asked a few questions, but the starry-eyed interviewer is much more interested in the real stars, who have already introduced a high-profile HIV theme to one of the long running soaps that are what all Malawians in the 1990s tune into, having very limited access to TV and no means of creating television on their own terms.

'Yes', says Ruth, 'We are most pleased to be able to employ Mr. Ali. The last Professional Development Programme was Spanish Guitar and although the man was very nice *indeed* (everybody nods vigorously) his system was not quite suited to our purposes.'

Interviewer: 'And what would those purposes be?' (He's so star struck it hurts.)

'We are ATOBA: a coalition of artists against AIDS.'

'Yes but what was the system?'

'Oh it was very good, very clever, wasn't it my colleagues?' (Even more vigorous nodding.)

'Then could it not be adapted as you are hoping to do with Mr. Ali?' (I'm keeping *shtum* here.)

'No, although the cardboard guitars were most ingenious and cheap too. We learned all the fretwork listening to a tape, and then we'd hear a piece from the Maestro himself – Villa Lobos, I think it was – and then we would replicate this on the cardboard guitars so as to perfect our fingering.'

'Actually' (this is another ATOBA delegate) 'it was just the neck of the guitar we used, to be precise.'

Ruth   'Yes, the neck. We didn't need a whole guitar to learn the fingering. Just the neck. Cardboard. Clever. Then he gave the concert and then he went home. He was a very nice man.'

Interviewer   'And does anyone in ATOBA still play the repertoire he taught?'

Ruth   'Oh no, Sir, not at all. None of us has a guitar, you see.'

Beginnings are such important times as I say. The next day I got out my very own cardboard guitar (the Handshake Forum!) and we had a ball. But there's no way I was going to determine the repertoire!

Straight away I was out of the comfort zone, from the moment I clarified what a Model was and airily asserted my confidence that as performance is a universal language we could go straight to making Models in the six languages we had preselected for geographical spread.

Someone should translate the basics to me when we came to running
our first Forums, starting with different Jokers (I was adamant we'd try
for male/female pairings of the role) and then we'd head to traditional
villages upcountry which was where the first iteration of the work was
headed. I would use cartooning and storyboarding as we went along,
and then we could create templates in the light of what worked, where
and why. A marvellous pedagogical strategy, I reckoned: collaborative
and egalitarian all the way through.

Frame Two
(Upcountry, Malawi; 1995)

George the Drummer and I are sitting under a tree. It's a huge
Cottonwood and you have to see one to believe it. I feel dwarfed,
hot and overwhelmed, but at the same time I've never felt more
welcome in a new place. The village is a long way upcountry and
ATOBA have really meant it when they've set up things either
to work in traditional rural contexts, or not work at all. There is
already good public education around AIDS/HIV in the cities, but
this is a very traditional culture we are looking at: beautiful mud

Figure 4 Forum Zomba 1. A Forum Theatre scene (Model)
looking at the impact of HIV on village women; Domasi village,
Zomba, Malawi.

houses like beehives, painted with dazzling abstract designs; each compound comprising several circles of them with open space between each extended family unit; a central meeting place for the community under this gigantic tree; the bush shimmering in the heat; the forest beyond. A wonderful, peaceful place. But a place where traditional cutting of both girls and boys (using the same razor, repeatedly) and other cultural and religious practices are one of the possible vectors of HIV infection that we will have to expose as doubly problematic in our performance and that in the ensuing AIDS/HIV Forum must now be questioned, however ingrained they are in traditional life. And that means Patriarchy.

I'm pretty confident I'm going to recognize the Patriarchy part when I see the Model in action. George is going to do his best to translate as we go along, but he's a confirmedly urban guy himself and he has no more idea how the villagers are going to react then I have.

And here they come, gathering.

The Elders gather first. They squat on woven mats, brought out by younger men. They clearly have a designated place, in maximum shade. Then comes the Chief, who alone makes eye contact with me as an equal (everyone else sneaks looks when they think I'm not looking). Very few white people have ever come here, George whispers. I've worked that out! The Chief has a chair carried out for himself: a rough, wooden construction that is very simple and beautiful. He indicates that he doesn't want me sitting on the ground as I'm a guest and so another one is found. There clearly aren't many chairs in the village. I sit next to him and he really is gracious: patting me on the hand, gesturing to the gathering crowd that I am very welcome. The younger men sit in front of the Elders and the women on the other side, quite separate. Finally, all the children gather and fill in quiet, orderly rows at the front. For a second I remember how much jostling and argument there would be in one of the London parks where I learned my trade, on summer play-schemes doing participatory theatre, *back in the day*. Not here. The village is orderly and organized and they clearly sit here often for debates, gatherings and all kinds of community events. I notice that children get to see and hear everything, but I'm pretty sure they won't speak.

As the Forum begins, I get a sense that we have met our first criterion of appropriateness pretty well: we will be complementing a culture of whole-community participation and spectatorship that is obviously well-established, in a tribe where performance isn't seen as a separate activity delegated to professionals. Indeed – as I am to learn – it is quite the opposite.

The first Model goes well: I can see that the Protagonist has contracted HIV whilst on business in the city, and he is now a threat to his family and his wives in particular, although as yet nobody knows it. The village/city dichotomy (the innocence of Home versus the fleshpots of Lillongwe) has become a key theme with us. It reminds me of the tropes of Restoration Comedy: Country and Town.

Suddenly, the actor falls to the ground and thrashes about, raising huge clouds of orange dust, while the audience gawp, laugh, point and cringe alternately. It's a truly staggering display of gymnastic ability, apart from anything else. His back arches at one point in a perfect bow, with only his heels and the crown of his head touching the ground.

Business-like, I make a quick note that if we are to display AIDS-related dementia so early in a story about its invisible progression, maybe we are undermining the point we are intending to make by creating a Forum. It's spectacular, but it needs to be dialled down, otherwise we've only made a Cautionary Tale and no one will dare to make an Intervention.

'Are you making a note of his superb performance?' asks George.

'Um, sort of. Why is he doing this now? I don't remember that from rehearsal.'

'He is being gripped by ancestral spirits. They are telling him the right things to do and say.'

'Ok, but that doesn't leave much for the people to bring to the Forum does it? I mean about trying out ways to change behaviour, when guys mess about with Bar Girls in the city and then come home?'

'He's being told to practise Chokolo.'

'George, I don't know what that is.' I'm trying not to hiss. The Chief is unperturbed.

'That's because we don't have it in Lillongwe! It's Wife Inheritance!'

The chief now realizes we are whispering urgently about something and smiles and nods encouragingly. He thinks we are enjoying the performance. The audience is utterly transfixed. The Protagonist is dusting himself off. The story goes on: he goes back to his wives, he sickens, he dies. The Joker stops the Model.

'George, I don't see what we can have the Forum about. He's dead and he slept with all of his wives. *Everyone's going to die*, George!'

'That's not the question we are bringing Mr. Ali. It is to do with Chokolo. His brothers are now obliged to marry the wives. It's their social security system!' He beams at me. He has the best smile ever, with a big gap in his front teeth. I love him to bits but my entire plan is falling apart and everybody, upcountry, is watching. I have no idea what to do.

This is the place I am revisiting now, to extrapolate what I understand to be the proper relationship between us, when we impart, recreate and adapt the techniques of Forum to communities we aspire to empower, but who are in the end the experts on their own experience, not us. Maybe a story about Malawi isn't the best way to do this, but it's the way I know. I tell it because it speaks to me as a crucial moment: an uncomfortable epiphany as all the best moments of truth must be, if I am to evidence the *not-knowing* (not the *knowing*) that is a vital part of learning what cannot be learned in any other way.

I was able to see (thanks to George) on this particular day, that what had been made – the Model – was nothing I had seen before, expecting as I had been to see an interaction between husband and wife about condoms, or a village debate (such as happened regularly under the Cottonwood, in airings of all manner of disputes over land or property). Instead of these knowns, the Model I saw had been truly taken out of my hands. The conflict was around something I knew nothing about, but in its making and performance here marked a tipping point, where this well-informed group of trainee Forum makers knew the most impactful Interventions might be made. And where I did not know. Even if I'd understood the mother tongue being used, I would still not have understood this.

Frame Three
(Upcountry Malawi)

We've agreed that we will Hotseat the main characters in each Model, so as to clarify who has the problem and who has the power. It's a strategy to build a bridge between the performance and what can often be reticent audiences: certainly this has most often been the case with those I have worked with on AIDS Education projects elsewhere. I first tried the idea in Uganda five years ago and in rehearsals here it has been lit upon with glee. The actors in the group know it already, as a kind of rehearsal game to enable character development and so it has been relatively easy to factor into the template so as to make sure the Spectactors know what is going on and begin to move in action as well as attitude towards a place of informed Intervention further down the line.

The husband is being Hotseated and clearly there is an order to who speaks and when at this community gathering. Only the Elders (male) are speaking, followed by the young men, followed by an opportunity for the women; female Elders first. Nobody thinks the children should speak at all, although to be fair all the children are there and are able to witness.

The troupe seem to have decided on a single Joker today and it's a man. He knows what he's doing and he pulls out the questions really well. I still don't really know what Chokolo is, but the traffic of ideas is energetic, each suggestion being greeted with roars of approval or a really striking, completely synchronized 'Uh-*Uh!'* from every single person gathered, so in unison it is to me quite uncanny: not loud but packing an *Oomph* of collective vocal power that speaks of a strong participatory culture and a shared vocabulary, signalling assent when it is deserved and an equally powerful silence when it is not.

'Mr. Ali, can you see that lady?' George is looking toward a woman, who the Joker is about to turn to. Correctly reading the village, the context and the shared community tradition of who speaks first, he is moving towards Forum without disrupting more basic traditions. Rome wasn't built in a day.

'That lady. Look. She is angry!'

Hotseating the male Protagonist has gone on for some time without any real disagreement about his dilemma. George has explained to me (we are still whispering behind the Chief's back like naughty schoolboys) that he knows he is going to die and that the point of the Forum is not to 'save' him but to see where and how the custom of Chokolo needs to be contested in the light of what the villagers know about AIDS.

They know plenty, it turns out. He (the Joker) works with public education and radio, after all and he knows what they already know. They know he will die, and that his wives are likely to be infected, and that if his brothers marry them and take over the care of his children (as they are traditionally bound now by Chokolo to do) that they will eventually die too. Right now, the advice he is getting in the Hotseat from first male Elders and then younger men is just that: advice. It is challenging nothing and will change nothing. The Joker is giving that advice space – he is a really good Joker and he has done his homework on this community' traditions – but the Forum looks set to be difficult unless …

The angry woman stands up. For an instant I'm reminded of one of Augusto's famous stories about the woman in Lima, who in the near-mythology of the origins of Forum was the first to march out onto the playing area and actually make what we now call a full Intervention.

But no. She is an older woman and commands huge respect as she straightens up. She looks to be near 60 and that is old in a country where even before AIDS the average age of mortality is under 50. It's George's turn to be bewildered. I think she's going to try some kind of Intervention and that she will use the Hotseat to warm herself (and other women) up, before trying things out and challenging the operation of Chokolo as I now understand it. But no. She is glaring past the Joker and looking very directly over the Protagonist's head.

Right at us. Or to be precise, at the Chief.

That day is vivid and precious to me, still yielding up its meanings to me 25 years on. It is a moment on the other side of *not-knowing* and of apparent failure: that moment where, through a necessary relinquishing of control or understanding, we learn the thing we could never have learned any other way. That moment is a gift. It is a moment where a hidden part of the pedagogy of the Theatre of the Oppressed revealed itself to me through interrelationship with my collaborators and was opened up to us through a radical disruption of our expectations, both of ourselves and the community we aspired to serve as artists and educators. It is that moment I return to again and again as it is held in a Now that only the making of performance can reach and no other mode or method can uncover or disseminate. Because there is only one Time in performance. The Now.

Frame Four

'She wants to talk to the *real* Chief!' George – who is one of the coolest people I've ever met – really looks rattled at this point. Dotted around the edges of the audience the rest of our group of maybe 15 are looking one to the other for what to do and how to help the Joker as we have agreed will happen if anything untoward crops up. And my, is this *untoward*.

'Let her', I say and it's the only thing I say while the whole iconoclastic episode lasts. George hisses at the Joker. The gap in his teeth is a boon at a time like this. The Joker invites her to carry on. Or will she make an Intervention?

But she stays firmly planted where she is, with a crowd of older women seated around her. One or two Elders look a bit discombobulated (and that has never done any harm in my book) but the whole community hears her out. Not just hears, witnesses.

As I later learn, she is using the usual setting, the Constituency of which she is a respectful and respected member, to voice from that place of the *status quo* a new truth and to make a controversial – even heretical – demand in a daring way. She tells the Chief (and George whispers to me as she does so) that it is in his gift as a spiritual leader and steward of tradition to address this dilemma, here and now, from the seat of power. It is moreover his responsibility to change the tradition of Chokolo so that if a wayward man comes home, neither his brothers not his wives should be condemned to death as a consequence of his behaviour. If he will sleep around in the city he must be told to use a condom. If he does return to his wives, infected or not, then he must use a condom still. If he hasn't used a condom and his wives sicken, then his brothers must honour Choloko as before. But condoms condoms, condoms, she tells the Chief. And where they aren't readily available, then let all the men change their behaviour and *let you be their example!*'

George finishes explaining. Silence falls. For a terrible moment I think we've exposed someone who will be punished after we go and it will be our fault. But the Chief doesn't react like that at all. He nods, and the Forum goes on, and although only men step up, every single Intervention has been shaped by what that one woman has said, from a place where she is strong and safe, breaking that theatrical convention of Hotseating but creating through her transgression (and the riskier social one it represents) a new channel for debate, directly between herself, the other seated women and the Chief, diverting the existing tradition of respectful public debate to make her points with Hotseating as the platform from which to make them.

Afterwards we realize the Forum we planned has failed, as a plan. *But the woman has succeeded.*

Allowing this vivid scene to unfold (as it has done for the twenty plus years since I was part of it), I realize as I recreate it and frame it to the present purpose that it is about *everything but the Forum*. The Forum was simple. We made it in a morning, which ran roughly as these things always do: two hours' discussion to one hour of rehearsal and, that Malawian speciality, a quick scene improvised in ten minutes designed for that village meeting under the tree. That latter task would of course take a UK troupe all day and so in every part of this cycle of making and testing and learning, unfolding itself more deeply as it is at the time of writing and remembering it, I am reminded that the idea of a Forum is simplicity itself:

- make a Model;
- check that it poses a challenge genuinely shared;
- stand up that challenge to your audience with the best theatrical skill you possess;
- choose a well-trained Joker who can democratize the flow of Interventions with minimal mediation;
- close down safely what you have opened up;
- ensure that your artistic disruption of a group or community includes your facilitation of a return to lived social reality;
- end with an invitation to your hosts to take what they want from what they have seen and done, integrate it into their lives and leave the rest.

A paragraph says it, more or less. I've already related as a playlet the last time I went through the whole system, in my office, twenty-three years on in 2018, in ten enjoyable minutes, one more time. But it takes a book – maybe many? – and a lifetime of trial and error to understand the rest.

So what have I understood? Firstly, the thing that can never be stated too many times:

- that the Theatre of the Oppressed is an exercise in solidarity with communities and not a reading programme;

- that I don't *need* to understand what is happening in all of the languages my collaborators might choose to use, if I have done the work of imparting the techniques as clearly as I can, setting them out for the perusal and experiment of the troupe with minimal mediation on my part.

And more than this, specifically from what was learned in Malawi:

- that my *unknowing* (whether of a language, or the detail of the host community's lived experience) requires me to improvise within the limitations of my role as Joker;
- that I must strive as Joker to open a safe space for Interventions that go (if necessary) beyond the system of Forum;
- that I am responsible for holding that space with a vigilant eye to the wellbeing of all participants;
- that I must not be tempted to mediate from any personal sense of appropriateness, sticking to the neutrality the role of Joker affords.

This opens up a new role: that of a listening Witness. An Ally. If I am trying to control outcomes, whether they be according to my personal views on how AIDS Education in Malawi should look or how a Forum should correctly play out, then I am in danger of imposing a fixed, pre-decided template for content and doing so by the covert policing of form. There is, of course, a form: it has only taken a paragraph to describe above. Its beauty (and it is indeed beautiful!) is its simplicity and it requires neither grandiose claims as to its artistic provenance, nor exaggerated expectations as to what it can deliver. It is simple and it is powerful and it is a superb system of artistic production that can be shared with all groups who have been denied access to the means of creative agency on whatever grounds. It is the enactment of a radically egalitarian ideology that inheres in the doing and not in the discussion or the analysis. Augusto always loved discussion and of course we require it to prepare and to share ideas, but it is to the performative Now of the village in Malawi that I always refer and return, shaping as it still does my words, my choices and the learning I have been privileged to pass on out of that shared making two decades ago.

I must be prepared, if I am to walk my talk as outlined in the two paragraphs and two shortlists above, to be changed by the Forum, as much by the woman whose name I never learned, but who handed me back, turned inside out and reconfigured, everything that matters to me about TotO, by seeming to reject it.

Frame Five

Whatever has happened, the Chief and the woman in the audience are smiling at one another as the woman sits back down. I look across at Isaac and he clearly isn't so happy. The Joker hasn't followed the agreed plan which was to fast-forward to the brothers' various dilemmas as they decide whether to follow Chokolo or abandon the women and children, as often happens now in Malawi, where the average life expectancy has been lowered by AIDS to 45. He looks angry in fact, and we are later to have a rather heated conversation about whether we have succeeded or failed. The next scene is far more to his liking: a father who finds a condom in his son's room, freaks out completely (even though they are being given out free in enlightened Malawian schools) threatens to kick him out and divorce his wife for abetting immorality in the home, etc. Real born-again stuff and not a Bible in sight.

A stock figure we have called the Uncle appears, whom all the men in the troupe seem to delight in playing and who is clearly a staple of the radio soaps. His appearance explains why I'm going through so much toothpaste too, as this is always generously used to give him pretend white eyebrows and a peppermint flavoured goatee. He is instantly recognized and after the disruption of the first not-Forum (this is Forum Number Two) he seems to replace the transgressive space that interchange temporarily opened up, with the reassurance that stock characters bring. He calms down Dad, wipes Mum's tears away, takes Son aside and gives him a quiet lecture on the facts of life, before shambling off (leaving a faint whiff of Colgate) to the loudest applause of the day.

That's it.

This time it's my turn to be exasperated! Where's the conflict? How do we make Interventions? But the Joker is on it: he rewinds to the opening argument and takes all kinds of ideas from the audience (again using Hotseating as a bridge to full participation) and then various Spectactors intervene, including an impressive queue of young people (girls and boys both) who use the Conveyor Belt to try one line each to both Dad and Mum about how this is what they are all required to think about at school and they need parental support. Their parents didn't grow up with AIDS. They are.

They've all sat down before I realize that they, too, have broken a convention by standing up!

Again, unpicking this, I catch myself using the term 'exasperated'. None of us can operate without expectation and it is in the nature of all human activity that we will find those expectations unmet. But I have to be merciful to myself, then as now. I needed to plan to be able to create the training and Isaac needed to do far more than that to put together the troupe and identify funding, resources and source villages that it would be safe to try our new work in. He needed to be a real Chief himself to marshal support for the sustainability without which the whole thing would be a one-off: parachuting with a cardboard guitar.

We must plan, but we should eschew *projection*. That's what my practice of letting go is about, when it is played out in relation to the expectations and agenda of the person or organization who is hosting me. I was hired to facilitate adaptation and customization and to do so with appropriateness. The reality is that somewhere between the first near-Forum (which Isaac thought wasn't) and the second (which Isaac was pleased with and I found predictable) is a fluid relativity around the notion of 'success' that must remain just that: relative. When we unpacked and evaluated later, Isaac said just one thing about that day to me, with a wry smile: 'We have seen the TotO succeed and we have seen it fail.'

He just wouldn't say which was which.

Frame Six

Before we leave the village, I notice that George looks disappointed. I try to reassure him.

'Look George, it wasn't at all what we planned, but it worked, right? I mean some things worked. If we take it apart and share what we learned tomorrow back in town, we'll have something really valuable to build on. There's no such thing as a mistake, if we look at it that way.'

He continues to shake his head.

'Mr. Ali, you've come from London and we've all taken the time to drive upcountry from Lillongwe and Mr. Chirwa has taken years to arrange all this. And we didn't see the Masks.'

'The …?' I might have missed a few things today but never in my whole career have I so much as mentioned masks. Hate 'em!

'Here we are in the most famous district for the Masks and they haven't visited us. They haven't come. I'm sad for us and I'm even more sad for you.'

'OK' (the air conditioned SUV awaits).

At that *exact* moment, the most terrifying moment of my performance life happens. There is a whooping from the edge of the forest, which looms, tall and ancient, a sombre curtain beyond the furthest huts. Something is thrashing through the seething trees – and fast! – towards the clearing. Some unknown thing is approaching us. Is it an elephant? I'm about to bolt. I feel a surge of primal fear. George grabs me by the arm, turns me back to face what's coming. He's grinning, but it's not his happy grin.

Out of the forest, first one, then three giant, gnarled, wooden masks appear, with only the legs of the people inside them showing. They have staring eyes and jagged needle teeth. They rush down the slope towards us, raising dust. The entire crowd parts in an instant, like a shoal of fish, in that unison I've heard ('Uh-*Uh*') but now I'm actually seeing. The whole community: gone in an instant, leaving an empty space.

The Masks dance. Their feet are pounding the orange ground. It's at exactly the rate of my heartbeat. I've a sudden feeling they're dancing in my head and their rhythm is thudding along my blood. Their dusty bare feet keep pounding, pounding until from the compounds comes a drumming that isn't an echo but an answer. I notice there are people peeking out from the thatch, from behind the woven goat pens, from the roofs.

They dance. Time stops. Dust rises and drifts towards us, smelling like spices, like life, like death. Then they're gone.

On the way home I ask who they were. I mean, really were, behind the masks. I would very, very much like to know! George is strangely subdued, but pleased we have all witnessed the Masks. Ruth, too, had never seen them before. I tell him that I think I maybe saw the Masks before but I can't remember whether in a book, a museum or a dream.

'A dream', he replies, 'if that's what you want to call it.'

'But who operates them, George? I'd swear I recognized one person's trousers under the Mask, I'm sure of it.'

'That's only information. The Masks decide when to come and who to come to. The owner of the trousers has no choice.'

Now I really know what I don't know. And so we go home.

GRAEAE theatre; 1995–8

'What do you want?'

Throughout the mid-1990s I was privileged to take up a role offered me by Ewan Marshall, the then artistic director of the longest-standing professional company led by disabled performers, GRAEAE, whose name comes from the Greek myth about the women who shared an ear, an eye and a mouth and helped Theseus on his way to slay Medusa.

The company have been strategic since inception in combining devised work made on their own terms (and often issue-based) with mainstream, innovative productions such as *Flesh Fly*, the first performance of theirs I ever saw at Oval House, South London, and to this day the most striking take on Jonson's *Volpone* I can remember. Always seeking to expand their capacity around the uses of theatre as a tool for social and attitudinal change, GRAEAE have for years accompanied repertoire productions with workshops, training and activism, and memorably, under the current artistic director, Jenny Sealey, gave an eye-popping heft of agency, visibility and pure performative joy to the Opening Ceremony of the Paralympics in London in 2012: a benchmark moment for anyone interested in making theatre by, with or for communities who don't normally see it, let alone make it on any scale or with any budget. Mat Fraser drumming with Coldplay and Sir Ian McKellen surrounded by flying wheelchairs. Marvellous!

I will take this tranche of my own Continuing Professional Development (CPD) work with GRAEAE as the second example of what for me across that decade was a cycle of the iterative practice-based research into Forum and Image Theatre that transformed it for me, in the doing as well as in the understanding of what that doing might mean, opened up to me by some of the most creative partners I have ever been lucky to work with. I was asked to train a troupe not of disabled actors (the fifteen people I worked were that already) but Jokers, so as to boost the capacity of the company to create their own work, on their own terms, with adaptation of TotO techniques to physical disability as only one of the political, educational and artistic starting points. The best bit of the brief was to this day the clearest I have ever been given and my favourite by far: if I knew I'd done my job right, it would be because they no longer needed me and were set up and confident to carry forward whatever template for disabled-led Forum we had co-created, without me.

I'd be fired!

Having said this, as I approached our training venue in Year One (the Winchester Project in North London) I was more nervous than I've ever been, anywhere. What a time of transition for all of us the 1990s was! What is still known (and vilified) in some circles as PC was, far from 'running riot', under concerted ideological attack from government and the right-wing press and the funding structures and organizational frameworks that I had been fortunate enough to develop my practice in – the Inner London Education Authority (ILEA), the Greater London

Council (GLC) and the Local Education Authorities (LEAs) – were under systematic attack as hotbeds of Loony Leftism. In retrospect they seem now havens for the nurturing and enablement of minority groups such as the LGBT community to which I belong. We need only look to the America of today to see how swiftly such networks and funding institutions can be dismantled and how the press collude in their depiction as hotbeds of Socialist subversion.

I walked into the rehearsal space (actually a community hall) in Swiss Cottage knowing that I would only have this work for three short bursts over three years; that it really mattered to me to get it right; that getting it right would mean quite rightly standing aside as disabled facilitators replaced me. That would be the logical (and indeed the 'politically correct') outcome of my leading this training, even if that meant not being able to work with a company I admired and, to be honest, envied any longer. A good dilemma on paper. A fantastic challenge artistically and ideologically. A pile of unpaid utility bills, in my personal social reality.

Frame One

The hall smells of cabbage. Why has the space my artistic development most often been conducted in so often smelled of cabbage? It's because I have come up through Educational Theatre, two shows a day, ten shows a week, three terms a year, 100 children per show, and the school hall is where it has all happened: where BREAKOUT used to happen. I'm on my own now, but I've learned such important things in Malawi that I can't wait to dive back into a new context, new people (smiling at me; circle of chairs ready; tea urn steaming in the corner; Ewan introducing me) and anyway someone has to cook cabbage and it might as well be a community centre that feeds a lot of old people at lunchtime.

I burble on about what I've been doing and stumble over my (PC) choice of words by saying 'differently abled' instead of 'disabled' to a group of actors and workshop leaders who know perfectly well they are disabled and don't need my use of a PC term (to make myself feel more comfortable) among my credentials as I summarize them. I'm being scrutinized in particular by the twinkliest blue eyes I've ever seen: Jamie Beddard's. They are full of mischief and humour. He's sussing me out and I'm floundering a bit, but basically everything's OK.

I'm going to do myself a favour, shut up and introduce the work by diving in. Since Malawi, Do-then-Talk-then-Do-More has been my motto and it's the way I now introduce the idea that our training should follow that iterative, cyclical path, with each choice I make being transparently discussed in the light of the previous set of exercises and makings. Even more so here: our aim is the customization of techniques and as the only able-bodied person in the room I will only know how to do that if the group Do First, then tell me how it has worked. It's exactly as Augusto taught me. The storyboard of the day's exercises and their ensuing adaptation will appear on the wall behind me, cartooned by anyone who fancies a bit of drawing and voiced for access by the two or three blind and visually impaired participants.

I've chosen the *Great Game of Power*, where the group have to negotiate and then create Images of what that word power means to them and how power structures are inscribed in even the smallest, most individual transactions of our lives. We are going to use a table, six chairs and a cup to make the Images and as yet nobody will add themselves in to flesh them out with a performing body: their own. I've used this game ever since I learned it in Nottingham and seen it explained further in *Games for Actors and Non-Actors*. It's one of Augusto's best, and I think that's partly because it was developed with the Paris CTO group in a context where translation and adaptation were already informing everything and everybody in the room that appears in the illustrations. I've never known it fail and it takes us into an always very grounded discussion about what power structures we might go on to expose and explore with actual scenes or – as I've decided to describe on Day Two – Models.

I explain the rules and invite people to make as many Images of power structures as they are able to, in ten minutes, allowing for both deaf signing and voicing for blind participants. Jamie's periwinkle eyes don't leave me for an instant.

'Are there any questions' I ask, brightly, rather fancying that there won't be as I've set the whole thing up rather well.

Jamie is a man of few words and the difficulty he sometimes faces with speech is not the reason.

He sits on one of the chairs, puts both feet up on the table with a crash and fixes me in his gaze once more. He says, loudly:

'Yes. WHAT DO YOU WANT?'

All great learning moments involve discomfort, I've found. This one reverberates with no less clarity but even more meaning than it did that day, as the room froze at what all knew was a challenge. And do you know what? I can't remember what I said! I knew I wasn't being attacked. I was being invited to restate, at the top of the practice, for all of us (myself included) why I was there, certainly, but this moment is far more than that to me. Nothing could have reset my way of just being in the room, not just talking about what my intentions were, but being made aware of how I was positioned personally, pedagogically and politically, right there, right now. Who I was being and what that meant. The able-bodied man, talking about modes of two-way learning as a democratized process whereby no one person knows everything and nor is any one person an empty vessel, waiting to be charitably filled. Of course I wasn't intentionally behaving that way. Apart from anything else, we hadn't even started yet and so I hadn't had a chance to show what my intentions were and how my pedagogical strategy aspired to enact them. Democratized. Egalitarian.

But what did I *want*? Just to work. Just to do my best. To get beyond my own preconceptions about what we might or might not be able to do in this particular setting. Just to be able to teach well, adapt well. *To be able*. Jamie shocked me into re-contacting my own sense of my own ability, not anyone else's in the room, all in that moment. What anyone else might be able to do was really none of my business, from that moment. He was and still is a man of not so many words as of striking, powerful, effective theatrical skill and especially of merciless comic timing. And he'd just used it to reset me into awareness of my own role and position: the power relationship that doesn't need to be spoken about by the able-bodied as they enjoy unearned privilege by default in all the rooms they enter, cabbage or no cabbage.

I never used the words differently abled again. We made Images and as ever the technique worked beautifully, and although the Images resembled many I had seen before in schools, in prisons, in theatres, these looked different. They looked different because I had been abruptly shocked, by Jamie's one precise and theatrically pointed gesture, into an awareness of my own position in relation to the system, the group, the room and the world beyond the room. Awareness of my unawareness.

Frame Two

In the break, generously and kindly, I am taught a little about disability as a socially constructed thing. About my choice of a technique of Image construction, however well set up and explained, as being informed by the ways that the world has always enabled, applauded and foregrounded my skills in constructing practically everything, unbeknownst to me and therefore unexamined. I've been looked at by Jamie's most seeing eyes and the action that he has performed has rendered me visible to myself. I stand, not corrected but educated. It's exactly as it should be.

Some things you just need to sleep on.

However, I haven't slept well, as although Day One has unfolded very well from that *initiation* – as I now understand it to have been – it has, equally, required a lot of processing. I'm going to keep to the plan (*plan but don't project!*) but stay quietly in touch with what I know in my bones to have been a true moment of Conscientization between Jamie, the group and myself. Scary for a few minutes, grounding and empowering for life if properly understood. I believe I have understood it. I feel right-sized and

I'm beginning to experience the amount of skill in the group for myself as I hadn't over the warm-up, to start learning some sign language, to incorporate a stamp on the floor alongside my stop/ start instructions in exercises (for deaf access) and so on.

I always move through Image Theatre towards the making of new Models for Forum. Images are the building blocks and to my mind (and this remains the case) their making, reading, ordering into coherent performance and then the rehearsal of that creative sequence as a whole are often far more democratized than the running of a Forum itself where so much of the ideological traffic is conducted by one Joker. I'm worried about that, but it's not happening until Day Five when we will present what we have created to an invited audience.

I always start with Granny's Footsteps. It's a playground game known by many different names all over the world and all over the world I always choose it so as to make our starting point what the group knows and not just me. The specialist games and exercises, for me, must always follow and not only seem to be 'mine'. I'm already well into introducing it, saying that although the whole system is games and exercises based, with a reclaiming of play – the ludic – as a political act in itself, leading to de-mechanization of the performing body, when I stop. No, I baulk. There are three blind and visually impaired people in the room. I haven't thought this through. How can they play when if you are Granny you have to spin round and send back to the starting line anybody you can *see* moving? I've no time to think. I can't admit I haven't thought about adaptation (that's Day Three!) and that's because, well it's because …

'Problem?' Kate Portal and Liz Porter have heard rather than seen this mini crisis. Multitalented, generous women to work with, Kate is blind and Liz is visually impaired. They've already tweaked one or two things we did together yesterday. We're getting to know one another and to like what we know and so there's no hiding this embarrassing glitch from them.

'Is it because I'm blind?' asks Kate. How can I say the answer is yes? Or rather, my answer is yes? Or rather my problem is my problem?

'Because if it is, Ali, please don't worry on my account. If something is going to be too difficult or too dangerous to adapt for me so that I can do it, I'll tell you. If the learning I'm going to get is smaller than the hassle of explaining it all just so I can pretend to participate, I'll also tell you. OK?'

And it is OK. We play. Granny has all the power and has always had the right to send you back, whether she does that out of seeing you move, hearing you move or simply glorying in her turn at being a total despot and pointing randomly it doesn't matter. That's what despots do and several of us are gleefully contacting our inner despot today.

Blind Granny is no different when it's her turn. The game is a hoot. It's changed though. Kate and Liz have changed it, not me. It's even more about power than before, now. And as the day goes on and the Images proliferate as they always do, the different ways we can voice them or feel them only add to the richness of empowerment through co-creation that this abundant part of the TotO always opens up to a group whose intentions are clear and uncluttered by unspoken expectations or secret power play.

Liz moulds Kate into an Image. Iona voices for Kate using Objective Description: a term I learned today for the first time. 'Her left arm is held at an angle of 45 degrees to her body, the hand palm open and up, stretched out towards the audience. Her face is tilted slightly downwards. We can't see her expression. Her right hand is clamped tightly over her mouth. Her left leg is tucked behind her right. She is balancing.'

It is a performance text already and its starting point has nothing to do with the disability of those making and reading the Image or the need for myself as facilitator to 'catch up' with adapting the techniques I am being taught, as I share those I already know. The starting point is just as I've said. It is the power relations that are normally not made visible, or voiced, inscribed in all the interactions in the room, whether they are part of the formal process or not. The Image is being voiced. Theatre is, as Augusto always said, knowledge in itself.

For those three years' galvanizing, transformative collaboration with GRAEAE I saw the system taken in directions I couldn't have imagined but had indeed hoped for, on paper at least. We made many different Models: a process requiring of me considerable unknowing of what I thought I knew (about TotO, about me), but through negotiation, playfulness and a shared sense that we were synthesizing new techniques rather than cobbling something out of old ones.

How hard it is for those of us who haven't experienced powerlessness to let go of power so that knowledge can come in! It is the essence of privilege that those who have it don't even know they do and so merely feel 'got at' when confronted with this abiding truth. That's why when there is a movement against unaccountable power, the Oppressor so often uses the language of a victim. The Oppressor knows far less about the reality of the society he dominates than do the Oppressed. Confronted with his racism, he says, weakly, 'All lives matter!' and doesn't understand how that statement is the opposite of inclusive or empathetic. Challenged about his sexism, he complains about 'toxic feminism'. Confronted with his own simplistic and patriarchal fundamentalism, he cries 'Terrorist!' And if he is gently shown how his able-bodiedness has left him deaf, blind and dumb to social reality, when it comes to discerning the operation of discrimination inscribed in all walks of life and institutional processes, he is tempted to fold up and fall in to self-pity: the most 'handicapped' person in the room.

Here, in these inversions, is the intersectionality of personal and political as it is played out around the Cabinet table as benefits cuts are discussed. Here too is the explanation for attacks on disabled commuters as they manage (after long years of struggle) to secure access to buses on ramps, only to be vilified as they travel to work. How this inversion operates in the human psyche remains a mystery to me: I am not a Jungian psychologist, although that is probably the direction I would look in for explanations for the way the oppressiveness of societies writ large is enacted in daily micro-aggressions by those who have been manipulated (with their own unconscious consent) into seeing an assertion of the rights of the Oppressed as a threat to their own, unearned supremacy.

That 'threatened' individual votes! How to lead them to a place where they can see how it is their own unfinished business that has left them feeling so vulnerable? That those who daily walk with true powerlessness and vulnerability can show the whole of society a way out? Where is that place where perception can be transformed, peaceably?

The Theatre is – for me – that place. Not for 'answers' but for the non-violent education of the Oppressor by the Oppressed; for direct confrontation with the structures of power as they play out as the othering and suppression of minorities; for the transformation, of what might otherwise merely turn to unwinnable, violent conflict, into a proliferation of palpable choices, rehearsed in this space that we can build anywhere we choose.

Frame Three

We're grappling with the trap inherent in the notion that a Model has to have a Protagonist and an Antagonist. This doesn't mean a Goody and a Baddy, although we've had a great deal of fun with those. Mat Fraser and Mandy Colleran are two of the most gifted, politicized comics I've ever worked with and my sides are splitting. The last thing I expected was this much laughter in rehearsals, but my expectations are being stripped away, faster than anywhere, and it hardly hurts at all. Apart from a stitch!

This Model (or Anti-model as the Academic in me seems to need to dub it) is all about hand-jiving. We all learn it together and that means that in line with our capacity-building there will be one more potential Forum in the Scene Bank to be brought out in workshops (schools for example) where the opening exercises such as Granny's Footsteps expose a lot of negative peer pressure, just asking to be flipped into positive, collective energy.

Three people sit facing us. The music starts. Very cool music. They Hand-jive. To the left of the row is an empty chair. One by one new people appear, wanting to join in (it's a very cool routine). But as soon as the left-most person 'gets' it, the hand-jive changes and they look like an idiot. Desperate to recover that sense of belonging, the newbie tries to crack the new moves. But who is leading them? They have to work it out. They sometimes manage.

Only for the whole routine to change again.
'How do we make sure someone making an Intervention knows what's expected of them?' I ask, once the laughter dies down yet again. 'We don't want to make anyone look too dumb!'
Silence. What have I said? Over tea, one actor, who is deaf, quietly lets me know. She asks me not to feel bad, but just not to use that word. Dumb. I honestly didn't notice I had.

In our second year of capacity-building, our line-up changed, we moved to an old church in Southwark, south of the Thames, and one of the collaborative processes in my life that changed everything unfolded. Nothing I have done since in the Theatre of the Oppressed has been uninfluenced by the gravitational pull of that five days, ending with the presentation of a new, disabled-led, flexible template for Forum sessions, to an invited audience including Paul Heritage (who founded the Drama Department at Queen Mary, University of London, where I still work) and Jane Plastow (who has patiently mentored the writing of this book). We knew we had come a long way towards adapting the systems of Image and Forum, not just to serve a disabled-led agenda but to hold a space where the socially constructed model of disability was brought fully into every aspect of the work for de-construction, as it surely must. At no point was the task around rescuing or even personally empathizing with the disabled protagonist as a victim. 'Being a Mother Theresa' we called it and we didn't apologize for the term.

I have already touched on intersectionality in this tranche of work that was enacted not across some imaginary boundary between able-bodied and disabled actors per se, but between notions of how the personal and political play out. We'd discussed this a lot as we made new exercises and adapted existing ones from the 'arsenal' of the Theatre of the Oppressed (arguing as we went about many terms, including that one). How do we show in an accessible way that the dominant point of view of the unexamined, able-bodied life, given the power to perpetuate oppressive political structures, is at play in even the mundane microcosm of daily, personal interaction with a disabled person? We had determined that even well-intentioned, charitable beings needed to be disabused of the notion that they were doing something other than just amelioration of the symptoms of oppression (by doling out money or 'caring' how Unfortunates 'feel') rather than addressing the commonality of oppressions created by the dominant structures of capitalism.

You wouldn't put *that* in a play and expect a laugh, but laughter had been a very powerful force in our room and we weren't going to exclude our guests from it. We had needed to create exercises about transforming perception. If we could do that, then we'd avoid the panacea of an empathy that leaves one feeling better but avoids any risk and changes nothing that matters in the macro-narrative of oppression. But if we changed perceptions then Spectactors would hopefully find out for themselves how it is that perceptions, backed by power, unconsciously shape choices regarding those we have been trained to see as lesser than ourselves. And if that new way of seeing is indivisible from an owning of the reality of how the able-bodied come by power as participating members of society, then a space is opened up to rehearse peaceable but radical change. In getting to that place, we must be ready to run the same risk as those whom we aspire to 'help'. We must act, not dream or empathize or become mired in sentimentality – towards the Other – or equally, self-pity, towards the person I now see that I am and who must relinquish unearned power before I can change.

We need new exercises.

Frame Four

Damn. There's an odd number of us in the church today, as one of the actors, who has multiple and complex health problems, has found the first two days extremely onerous. He isn't here. I'm being completely selfish as I recount the heads (OK, not quite like primary school, but I'm trying to make this thing happen!).

I expected to make pairs.

We've agreed to take one of BREAKOUT's best inventions, believe it or not, known as The Wheel, first devised with Simon Floodgate and Sally Ellsbury some years ago in the Berkshire school halls I used to frequent and now inhabit no longer. Two concentric circles face one another and the outer take turns to sculpt the bodies of the inner into any set of Images they agree to look at. Then the outer circle rotates and the effect is that of intensely individualistic meanings strung together into a flickering comic strip, strobing into a collective vision.

Usually, that is.

But it's best with equal-sized circles and that means there's nothing else for it but for me to join in. I'm happier not wearing the facilitator hat and the participant one at the same time (maybe too happy?) but here we go. We need to get the invited audience up on Friday, each making one personal contribution through an Image, sculpted with another's body. It is clear that we won't be even considering who sculpts whom: blind/sighted; wheelchair/not wheelchair won't matter if we get this right. And to get it right on Friday we need to try it out today.

I end up with Jamie. He winks. He's choosing to sit today for this part so he's got an ordinary chair with him. We propose a Wheel of Childhood Memories to start.

I don't remember what I sculpted Jamie into, now. I do remember that the sense of being able to work with his body was very important to me. The structure of The Wheel is something I'd had a hand in creating and I trusted that structure to keep things intimate but at the same time, paradoxically, impersonal.

I make Jamie into an Image (a self-portrait) and he adjusts it so that he can hold it still with today's troublesome legs, and we spin around to see the collectivity of it all. From personal to political. Spin, spin. Sorted.

Now the circles swap, inner to outer. We repeat the sculpting. My turn to sit. I don't need the chair, obviously. I'll push it back. Isn't it obvious I don't need the chair? Not to Jamie. He plonks me down on it. We are doing a second circle of looking at childhood and already some surprising non-verbal meanings have begun to fill the room: bewilderment, mischief, fear, mishap, pain.

He pulls my jumper up to cover my whole head. That's it.

Mandy is now facilitating: the agenda that facilitation should become increasingly devolved away from me has been kicking in, but at this moment – one of the most important in my whole performing life, as I am about to discover – I can't observe her as she instructs the outer rim to spin. I'm sitting with my jumper over my head, unable to see what's going on.

Or not quite. It's a thin jumper and I can see the ten or so people in the outer circle as they spin past, some at walking pace, some with sticks, some stopping to read me with their fingertips. The Wheel speeds up. My mind is racing. This isn't feeling as I thought it would feel. I was on the verge of trying to imagine being Jamie but I'm not Jamie.

I'm not Jamie. I'm not Jamie. I'm not.

When suddenly, I feel this surge of power. It's exactly halfway between dread and excitement. Visceral. Inexplicable. Unexpected.

I've run this exercise often and I've seen some true moments of revelation in the bodies and faces of others (as I've intended, as I've expected!) but I didn't plan this today. I was intending … I expected …

In this turning of The Wheel plan, expectation and intention have evaporated. I feel this surge of power, from the ground up, coming up through my legs into my gut. Someone is reading me by trying to find my face and she can't. She's giggling. I can just make her out through the weave of my jumper. It's … no. Doesn't matter who it is. She can't read me. She doesn't know me. She can't find me.

I'm liking this unknowability!

That day, as often happens when a frame chooses me (not me the frame), is otherwise rather dim now, twenty years on, although I could no doubt give a diaristic account of it. The notebook must be somewhere. But to diarize would add nothing but information about time and place. This moment is alive to me now, as is the conversation I had with Jamie afterwards over tea. He explained to me that in fact his idea for an Image of childhood had popped into his mind through the sculpting itself, which he dove into intuitively, that, as we've been learning, proving to be the best way. He had in mind something along the lines of how he just wanted to fit in and how his childhood idea of that looked, before he had become an actor, before he had joined GRAEAE, before he had become politicized, was that to fit in would basically mean to be invisible. Furthermore, by being funny, smart-arsed and lippy his smokescreen persona (like my jumper) had fulfilled that unwitting self-erasure, for a time. It was clear that as for so many young people the discovery of Drama had been hugely empowering for him and all the skills he acquired were now, in this work, in evidence, in all their deft, professional glory.

But Jamie's childhood wasn't all like that and to fit with the peer group didn't mean that application of performative skill at all. Far from it.

That's not the point of this frame though. The mystery to me was how I'd not yet heard any of that story before I joined in, and I'd only done that because I had to, to make up the numbers. The point of this frame, urging me as it has to be unpacked twenty years on, is what happened when I felt the surge of power. It is a point I can only now make auto-ethnographically.

I reject a superficial 'identification' with Jamie or any other person to whom I might say 'I know how you feel' so as to make *myself* feel more comfortable around them and less guilty about my unearned position as an able-bodied, white, cis male in the political North. I have no time for 'sympathy' or sentimentality in my professional work, although I endure wave upon unreliable wave of those in private, and in the case of GRAEAE, often retreat to the toilet of that church in Southwark at breaks, to worry, to rage and once or twice to cry in my own bewilderment at how I could get things so wrong, feel so much and seemingly accomplish so little.

But there, in The Wheel, I didn't feel personalized emotion. I felt power. I told Jamie and I could only add that it was as if there had been a direct spark of meaning, jumping from him to me. He had charged my body with meaning and I had, as The Wheel spun, felt it without knowing what it was. Yes: it was a spark! I call it *identification* today because that word suggests both personal truth ('identity') and a process ('-ation') whereby we are enabled by intimate contact with another person to name, to recognize, to own and reassemble those unspoken parts of ourselves that we cannot *identify* alone. Applying this understanding now, to this moment, allowing for the ultimate unknowability of any of us by another, I can only say *now,* as I did to Jamie *then,* that for a few seconds I knew in my body, not in any part of my conscious, personal mind, not how he had felt as a child trying to fit in but *the power he had imagined that this fitting in might lend to him*. I didn't experience past invisibility but present agency. One was enacted and transformed into the other through the technique itself.

We don't do this work for some hazy notion of enlightenment. It is the misplaced (and much manipulated) expectation of 'personal growth' that has caused such heart-breaking conflict through the processes of translation of the TotO into contexts in the political North, where a culture of identity politics and therapeutic personal development has allowed for specialist workshops and conferences to open people up to a complicity in their self-exploitation in search of a promise that TotO seems to offer: what looks like, to hungry Western eyes, healing, belonging, connection and redemption.

Those are there for some maybe, as they are in a hundred sundry modes and methods of personal development, many of them factoring in the panacea of making us *feel better* about being able to afford them and thus acquiescing in the inequities that uphold that spending power.

This other kind of power, shared with a powerful friend, was non-verbal, raw and transpersonal. It was a surge of what we needed to transform the system of TotO into one that was disabled-led and not just 'about' disability. I couldn't explain it then, although the discussion (cut short by the need to get back to work) was a rich one. And the fact that I couldn't explain it away is precisely the reason that it is speaking to me today.

The fact that I don't understand what passed between Jamie and myself was what opened up a place for something new to be understood.

Frame Five

It's Friday and we've decorated the space with pink everything as it's Valentine's Day and we have gone for the trademark iconoclastic humour of GRAEAE to make our mark. I'm co-facilitating with Mandy Colleran who is one of the funniest people I've ever met. Birkenhead and Glasgow humour have much in common ('gallows', basically) and it's all about transcending grimness, if you ask me. That and a merciless attention to detail. For this reason her favourite stand-up is Lily Savage and mine is Billy Connolly.

Stand-up. That's what cracked it. Mandy does stand-up too and who wouldn't deploy that skill-set at times like these? In file our invited audience, into our screamingly camp ante-room (we're holding the audience in the Vestry before we unleash the Main Surprise) and they look so nervous. Paul and Jane are late. We wait for them and of course wise-cracking is the way to do that, whilst breaking the ice.

There's a lot of ice to be broken. Here are funders and researchers and Ewan the artistic director and it all really needs to 'work'. Co-facilitating (it's going to be co-Jokering next door when we move to the Forum proper) is a real business here: one of us can scan the room for that shy person who nevertheless clearly has a contribution on the tip of their tongue. Or put more simply, it means that if either Mandy or I blank out with our own nerves, we can use our outrageously ham set of secret signals (fooling nobody, ever) that help to throw the ball back and forth while we Joker or work this busy room.

Everything's pink. Mandy's ghastly choice. Images of straight, cis, white, able-bodied lurve everywhere you look. Lots of cake. 'Let's sweeten them up first,' she quips as we unwrap pink sugary treats in a hundred lurid forms.

'Welcome to GRAEAE's Valentine Special!' pipes La Colleran, reversing neatly into her place by me. She sums up the capacity-building agenda of our week together (the second in a three-year series) and makes sure everyone knows that if I've done my job right, I won't be here at all in Year Four. One or two guests look to me for a reaction. Do I see SYMPATHY?

No time to wonder. Into the lovely old Victorian Church proper we go, led by Mandy's chair and directly into eye contact with ...

Mat Fraser, Seal Boy himself, high above us on the ledge of a huge stained glass window. He is positioned so that it seems a Pre-Raphaelite angel has accidentally lent him wings. He beams beatifically down. Others are in correspondent Images of power: their own power, shaped as they see it, placed where they want it, not dominating the space (with power-over) but charging it (with power-with and *within*).

There are no chairs. There is no back row to hide in. No best place to watch from. No sedentary option. Mandy explains who the GRAEAE were, with a most erudite grasp of Greek mythology, but winking at me as she does (she has told me privately she thinks we should re-name the company *The Performing Crips* for 'Disability Awareness' workshops in future).

We all work on The Wheel: safe but fun and an ice-melter rather than breaker as people's worries about being around so many different bodies give way to joy and skill. We challenge everyone to make Valentine Cards: Images using all the bodies in their group and they truly are a wicked delight. Then and only then do we invite our Spectactors (having shown them what that means in Forum) to sit in the chairs we have hitherto denied them.

I am describing here a disabled-led workshop in a disabled-held space and the unique opportunity this afforded to all participants to catch up with whatever the dominant order beyond the performance space had up to now only seen and consequently imposed as limitation. It's the imposition that must be overturned in this work, and disability awareness (whose, exactly?) has nothing to do with it.

Frame Six

The *Tour De Force* or is it the *Coup De Grace?* (something French anyway) is the notorious *Coke Can Forum*, originally created by Jamie in a different, satirical context and requiring only a tweak or two to bring it to the task of modelling what our collaborations have achieved in transforming some of the techniques (and hopefully many of the distorted expectations) that are the strength and weakness respectively of the Theatre of the Oppressed from a politicized, disabled-led point of view. Mandy's going to be the Joker but with one other supporter – me – if she needs to call on me (she doesn't) and as the now happy and relaxed audience arrange themselves for what is apparently going to be a bit of 'proper theatre' I position myself where she can see me and we can wink or use other signals such as the Very Deliberate Nose Rub. I can't remember what it's for but it's reassuring if you get stuck.

On comes Jamie. The Model (or Anti-model as we're calling it) is based on what happened on the pavement outside an office he was temping in one day, not so long ago. He's gone outside for a bit of sunshine, a sarnie and a can of Coke.

Jamie sits and munches away. He twinkles at the audience. I swear: everything this guy does, *every single thing*, is seriously funny. He maintains eye contact with us throughout what follows: a crucial, strategic detail. He eats his lunch and drinks his Coke.

A Nice Lady goes by. She's smiling vaguely ahead until she notices him. For a second she wavers as she clocks his disability. She makes to walk by, hesitates, puts on the Mother Theresa Face (we've seen it a lot this week) and turns back.

And drops ten pence in his Coke.

A third character is passing, walking in the other direction, and has seen (witnessed?) the exact second of the coin-drop. They make eye contact with Jamie and then – again crucially – they look out of the Forum, directly at us. Mother Theresa (played by Liz Porter) toddles on by, oblivious, saintly and clearly feeling that this charitable act and the accompanying release from discomfort is ten pence well spent.

STOP!

Mandy has a high time of it, Jokering this. We are at no point inviting Interventions replacing Jamie. Gradually it dawns on the Spectactors that their Interventions are not about him but about *them*.

It doesn't matter what happened next, save to say that without too many hurt feelings (and there must have been some) we are able through this anti-Model to invite anyone who participates in an able-ist society, to identify with not Mother Theresa but the Witness. We have all seen this kind of interaction and it is in these moments, gone in a blink, where the micro-aggressions of an entire societal power structure are not only inscribed (Augusto's excellent term) but reinforced, maintained, internalized by all of us. By me. By you. I don't remember the Interventions but they were a huge stretch for many people to make that day and (if that Model is still out there) I trust they still are. What that character of the Witness does, looking outward directly into our eyes as Jamie's character does, is to turn over clearly and cleanly to us, without fear or favour, without blame or shame, the business of owning our received and unconscious perception of disability, seeing and owning it for what it is – an operational part of an oppressive society – and then transforming it, as a precursor to collective right action. We are being hooked in through the notion of Charity, however innocently held, firmly but gently having that turned around so as to expose it for what it is and point to where it sits in the structures of power that authored it. Even if the best intentioned among us don't see ourselves in these acts of complicity (*pace* Mother Theresa) we are nevertheless instrumental in their perpetuation. We are being invited to claim agency, through personal Intervention, whoever we are, in a collective revolution, informed by the social model of disability and incrementally moving towards its replacement with one predicated upon equity and social justice.

Thus ended, in that lovely old church, the most universally applicable, the most valuable, the most fun-filled and the most lasting lesson of my whole TotO career (so far).

To sum up that shared learning then, if such a lengthy and complex process can even be summed up:

Each iteration of an investigation, conducted with others and through the practice itself, should, if properly understood, leave us in the right place to formulate and clarify the next set of emergent questions and however daunting these might seem, to move concertedly towards them. I have in my accounts of the work in Malawi and with GRAEAE sought to show how this process arises from and ends up integrated back into the work and rarely is about 'answers' – certainly not about anything fixed. 'Rules' carry the danger of being taken out of context and the even greater peril of being imposed within a new, inimical context, without a sense of where they came from. I prefer to talk about *recipes* when I describe the makings generated by these intense periods of reflexive practice, not least because the clear purpose of that investigation was to customize the principles of Image and Forum in egalitarian collaboration with others, not to showcase my own done-and-dusted take on Forum.

A recipe is learned at someone's side or through a YouTube video or indeed through a gravy-spattered book propped up next to a bubbling pot. Or it might be told as a kind of teaching story, with Oracy as the mode. It's a side-by-side thing. You are given a wooden spoon by your mum and you have to stand on a stool beside her as you learn how she cooks, by absorption and mimesis. A recipe is by definition not a complete thing: it is a set of steps whereby ingredients become something else. It is given away by someone who doesn't say: 'I made this in 1995: if only you'd been there!' but in a spirit of generosity and within a culture of Gift.

More than this, a recipe allows for customization and adaptation, within reason. For example, my aunt, who is now 94, passed on to me her renowned chutney recipe thirty years ago at around about the same time I was working with BREAKOUT and first beginning to explore radical participatory theatre. The non-negotiable principle underlying the recipe was easy: she simply told me it over the phone. You need to have roughly the same amount of sugar to vinegar, but the sugar content can go down if the fruit or vegetables are sweeter and the liquid content likewise, if the fruit releases more of its own juices. But roughly 50/50 sugar to vinegar is all you need to know, plus jars as clean as you can get them and heated up so that when you decant the boiling chutney into them they don't crack. Last year's chutney was mango, apple and ginger, but this year's is going to be based on pears as we expect a bumper crop again in rural Sussex. I will use hard ones, but if they are softer then I won't need so much liquid, and so on. I am free to adapt as long as the principle (that of preservation through heat, sugar and vinegar) is followed.

As with good games and exercises, the transmission and dissemination of recipes is part of a larger, acculturated relationship.

But today, if I'm not careful about holding on to that living, open-ended pedagogy, I might fall into a delicious trap. Today, if I buy the Sunday papers, an entire glossy supplement, featuring chefs as celebrated as movie stars, will fall into my lap, leaving me wondering how to source ever-more exotic ingredients to get it right or – dare I day it? – perfect. I must find harissa! Otherwise I can't make the whatever!

It isn't the celebrity chef's 'fault'. They have books to sell, a restaurant to fill with people who are probably hungry for much more than mere lunch and a brand to maintain by dint of its exclusivity. If we buy this demi-god's books, we are to replicate, not improvise. If we can't find the exact right ingredients, then the book stays on the shelf. And that is why, on my bookshelves, recipe books jostle for space with unread books about theatre games (with one or two honourable exceptions) and for a similar reason. We can bone up on all the recipes but still be completely flummoxed when it comes to a day when we can't find aubergines (for the lasagne) or harissa (I don't know what it's *for*, still). And we can have read a hundred games without ever having played them, or learned how to sequence a few of them to a desired end, or what to do if the exercise that flew on Monday goes down like a lead balloon on Tuesday, even though the group and the intention are seemingly identical. No: we learn the sequencing and the 'what ifs …' by doing, by improvisation and by trial and error in the relative safety of spaces we are familiar with or into which we have been invited.

I have only ever called the sequences of games and exercises negotiated and then documented with each group I start with afresh: **recipes**. And I hope that this simile explains why.

More than a simile, it's a practice. In that second cycle of practice-based research, threaded through my three years' task with GRAEAE, I developed a shared cartooning diary which was created first by denoting a page for each day on a large flipchart sheet on the wall, then by dividing it vertically in half so as to show RECIPE on the left and TASTE on the right. Anyone could take a marker pen from the pot and notate the recipe on the left. We agreed that we would try to write down only the steps absolutely necessary to make that game or exercise happen, in another place, with another group, as if only the person holding the pen was the one who knew it before playing.

On the right, under TASTE, we could put suggestions and 'what ifs': if the children are too small or too lively; if the group refuse an instruction for whatever reason; if I hate playing this (that's the easy one: don't!) or best of all, if it takes off in such an abundant, energized direction that I can leapfrog directly into Image or Forum without any further incremental steps or warm-up. This, the right hand column, is subjective. But the diary as a whole is collectively written, transparent and democratized. It departs from Augusto's pedagogical practice only inasmuch as I **do first, talk after** as a rule: the game is played first and after a sequence and a debrief as he taught me ('How was it?' 'What do you see?') the documentation happens.

Documentation alone is not the solution to the quest for principles in practice I found myself on, however. Here, with GRAEAE, came my own epiphany. There were many surrenders and a lot of letting go of my own preconceptions before it happened, but in the way we worked together in the training (documentation included) and in the way I was quietly taught what being an able-bodied Ally should be like in action, I found myself on the other side of that so-formative time with a set of techniques that had been taken apart, sometimes rejected, always polished up (and deconstructed for access and appropriateness) and without fail, scrutinized for how they would sit with a new troupe of facilitators after I had successfully made myself redundant.

An example will close this section and point me on, as the iterative cycle does and must, to a fresh set of questions and makings, offered as before in a spirit of questing for principles open to adaptation according to context and Constituency, just like recipes. With a principle of *reculer pur mieux sauter* as before, I will take one quick look back at GRAEAE before I show you what I cooked up next.

Frame Seven

Mandy and I are Jokering. It's the Coke Can Forum and we know we are no longer using a Model where the apparent Protagonist is to be replaced. The 'problem' is not Jamie's disability. It is how that has been socially constructed in the eyes of the Charitable Lady and the Witness, one of whom does the 'wrong' thing and the other, so far, nothing.

How does that Witness feel? We are working in a secondary school in Dagenham and it is indeed 'Disability Awareness Week'. Mandy has muttered her preference for *The Performing Crips* over GRAEAE as a moniker as she reverses adroitly down the ramp into the arms of two beaming prefects.

The workshop template as it stands is reproduced below and is offered, as I have said, as a recipe, forged collectively over that three years' work and intended to be recycled by teachers. There are several of those in attendance today and as often happens it isn't necessarily the drama teacher who looks as if they are 'getting' the use of Image and Forum in what is called PSE (Personal and Social Education). The PE teachers and one or two others are really engaged too. We have stripped down our template so it is a neat 90 minutes long: a double period. We have assumed nothing on the school's part (the Constituency) other than they have agreed that an experiential workshop looking in a safe way at disability is a good thing. We are making no assumptions or projections about whether our recipes will be recycled or applied to other kinds of activity after we leave (the whole tour is a series of one-offs and that's the way the LEA funding is going). We will give our best, invite people to take what they want and leave the rest, and move on.

The template, in brief, is as follows with 'Taste' in bullet points:

Granny's Footsteps:

- Have fun creeping up on people.
- Develop 'freezing' skills needed to win but also required to make Image Theatre (next).
- Creeping up in joined groups of twos and threes, so as to work and make those Images collectively.

Crystal Ball:

- Use Image-making skills to create scenes from everyday life, including those of peer pressure and difficulty.
- Replay, hold and embody the experience of others.

The Wheel:

- Create collective Images using the whole group to move towards the universal and societal.
- Name what we see and take responsibility for that naming.
- Use laminated 'Thought Bubbles' and 'Speech Bubbles' as in a comic, to dynamize key Images that taste personal but resonate universally.

The Model:

- 'Here's something we made earlier at home' such as the Coke Can or the Hand-jive Model is offered, now that the whole group has demonstrated their own performative and authorial skills.
- Mandy introduces the Model as not a question to be answered correctly or a story about an Unfortunate needing to be rescued.

The Forum:

Young and (in this case able-bodied) people are invited to replace either the Charitable Lady or the Witness and to explore their own behaviour.

The Rainbow:

- Several young people can come up and surround the Charitable Lady or the Witness, applying their Image-making skill to creating a collective 'X-Ray' of what is going on inside individuals in society when they see a disabled person and feel those flashes of pity/anger/indifference/wonder towards them (or simply ruin their lunch by putting ten pence in their Coke).

It was always a wonderful 90 minutes, filled with a great deal of self-honesty on the young people's part.

We had reconfigured the central tenet of Forum, namely that a Protagonist has to be replaced in solidarity, using an Intervention from a Spectactor, to rehearse strategies for a revolution in the power relationships upheld by their oppression. We had explored what it might mean to be an able-bodied person using the techniques not to empathize but to *inhabit* a part of that inscribed societal power structure, without pretending to 'know' how that disabled Protagonist 'felt'. We had brought the Toolbox of the Theatre of the Oppressed into an alignment with new knowledges about socially constructed Models of disability and by deconstructing and then reconfiguring the system, we had brought it into the service of that project with neither compromise nor dilution.

Same recipe, new taste.

Chapter 5
Ten Top Tips

I have explained the strategies and adaptations created through my personal search for a pedagogy of the Theatre of Oppressed, customized for and with the groups I worked with throughout the 1990s and, as I hope to have shown clearly in Chapter Four, the proof of those new and/or remade recipes was in the tasting.

The third iteration of this process was the creation with the TIE team from the Redgrave Theatre in Farnborough of *Poor Ted,* a self-contained touring project for 9–12-year-olds exploring issues around substance abuse. I created the piece from scratch with a group of that same age in Burgess Hill School, West Sussex, early in 1995, knowing that as the infrastructures of LEAs and arts funding organizations were rapidly shifting (mostly in a downward direction, it must be said) that the best way to apply what my investigations had brought into my practice thus far was the following set of principles in practice:

- that the piece would include a fully scripted play, crafted by myself from the stories of the children;

- that the project as a whole would require as an indivisible element a short training session for teachers of all disciplines;

- that the Constituency of the project would be the temporary community created over a 90-minute format;

- that the package would empower the children to experience their own authorship and agency through a sampling of the techniques of TotO;

- that the play itself (45 minutes in length) would be a high-quality aesthetic experience, as it was often the children's first and only encounter with professional theatre;

- that the Forum would not be a simplistic one about 'saying no to drugs' but would look at all the pressures, internal and social, that might lead to substance abuse on any given day, by any single person, in a fully realized social context.

The indomitable adviser for drama for West Sussex, Anne Fenton, had already brought me into a training relationship with teachers, during the period when her own department in the LEA (Drama Advisory and Support) had the political will and resources behind it to bring together one teacher from almost every school across the county three or four times a year to look at ways drama could serve not only the national curriculum (which marginalized it as a subject in its own right) but personal and social education (PSE), health education and initiatives such as child-led campaigns against bullying. I can't stress enough what an important set-up this was. In Sussex, I was able to reach one teacher per school, three or four times a year, through residencies in Pulborough, Sussex, in a building (Lodge Hill) then still owned by the county council and capable of housing up to thirty teachers on – for example – a training weekend, looking at how to use Image and Forum Theatre across the whole curriculum and to tackle issues such as racism and sexism that often one isolated teacher, determined to open them up in a school on their own, ran the risk of being seen to be exacerbating things better ignored.

I had a Constituency! We brought in four professional actors and made a play, which with its workshop format (pre- and post-, with a teacher/parent evening per week) was the last time I ever wrote a 'proper play' as it happens.

Everything GRAEAE had given me and every journey in Sub-Saharan Africa came home to me in this process, in that temporary haven of a month's devising space: an oasis (it now seems) of creative freedom whilst elsewhere the TIE movement saw its remit, its platform, its commissioning structure and its educational credibility systematically undermined.

We looked for a charity to sponsor us, given the cuts to core funding that characterized that strategy of undermining, and we found one – paradoxically – in BAMA, the British Aerosol Manufacturers'

Association. Nowhere in the *Poor Ted* project did we ever mention or show a particular drug, seeking as we did to allow the children to project their own experience of substance abuse onto the central character ('Boy') and so come from a place of collective expertise as Forum requires. But how strange, looking back, that the purveyors of one of the most common of those substances (globally) abused by children saw the need to support a month of research, development and devising and the cost of four actors' touring, accommodation and delivery of the project to the tune of two shows a day, ten shows a week, across the UK, for two terms a year, over ten years! They weren't in any way our only partners but where most schools had no choice but to put on a video or create a 'Say No To Drugs' poster competition, this seemingly extravagant medium, understood and supported as it was by many non-governmental agencies and placed by LEAs who didn't need to carry its full cost, was seen by over a quarter of a million children over that decade until 2005. I am proud of that and the many troupes who we trained, four at a time, to rehearse the play and to take turns delivering the participatory template exploring Boy's story so as to attach a participatory technique to each scene and, as I had learned with GRAEAE, to keep the focus on the child; on their experience and skill in understanding a complex issue; on their ability, not to *empathize* with but to own their part of the peer pressure that is always the context within which substance abuse at that age operates; and finally, to make Interventions which went way beyond 'Just Say No!' and looked at how parents, 'frenemies', allies and teachers are all either part of the problem or of the solution, depending on what you chose to try out in the role as Boy or as someone else from his dysfunctional world.

Frame One

A day in the life of Boy.
   It's a school day. Boy dreads school.
   Boy has a bear called Ted who he tells everything. He feeds Ted chocolate, in secret. When his mum hurries him up, shouting, fag in hand, he hides Ted. And stashes the chocolate.

His 'frenemies' meet him on the way to school. They play Granny's Footsteps, Modelling the technique that will later be used as a key to the Image-making that will enable the Spectactors to enter into the world of the play later on, in the final workshop component.

It's 'Say No To Drugs Day' and Boy's essay about how he feels inside has won a competition. The teacher makes him read it out and he ends up looking like a creep. His frenemies make it clear he is now a marked man.

He meets a Girl in the break who isn't like the others. She has a nest of Russian dolls: Babushkas. They take them apart and wonder about what the real person nesting inside us is like and how they sometimes hide from life.

They are caught playing with the dolls by the frenemies. Boy's now the class creep (for being unwittingly set up by the teacher to read his essay out) and a sissy (for playing with dolls and that weird girl). He can't still be in the gang unless he tries … something. (We never see the substance.) Desperate, cornered, he tries it ('If it'll make me fly. I'll try it!') and he's sick.

The frenemies dump him on his doorstep. Mum is too distracted to take in what's happened. No adult can. He retreats to his room.

And he punishes Ted.

Where and how did his day go so horribly wrong? Long before he picked up a substance, that's for sure.

In numbers of Forums and in terms of its national reach, I suppose that this has been in quantity the most impactful piece I have made in any collaboration. *Poor Ted* achieved this in a setting and with the resources required for its delivery as a self-contained package, by training the actors in the techniques of TotO, negotiated with the children themselves for hands-on efficacy. I'm proud of that, but my pride in retrospect is to do with quality, not quantity. All of the principles operating within Boal's techniques that I had needed to explore so as best to deploy them, were to be found in that body of work: made, remade, shared and deconstructed many times and by many troupes across the UK. No enterprise in our field can go beyond ten years (in my opinion) without a rest, even if re-rehearsal and remaking is actually an in-built dynamic, integral to the project as a whole. But what that huge scope in terms of audiences and the collective body of experience garnered by the number of troupes who delivered *Poor Ted* taught me is itemized below. I list these findings in the form of an exercise we would conduct as part of the Joker training with each fresh troupe, always seeded into conventional rehearsal time so that each actor, no matter what their previous experience, could pick up the participatory tools they felt most comfortable with, make them their own and work out who would conduct the traffic of ideas in the workshop that preceded the performance and into which it then returned, as Forum.

Ten Top Tips, ostensibly for conducting Forum Theatre with 9–12 year olds

- Theatre IS knowledge
- There's no such thing as a wrong answer
- Don't just tell me, *show me*!
- Assume nothing on my behalf
- You don't need to understand all the Images I make
- Don't open up anything in 90 minutes that you can't safely close back down
- If an Image gives you the goosebumps at any point in the workshop, move towards it, not away
- You are in a two-way learning relationship with me, the child
- As a Joker you are a conduit, not an editor
- *Smile when you walk into the room! (Or leave it)*

The last one also serves as zero and sometimes doubles as eleven. It's before the beginning and after the end, you see.

Often as I sat at the back of a school hall (cabbage again!) I would witness moments that stay with me still: not from the performance, although there is nothing quite like seeing your own play performed by the wonderful actors who took turns to deliver *Poor Ted,* but from what happened with the children.

Frame Two

Ian Barrans (who plays Boy) has been surrounded by a Rainbow, as first adapted from that section of TotO methodology with GRAEAE a couple of years ago. Sam Jones is temporarily in the Joker role, although we have found it (as the Leeds-based, North of England troupe) more comfortable to use the term Facilitator.

That role in turn has, through experiment, been split into two, as I have discovered alongside that notable stand-up Mandy Colleran. The two complementary energies are called Sparky and Moley.

The energy of Sparky derives from the feistiness of stand-up: you zap people with provocative challenges to put their ideas on legs ('Come out here and say that!'), to have a go, to take a true risk and jump into Boy's world.

Out they come, ten of them, to form the spectrum of at-first-frozen Images we call the Rainbow, each of which is made with what for some of the audience is a newly minted skill first brought into the room by an uproarious game of Granny's Footsteps, but now applied to a purpose.

Sparky puts the Rainbow on Standby. But who (and where) is Moley?

Moley is the other half of the facilitation role. We have split the Joker, in an act of joyful iconoclasm, much as we have taken apart the constructs (and the operation) of Model and Protagonist. Moley spots the quiet people at the back. Moley burrows through the audience and notices that person who has something brilliant on the tip of their tongue (or their fingers, or their elbows: doesn't matter) and then Moley sidles up to you to ask you what you've got. Moley won't take 'I'm no good at acting' or 'Ask her: she's good at drama' for an answer. Moley asks you to whisper the idea (if it involves words) or to give a Private View (if it's an Image.)

The task is to respond or react to or confront or negotiate with or in other ways *deal* with the frenemies. You have just had the worst day of your life (in Boy's shoes, that is.) You have been quietly bullied into playing an exposing game on the way to school. You have been set up by a nice but oblivious teacher to expose your private feelings in front of a class who will now weaponize them against you. And that's what's happening now, as you are dared to try some substance that you know very well is poisonous (it's 'Say No To Drugs Week', after all) but that doesn't help at all, not right now.

Moley brings out the Ideas With Legs. Sparky zaps the Rainbow into shape. Sam and Ian bounce off each other: it is the improvisational, stand-up energy of the double act that is carrying this and it's infectious and very can-do: there's much laughter being brought to what has been initially performed as a scary and painful moment in Boy's day.

The Rainbow has two very quiet people in it. One is a boy with a single word to say. The other is a girl with an Image. The word we are yet to hear, as Sparky puts the queue on standby, ready to take their turns in trying their idea against Big and Small (the frenemies in the play, all set to get you).

The boy just says 'no'. Walks away. I swear Small who is the clever one – the manipulator – gets even Smaller and visibly loses all her power. A few more ideas are tried, Sparky bigging each up like a film director (Standby! Action! Cut!) and Moley helping people back to their places amongst their often open-mouthed friends, who haven't seen that boy ever stand up for himself like that before … except that now they have.

It's the girl's turn. She's tiny and the actor playing Big is really huge. She has her arms out behind her, outstretched like wings. But it's her face that's fantastic. Any little girl who can gurn like that is truly a terrifying thing. She's one of those children who can turn their eyelids inside out and unbeknownst to her, that's exactly the thing that the guy playing Big today can't deal with. For real!

But we don't know that yet. Moley is holding the last few in the Rainbow on Standby. Sparky is preparing for Action, although this strange, intent little being, intently holding her

Image, eyes not yet turned inside out, is unfathomable. We truly have no idea what she's about to do.

Action!

Gurn.

And Big falls over, for real.

Result!

Afterwards, Sparky asks the little girl what she was doing, 'just to help us understand' and to give the floored actor playing Big space to pull himself together. (He's a mess. She really got him.)

'I'm a Dragon. That's how angry I get at bullies. And that's *not even my worst face.*'

She doesn't need Moley's help to flounce triumphantly back to her seat either.

We can all recount wonderful Forum moments and of course the risk of that is either telling your reader 'you had to be there' or 'didn't we do well ... back then'. I love those stories of course and telling them as a core element of the pedagogy of the Theatre of the Oppressed is a seed that Augusto planted in me. But a *principle* needs to be shown as emerging as much from 'failure' and a *principle in practice* must point us forward.

Indivisible as I have said from the touring and capacity-building of the *Poor Ted* format, designed as it was to set up teachers to reuse techniques like our customized Rainbow in other settings and towards the exploration of different content, we always made one mandatory parent-teacher evening performance a condition of an LEA booking, completing the week-long package. Our partly independent funding prevented cost from being an excuse to reject something that a school might recognize as powerful work but would rather not 'make the problem worse' by performing and exploring issues including the complicity of teachers in the problem, perhaps, or that showed a (carefully staged) moment of substance abuse so as to 'teach children how to use drugs when they didn't know before'. And all attempts at empowering children (and the play had been written with them after all) attract one rejection more than any other: that we as adults with a (left-wing) agenda have 'put words in their mouths'.

At the time of writing (2018) members of the US Republican Party, funded to the hilt by the National Rifle Association (NRA), are accusing the survivors of yet another school massacre of being actors! Having had enough of their schools being places that they might be killed at random with guns you can buy at Walmart, a rapidly escalating protest against gun culture and the way it funds politics is gathering momentum, led by youth. The US government is sufficiently threatened by the passion, the clarity, the bravery and the motivation of these excellent young people (whose friends were shot as they watched) to call them actors.

What an inadvertent acknowledgement of the power of young people's voices that is! So it can be too (in microcosm, in a quiet way) with a workshop in a primary school, on a rainy day, with a teacher who feels she has been forced to attend, who is covertly marking essays at the back of the hall because she has been robbed of her time by being required to chaperone her class into some piece of shenanigans that she doesn't fully understand and which, furthermore, includes a portrayal of a stressed, blundering, well-intentioned teacher who is only doing her best … **(Top Tip Number Twelve: You spot what you've got.)**

'There really isn't time in our busy school for this … sort of thing. We've an inspection coming up and here were are, playing Granny's Footsteps! It's manipulative. What's wrong with a perfectly good poster campaign? They're putting words in those children's mouths and making the problem worse. I blame the parents.' (Etc.)

Those evenings with only adults in the room were one of the most important parts of my work in the 1990s and those experiences took forward what I had learned about how and when to devise and use TotO, essentially unchanged, into all the subsequent settings where I have agreed to disseminate it, across a wide array of diverse Constituencies and partnerships, as I sincerely hope to have shown in this and the previous chapter. Not because I want to say: 'This is how it's done' but to relate where the recipes came from and to tell what happened both when they 'succeeded' and when they 'failed'.

As, in my last frame before I hand this book over to the voices of others, I discovered one night in Burgess Hill, at just one such parent-teacher evening. Success or failure? Quantity or Quality? I leave that to others to decide. Making the best of bringing these frames to an evidencing of Principle has been the task I have set myself and I trust that

I have contextualized and structured those frames in such a way as to point the reader forward – homeward – towards their own practice. The work arises from and returns to performance, every time. And nobody can predict how or when we might be shown the thing we need to see, enabled perhaps by the space we have held and the theatre we have offered, but ultimately performed back to us as the thing we had no idea we would learn, if, that is, we hand over the tools of production to those whom we aspire to work with, in a spirit of service and solidarity.

The Last Frame

The play ends as it always does, with a very powerful moment, given to me during the devising process some months back in this exact same hall by a little guy who didn't realize he was becoming the person I was to call Boy. (I didn't realize then, either!)

Boy has made it back to his room, slipping past Mum who, fag in hand, hasn't noticed that something is very wrong and has chased off Big and Small: 'Scallywags!' She's not a 'bad' Mum. She just has no idea. It's not her fault she has no idea either.

Boy is at a moment of true crisis. He holds onto Ted, sobbing. He has always told Ted everything and always shared his chocolate stash with him. But now the stash has become a poison and telling Ted isn't working. He punches Ted, harder and harder, raging and crying.

(Pause)

Mum: 'Are you alright in there?'

Boy: 'Yes Mum.'

(Pause).

'Sorry Ted. Sorry.'

Sparky has frozen this pitiful moment. It's a very strong Model and although it's never about 'fixing' or rescuing Boy, it is clear that something needs to happen and for this moment of Forum we have chosen the full original, unadorned technique of the Spectactor shouting 'Stop!' and substituting for Mum. It's a parent-teacher evening, so that is the choice we offer. In a daytime show, it's Boy who can be replaced, as the basic formula of Forum, no matter where it is used, however imperfectly we understand the lived experience of today's audience, must surely always be that the Model approximates to that lived experience; poses a challenge that can only be met through Intervention and requires that a Spectactor runs the risk of coming out and trying something that might ripple out into a transformation of the underlying power structures that have been part of the oppression. Here, tonight, that is the oppression of the Boy, yes, but more importantly, the unavailability of the parent.

Moley has quietly removed the front row of seats. It's a strategy we discovered long ago. We bring the adult audience in, perform *Poor Ted* (the play) to them and the front two rows are always, always empty, even when people need to sit around the edges, on the floor.

This is England. We know what participation means, whether it's got a fancy name like Forum or no. It means the actors (swanning down here from bloody London) are *going to make us do something.* It's been a lovely play and very emotional (in fact I've got something in my eye, watching that last bit with the bear) but no way do I get made to stand up in front of all the other parents, let alone that Geography Woman scowling at the back.

Boy thumps Ted, his beloved bear, again and again. It's heart-breaking to watch. It has never lost its power. We have to watch it again, as the Forum always requires, and it's a tough watch as Mum again comes to the door, distracted, fag in hand, hesitantly knocking but perhaps not even wanting to know what's going on in Boy's room, his life, his heart, having so much on her own mind …

'Are you alright in there?'

STOP!

Sparky is momentarily taken aback. It's a big guy, in tracksuit bottoms, with a shaved head, tattoos and trainers, now sitting in the front row (because Moley has removed the chairs!)

Sparky   Well done Sir! And what's your name.

Dad (*not happy with stand-up*)   Doesn't matter.

Sparky   And as you know here we have a motto: Don't just tell me, show me! Do you want to show us what Mum could maybe do next to improve the situation?

Dad   No.

Sparky (*colouring slightly*)   Riiight. What would you like to say then, if it's a line rather than an action you have for Mum?

Dad   I want to be Boy.

(*Pause*).

Sparky (*well done, that Joker!*)   OK.

Standby and Action!

The Dad takes the bear from the actor. He has been very quiet, so very still, through the show. That's how he still is, coming out, taking the moth-eaten bear and now curling up, really small, holding the bear very tight.

Sparky   Action!

Mum   Are you alright in there?

Dad   No.

That was a moment, if ever there was, that I didn't choose. It broke the frame forever. It chose me for the telling now, to bring as a moment of truth to those perennial, too-diverting arguments about whether we are doing Theatre or Therapy; about the role of the Joker; about whether we can only substitute for the Protagonist, and on and on. I haven't any answers. I have these: these bright gems of evidence gifted me over three decades, to bring to the discourse and to extend and to evidence it in ways that return its power and multiplicity of viewpoint to the theatre, using the language of performance itself to do so.

That man moves – still, today, for me – into the middle of all of these questions and considerations and he says *one word* and that word, to me, justifies a whole ten years of struggle and failure and renegotiation, against the odds, in an education system being undermined by those we never meet, in a culture of fixing where children are reaching out for a substance in the absence of an available adult. That man speaks for me.

PART TWO

Companies and Conversations

Figure 5 Jokers. The author with Andy Stafford, one of the Lawnmowers Independent Theatre Company; Gateshead, UK.

Introduction: How These Four Studies Were Created and Why

In 2017, once this study had been commissioned and having already asked Professor Jane Plastow (Leeds) to be my writing mentor and Professor Jen Harvie (QMUL) to be the go-to person in my own department as to how to design my research, I found myself looking for appropriate ways to meet the requirements of that commission: to open up Boal's work to an intended readership of early-career researchers and practitioners seeking to understand, as much through example as possible, the principles in practice of his work. As I have shown through my account of many collaborations and discoveries over my own career, these principles had become gradually clearer to me only through collaboration and were provisional and relative: dependent for any useful pedagogical exegesis as much on context as content.

By **context** I mean what I have been calling Constituency: the places the work happens; the ways that our theatre is built, wherever it happens, out of negotiated relationships; out of a two-way exchange of what an enactment of meaningful solidarity can be and do in action, in the world of social reality that TotO reflects, takes apart, seeks to transform and ultimately returns to.

By **content** I mean the ever-shifting, emergent understanding of what oppression means to any group I seek to collaborate with and that (to begin with at least) they are the experts on, not me. We don't always meet around single issues and even if we do, one of the most powerful things about the 'prospective techniques' of Image Theatre is that we discover more and more where the true oppressions inscribed in lived experience lie. It is then, using the Toolbox of techniques to delve deeper, that we begin to open up knowledges that can be accessed – literally, brought into the light – only to find in so doing that we must look further, trying new kinds of making along the way and thereby customizing our shared tools and the ways we use what we make with them.

This is an inexact science. Perhaps because performance is, at once, a mode of research, a means to stand up ideas and a method of dissemination beyond language, TotO has been theorized more than

↳ the core of his research!

most contemporary theatre practices and has attracted many attempts to pin it down, often by importing an instrumental and pseudo-scientific lexicon in an (understandable but paradoxically, obfuscating) attempt to do so. Much talk of measurement and impact!

What was to be my solution (I asked my patient mentors) believing as I do that it is both an invigorating artistic challenge and an educational responsibility to open up Boal's principles through the examples I have selected and the design I have had to craft, so as to lend to those examples an appropriate, developmental ordering? How to advance my thesis by means of recreated performative material, as unmediated as possible, so as to maintain the centrality of making in my account of my practice-based research?

Above all I have sought to demonstrate how learning has been generated by a making, not discussion. Who made these discoveries, what was my relationship with them and why they could have been made in no other way? I have attempted to honour an iterative shape as much in the structuring as in the selection and sequencing of frames, because we are constantly seeking to reapply our fresh questions to each new cycle of work, if we are at all able to, rather than ever thinking it is 'finished' or the oppression that we have joined to work against 'dealt with'. For the most part, my path has been made by walking. And in 2017, by both design and impulse, I did.

Within the space of that year, afforded me by generous and ever-supportive colleagues (especially my then head of department, Bridget Escolme) I was able with research funding to clear from most other academic duties a year-long space in 2017 and to craft within that year my most ambitious frame: a design for auto-ethnographic research into exactly how, across that year, the content and context of my professional relationships, collaborations and evolving insights into TotO stood. A living, moving, annual inventory, if you like.

One of the sides of this 365-day-wide frame would be that very *Time-span*. I have held to it, although the processing and writing up of many things has flowed into the first quarter of 2018. The second side of the frame has been *Geographical*: I took myself and the guiding questions of my TotO life thus far, across five continents.

The third side is *Relational*: whether I have known them a long time or not, the people you are about to hear from are all, without exception, those with whom I have had a heartfelt connection that doesn't need to be explained (or explained away!) but simply followed, so as to lend a texture and a depth to our conversations. Depth (not duration alone) characterized my own relationship with Augusto, who was so much more than a teacher to me and who never failed to bring emotion into any room he held for rehearsal or teaching. It's how I was taught and today I'm still that way!

Lastly, I would term the fourth side of my frame *Identification* and that is the hardest to define of all. I mean that as I have listened to the many people I am connected with, across five continents, working with TotO, *whether I agree with them or not, or they with each other*, I have attempted to honour in both the construction and the editing of this part of the book, genuine intersectionality where it comes up. As a Quaker artist, I try to listen *to where words come from* and I have looked, even in the more 'conventional' interviews, to hold a deep listening space between myself and the other. That is where lasting meaning is made and where, on this printed page, you, our reader, are invited to be an actively listening third.

I have tried to delineate my role in each creative encounter, so as to allow a considered breathing space to appear between the present writer and that person who worked with Jana Sanskriti, who underwent Level Two Joker training with Theatre of the Oppressed NYC, who made his annual trip to Gateshead to create workshop formats for the Lawnmowers Independent Theatre Company and who joined the CTO Rio Summer School exploring the pedagogy of TotO with University of California Los Angeles (UCLA) students, wearing the hats of **collaborator**, **learner**, **company member** and **co-researcher** respectively. It has been through that standing back, in relation to these exceptional manifestations of TotO internationally, that I have sought that crucial fourth angle on what follows. By virtue of that distancing function, I have striven to reflect critically upon how it is I have come to the understandings I share, as well as to share them.

With Jana Sanskriti, as a long-time member of Sanjoy and Sima Ganguly's extended family, I will describe a working retreat I made with them at their compound at Badu, near Kolkata and (a retreat within that retreat) five hours away in the peace of rural Bengal, in the village of Digambarpur, where my friend Satya's father lives and where the beautiful open-sided Mukta Mancha Theatre stands in the middle of their compound. There, some profound realizations arose between us all about the company's Constituency: as it were, in the field.

With Theatre of the Oppressed NYC (TONYC) I was able in the middle of their busy schedule to reflect on their remarkable strategizing around **capacity-building** (especially the training of Jokers and creation of new troupes) and to be gifted very precious time to do that, during their busy strategic move of headquarters to the heart of Theatre-land in Manhattan. I had been their student in 2016 on an intensive Level Two Joker training and my position had been one of complete immersion in it: now I had a chance to go into some of the questions that galvanizing experience had provoked in me, with TONYC's bracingly honest executive director, Katy Rubin.

When I go every year to work with the Lawnmowers Independent Theatre Company in North East England, I go home, to my oldest friend in TotO, Geraldine Ling, with whom I have shared all of my early learning experiences alongside Augusto and many others: the class of '89. Her sons Sam and Joe are my Godsons. Her company has flourished over the following twenty-five years and as I spent my annual week with them as workshop co-designer and company member, I was able to have over that week's collaboration a three-way conversation about ways forward, as Gerry stands back (we are both in our mid-sixties now) and hands over to a vivacious new artistic director, Claire Hills-Wilson. As ever, we spoke about improvisation and what learning-disabled performers give to their work and their research partners, specifically through the **adaptation and customization** of TotO, currently to the enormous challenges of delivering training within the beleaguered National Health Service (NHS).

Finally, I worked with Geo Britto in December at CTO Rio, Boal's original company, now hosting a month-long pedagogic exchange with UCLA that brings together experienced scholar-artists such as myself with the full range of groups CTO has worked with for thirty years across Brazil: in schools, hospitals, prisons and of course the *favelas*. Our conversation brought together through metaphor and example, many of the questions arising in the previous three journeys of a telling year. And as this study has often shown, what began as a two-way discussion about pedagogy naturally extended to include the whole 2017 student cohort exploring an **emergent TotO pedagogy** with myself as co-researcher, using as a performative platform that same practical session I ran with Jana Sanskriti earlier that April, through our shared language: the techniques of Image Theatre.

What goes around, comes around. And so it is with cycles of practice-based research.

None of what follows, therefore, will be conventional interviews! All four begin with, refer to or illuminate in bright verbal Images our shared practice as Theatre Workers. There is little of what I once heard described as an *extractive methodology*. The one-way nature of that kind of encounter wouldn't have synergy with the way our work and our working relationships are shaped and co-designed, whatever specific topic we might agree or disagree on. And most of all, guided by my core questions, enabled and mentored by discerning (and patient!) colleagues, I have been able to offer – hopefully – a shape to this section of the book that is faithful to our work as iterative, as transitive, as evidencing theatre as a form of knowledge in and of itself.

Time, Place, Relationship and Identification are, then, the four sides of my frame. Within it I will introduce the four outstanding TotO companies that I was able to engage with, in four different roles, in 2017, enabled by an auto-ethnographic research design to stand back from my experience with them so as to extrapolate more universal principles of TotO as they appear within the frame.

Or, as I do now, to step through it.

Very much in-the-field
He's an insider talking from the is inside,
just one-part of an ethnographic approach
No critical perspective

Jana Sanskriti: Field Work

I have known Sanjoy and Sima Ganguly, co-founders of the internationally celebrated company, Jana Sanskriti, ever since we first met in Paris in 1991 and subsequently in 1993 in Brazil. Since then, I have never lost touch with them, and my visits to their base and training hub at Badu, West Bengal, have always been pivotal to my own Theatre of the Oppressed journey: times of radical review and an essential rebalancing between tireless rolling out of the work on the one hand, with shared reflection on its core values on the other, in the peaceful retreat and life-changing hospitality that Badu affords.

The company holds a unique place in the movement of the Theatre of the Oppressed today, as it always did with Augusto, not only exemplifying abundance but integrity. Their prodigious output is a unique example of both invention and adaptation, supported by the training of new generations of Jokers and troupes and – in harmony with that endeavour – practising an international hospitality that brings together the motley diaspora of the TotO movement to the Muktadhara

Figure 6 Composite. The Mukta Mancha Theatre being used by actors to thresh rice (followed by an evening performance); Digambarpur village, West Bengal.

Festival in Kolkata every two years. There, in the Maidan, at the centre of one of the fastest-growing and most overcrowded cities on the planet, we participants and the wider community are afforded at Muktadhara an overview of the diversity and multi-applicability of the many forms TotO can take, whilst a short journey away to Badu – the world's worst traffic permitting – finds us looking inwards and working practically together on fresh techniques and emergent challenges alike in the famous mango garden where we come together to dig deep and re-source ourselves and each other in a reflexive space that is all the more precious for its rarity.

It is one such retreat – in my time-frame of 2017 – that forms the heart of this section about a Company who have only ever asked me on my visits to share my new ideas and techniques with them in exchange for my keep. Sanjoy has always said to me, 'While you are here, Ali, you will not put your hand in your pocket', and that statement takes into account a daily exchange (for room and board), whilst reminding me of the deeper values that this arrangement – for myself at least – exemplifies in action in our lived, social reality.

Jana Sanskriti have given me and taught me more than I can ever say (or they will ever know!), and just as Badu is at the heart of their astonishing output, so my writing about the last time I spent with them, working with the core company, will be unashamedly personal. Writing from the heart can be hard to find in the volumes of analysis about TotO, but it was never absent from Augusto's books or stories. In writing about Jana Sanskriti, I have been challenged to ensure that the head and the heart are aligned.

To help balance the inevitable subjectivity of my mode of telling, Professor Ralph Yarrow (one of the Company's doughtiest allies and commentators) has kindly worked with Sanjoy Ganguly to contextualize this section with as objective as possible an overview of Jana Sanskriti's work, resulting in the admirably concise overview (italicized below) that precedes my own account. I am deeply indebted to them for this, as I am for their additions to the Suggested Reading at the end of this book. I trust that these complementary ways of bringing Jana Sanskriti to the attention of a new readership inspire students and early-career researchers, like the young woman on the MA programme at Goldsmiths, who, in the middle of a workshop I ran recently (just as the final proofs of this book went out), came up to me during a brief break in our Forum session – radiant with excitement! – and said that she had just secured funding to attend this year's Muktadhara in person. That is what the Festival in both its public abundance and its inward-looking reflectiveness is all about.

Jana Sanskriti (JS) are the leading practitioners of Theatre of the Oppressed and Forum Theatre in India and the East. The movement has worked continuously with rural communities in West Bengal since its beginnings in 1985 to reconfigure social and political relationships through theatre, achieving both a solid regional presence and an international reputation. The company has performed and taught in Europe, Africa, the UK, the USA and Asia, hosted eight international festivals and established an international research and resource centre. Its director, Sanjoy Ganguly, has published two books and a collection of plays, which together exemplify key aspects of the company's history and practice. Augusto Boal regarded Jana Sanskriti as a leading representative of the practice of Theatre of the Oppressed and, in many ways, as the international icon of his vision.

Jana Sanskriti's practice is characterized by a unique way of working with performers, audiences and communities. Rooted in an amalgam of Indian folk practice and Forum methodology, it can be understood as a training in embodied agency and an enhancement of the intellectual capacity of 'the people'. Sanjoy Ganguly describes how the theatre space becomes a space for reflection and collective research which reflects and recognizes the capacities of all present and an arena for dialogue and a mirror in which participants both on- and offstage become 'the Spectators of their own actions'. The performance aesthetic incorporates a wide range of forms, including dance and music, creating meaning and provoking structural analysis through metaphor and symbol. Latterly, this has also included work with pre-scripted 'classical' or foreign texts (e.g. Brecht, Ibsen), which has led to more formal innovation and to different challenges to the audience to recognize the specific issues they face through a framework of widely applicable propositions.

Major issues which are frequently addressed include gender relationships, land and tenure, education, health provision, trafficking of women, production of illegal alcohol, political power structures, displacement, migration, employment issues, etc. The group twice cycled from West Bengal villages to New Delhi (1989, 2005) to raise the issue of rural unemployment, performing their landmark play on unemployment (Gayer Panchali) at each halt during the rallies.

Jana Sanskriti never perform plays only once. The Forum event is repeated at least three times at intervals of 1–3 months for the same audience. Subsequently, the same Spectators engage repeatedly with the issues from increasing degrees of understanding and with increasingly sophisticated critical and imaginative levels of response. Within villages and districts, they then form Human Rights Protection Committees, the forum of **Spectactors**. For Jana Sanskriti, doing theatre has always been to engage in politics; through this extended interaction, acting and activism, onstage and offstage, form a continuum.

For Ganguly, theatre is an art of creating connection. Connection is a Praxis, operating at all levels and rooted in recognition of the intellectual and aesthetic intelligence of people who are often presumed not to possess such qualities. Jana Sanskriti achieves this by creating an aesthetic of relationship in training, rehearsal, performance and ongoing offstage activism.

Here, aesthetics means the extension of sense, of possibilities of meaning, of different approaches to issues and situations materialized in practice. The results of this development (a form of Freirean literacy, a Pedagogy of the Oppressed which has respect for intellect and rationality at its core) can be seen in Spectactors' communities and is equally embedded in JS's management structures. **It is a form of democracy in action**. In this aesthetic journey, actors and Spectactors evolve as critical thinkers. This critical thinking breaks passivity in a responsible manner and turns actors into activists and Spectators into Spectactivists. Though the latter term looks like a synergy of Boalian concepts, it was born in Ganguly's awareness over 22 years as a result of making theatre a space for critical thinking as opposed to problem solving and subsequently observing offstage political action.

This iterative theatre-making process operates as co-creation. The plays Sanjoy Ganguly and his collaborators create are derived from and firmly rooted in the lived experience of the communities they work with, and the methodology of creation ('scripting the play, not playing the script') encompasses this process and is built *into his workshop method. Ultimately, he sees it as 'a journey from "I" to "we"'.*

From the above, it is strikingly clear that, for Jana Sanskriti, their theatre-making *is* their politics, and vice versa. At the time of writing, they are touring a world-class production of Ibsen's *A Doll's House* throughout India, bringing one of the most celebrated examples of naturalism to often first-time audiences, who will simultaneously encounter both the Forum and an aesthetic experience of the highest standard. The theatre *is* the politics: in form, in means of production, in content and – indivisibly – in the extension of debate. Through performative means, the audience is empowered to connect with the issues raised by a classic and can, through their *Spectactorship*, explore these issues with the aim of rehearsing realistic social change and integrating that into lived reality. Naturalism indeed!

But how do Jana Sanskriti manage all this, sustaining it and supporting it whilst training the individual Jokers and the ever-growing numbers of teams who deliver it? Nobody reading the above account could fail to arrive at those questions, and it was with the aim not of 'answering' them but of *walking with them* that I visited the Company in 2018 in the spaces at Badu and Digambarpur, where delivery and discovery intersect.

With that, I step back into 2017.

It is April. I am standing with my old friend Sanjoy in the middle of the company's experimental organic field at Digambarpur village, about five hours' drive and a whole world away from the intensity of Kolkata. To work on one of the Forums that they tour to a network of over 300 villages across West Bengal (and internationally, when they have the time!), the company have begun to experiment with organic crops, so as to be walking their talk with respect to their audiences. Why? Because the show is called *Monsanto* and is aimed at opening up the dilemmas posed to subsistence farmers (the audience) who are sold patented seeds, fertilizers and other products that seem to offer magical short-term yields. We all know they don't, but the company is doing far more than performing as a well-intentioned group of apparently urban sophisticates preaching to the Poor. They formed, have worked with and still – in all kinds of ways – model and enact solidarity with their audiences at every level of making, of governance and in their training of new troupes (always three men and three women in each) in techniques of TotO at their main base: Badu, just outside of Kolkata.

That training, during which new troupes live, eat and work together in the dormitory accommodation at Badu, covers far more than how to run a Forum back at your own village, on your own concerns, through TotO techniques. To build the actual theatre that Forum and other gatherings will be held in is equally a part of Jana Sanskriti's methodology of training and dissemination.

I look across the field we have just crossed, back to Digambarpur village, across the verdant rice paddy – the most vivid green in the world! – to the Mukta Mancha Theatre, which is a rounded structure with a waist-high circular wall made from local mud bricks and supporting, on wooden pillars, a thatched roof made from the straw left over when you've winnowed away the rice in a long, exhausting process I am going to learn later today in that very theatre, roofed by … a rice paddy! The roof is like an umbrella, or maybe a huge mushroom. The theatre looks like it grew in the middle of the compound; the compound from the village; the village from the fields.

One day, years ago, Satya, whose father's compound the Mukta Mancha stands in, suddenly left my side as we were walking along one of the raised causeways linking villages during a break in the international TotO Festival of Muktadhara that Jana Sanskriti host bi-annually. Down the steep causeway slope, between wet paddy fields, he slid towards a stack of what looked to my Scottish eyes like peat, piled up in rows in the hot sun, ready to dry. I was half right, I realized, as he came back up grinning and presented me with an as-yet unbaked mud brick. I held it. I thanked him. It was heavy. I could *feel* how long it might take to cut, stack, dry and carry a pile of them. I could work out how many it takes to build a theatre. I could see beyond us a man with a seemingly impossible stack of rice-paddy thatch balanced high on his head, jogging along another mud-brick causeway in the distance. I could *see* everything you need to build a theatre according to Jana Sanskriti's design, which goes back to each new village with each new set of trainee Jokers. If you can't give money, you give bricks or thatch, and if you can't give that either, you give your time by working on the building as well as attending the Forum.

I can see how the Mukta Mancha is built because I'm holding a part of it.

'You lost your own field, Ali', says Sanjoy today. We've been talking about the aim of this retreat I am taking with the company. I haven't been allowed to put my hand in my pocket for food or rent. I am to give workshops and gather what everyone wants to tell me for my book in return. 'You had to do so much to please the funders that you lost your field.'

That alone is worth the journey to India to hear, from a friend you love.

But what's happened to these potatoes? All the other rows of experimentally grown organic vegetables look like what my mum (one of a long line of great gardeners) would have called 'happy', but these tatties are a disaster! Which brings us back to the devising methods of the company and how they fit into a way of life that is, in itself, in solidarity with the *Spectactors*. Sanjoy explains that to make the show they knew they had to try organic techniques themselves. As I can see, not all of them worked. But the okra, aubergines, chickpeas and some other thing I can't identify (with long, thin, dry pods) all seem to be thriving on traditional organic techniques learned from older farmers. And the rice in the distance is eye-poppingly green, which is, I imagine, good. But what do I know?

We walk back to the theatre, and, of course, my perceptions have been changed, as they are by any conversation that gives space to rigorous discourse, as my quintessentially Bengali talks with Sanjoy always do. Satya and two actors, their mouths covered so as not to inhale dust, are sifting rice on the smooth floor of the Mukta Mancha itself. No performance today. Farming is what these actors are doing. They wait for a gust of wind through the open-sided walls (today being a good day for that) and they hold the baskets high so that the half-winnowed chaff is carried away and the grains fall directly to the floor. This happens over and over, between two washings of the separated grains. The company, here in their haven of Digambarpur and home in the busy-ness of Badu, are largely self-sufficient in rice. I've often joked, as we work on the open dais in the mango garden at Badu, that I can not only smell my lunch (from the communal kitchen at the bottom of the garden) but *see* exactly what I'm getting, growing all around me as we make Images.

Satya mentions that if I keep talking in the general direction of the rice everything will go quicker.

Sima laughs from the pipe well, where mustard seed is being washed. And shows me what the long pods are. Dhal. I'm so taken aback! I've only ever seen lentils in a one-kilo bag, cleaned and dried, processed and wrapped, in the supermarket. I had no idea they came in long, thin pods.

That's what I learned today at Badu about how you make the Forum about Monsanto and build a theatre and train the village troupes and winnow the rice to feed the company.

Back at Badu, we are at the top of the dormitory and admin building: a third story that has been added on the last time I was here. I've got my own room, and above me, with – a luxury! – *air-con*, is the Augusto Boal Auditorium, where I now earn my keep in exchange for so much leaning. I work with the children's group and the trainee education company, who are beginning to roll out a programme in more than 300 schools in the Sundarbans. I work with a truly adorable youth group. Two days each per group. Then I hold a collective visioning for us all the longstanding core company, reflecting together on what TotO means to each of us, using performance as the language to do so and ending with a labyrinth walk: the first that I have created for the company for many years and that they have requested now, to end our time together.

The visioning is an Image Theatre session where I ask everyone to think about their work with the company as a journey of specific length and purpose, just as I have taken on this journey to India, or the one of five hours to Badu, or the one across a single field with Sanjoy. Whatever the length in time and distance, that walk will first be shown as five Images per company member (we are 12) using the Stroboscopic Image. Then, these images will be shown as a movement sequence with minimal words. Next, each of us will create a personal manifesto, using words as economically as possible, directly out of that shared performance, saying exactly what Jana Sanskriti is and does through the frame of that most individual journey. And finally, after six days' earning my keep, I will have some text for this book, generated by all of us, opening up what we can only re-experience as knowledge by performing our journeys together, collectively. Those manifestos appear as the penultimate part of this section, unmediated, translated by Sanjoy's son Sujoy, and speaking for themselves.

With considerable grace and the straightforward trust of a good friend, Sanjoy quietly steps out of the process, saying, 'I don't want to inhibit the others'. His words and Ralph's contextualize this section, but it is this statement of Sanjoy's that sets the tone of the chorus that follows. To stand back so that others can speak freely is a sign of true humility. If there is a quality that underpins Jana Sanskriti's 30 years' service to the Theatre of the Oppressed movement – to all of us – it is this. It isn't a secret ingredient – it is evidenced throughout by the whole company's words and lives – but it is such a rare one! First, though, and from the heart, I offer a Frame.

Frame One

Augusto is showing me the Stroboscopic Image at my house in Camden Town, London. He had been developing it in Paris and is lit up with excitement. He gets us all to close our eyes in the middle of dinner, and my slightly reverential guests (this is the maestro after all!) aren't quite sure what is going on.

'Open!' He shouts. And: 'Close!'

And as we open our eyes we see, as in a series of freeze frames, stop-start animation style, the chicken-leg in his hand slowly disappearing, bite by bite, Augusto's mouth getting fuller and fuller with my celebrated Ugandan chicken. As he says then (and I say at Badu today): 'I LOVE this technique!'

Every member of the company has made five Images each in readiness for the Stroboscope and now we open and close our eyes ('KHOLO!' 'BONDU!') as those meanings, distilled from each member of the company – 12 people's journeys – multiplied by (for some people) thirty plus years, move and resonate and interconnect in the Augusto Boal auditorium.

Mixed in every-how with Images of transport, rehearsal and technology (lots of mobiles and laptops), I see again and again the Image of a tree. I remember this is one of Barbara Santos's abiding metaphors for what the Theatre of the Oppressed means to her, and the biggest question of all, held since I first thought of this book, is answered to me. That question was, once, 'Are we a movement or a method?' It evoked a false dichotomy, I can now so clearly see.

Like a tree, we are indeed growing like a movement. But, just as we use the Stroboscopic Image to sift our experiences of that growth – like winnowing rice in the Mukta Mancha – we have selected and harvested the fruits of that growth through a method. Everything I have learned with the company that Augusto loved (and indeed blessed) most, after his own, inheres in this. We are all (if we are truly walking our talk and finding ways to nurture those we work with) engaged in *propagation*. And that, as this embodied tree is telling me, is both movement and method, both the *who* and the *how*, together.

The Images flow by me, and I am flooded with gratitude. Sanjoy and I often cry when we work. Why wouldn't we cry, seeing what we see, in prisons, in slums, in inner-city schools and *favelas*?

Here, then, are some of the voices of Jana Sanskriti (those who were happy to be recorded, that is), directly after that long visioning, as one by one they took their places under the real trees that shade the open-air dais at Badu. Each of us explored, first through the Stroboscopic Image, then through collective movement, then through text, three questions:

- What do you do today in Jana Sanskriti?
- Where do you want to be in the future?
- What do you need to do to get there?

And after saying these to Abby (the lovely student who helped me in everything I did) we went right back up those stairs, back to that place with no need for words, to walk a beautiful labyrinth made out of lit tapers by the youth group as a gift to us.

Our path is made by walking.

Dipesh

The first thing I'm going to talk about is struggle. TotO is done through a lot of struggle. For example, we are trying to make all these troupes, and we have to work with women's teams, and very often the character of the women is questioned.

My second point is about sacrifice. Sacrifice is about the fact that we are sometimes unable to look to the needs of our own children. We don't have the time to talk about what is good for them or bad for them. In order to be able to do TotO, I am unable to attend to the needs of my ageing parents, so there is also sacrifice.

So, if you don't love honesty and dedication, it's not possible to work for the oppressed. The more dedication you have, the more complete your work becomes.

I have been working with Jana Sanskriti for ten years.

Brindabon

I want to talk about values. When one cultivates human values in oneself, one can create those values in others.

Just as we try to bring about a lot of awareness in ourselves and we try to transmit that awareness among the people we work with, this awareness is important to complete a work properly. Without awareness, a person is going to make a mistake even in doing the things that he knows. So, a great part of the work of Jana Sanskriti is to create awareness.

We try to give the people we work with the same kind of love that exists between members of Jana Sanskriti. We learn a lot of unknown things from them. We take something very small to them, but we receive an enormous amount of knowledge, and, therefore, this creates an opportunity for us to emerge as knowledgeable people.

Through Images, we try to explain ourselves: not just through words but through our bodies.

When we go to a village to do our plays, we don't just rely upon words; we rely on Images as well. This is a huge gain.

Pradip

I'm a full-time worker at Jana Sanskriti. I have five words:

Place, Debate, Unity, Thought, Acting.

About Place: In society, in politics, in the family, there are a lot of things that we want to talk about, but we don't get the space to, so, even if we want to, we can't. When we ask the Spectactor to come onstage, they get that space. This is a big issue to me. They're not just going to listen to the play and walk away; they're going to come and say something. As a result, what happens is debate. In this debate, there is no monologue. I'm not instructing somebody in what to do and how to be. We say, 'Come: let's talk about what can be done. How will this be? What will that be like? Is this a yes or a no?' We ask, 'Are you accepting this, or that? What next?'

In this debate, people are not going to remain passive.

The Oppressor says: 'You come behind me. You don't have anything to do. You don't have anything to say. You just follow.'

In our Forum Theatre, we are trying to re-include them into the world of thinking. When they've been to a show, they come back with a feeling of being disturbed: 'Is this right? Is this supposed to happen? Is this to be done or not to be done?'

When people question the reason for the way things are (for example, 'Why is this happening?'), they start to think about how they can solve the problem. Whether they will blindly accept it or if there is a road away from this.

And that is when they start to think about how they can solve the situation. And then we take these people and start thinking and planning how to act offstage.

There was a curtain behind which I used to hide myself. Then I came here, and now my potential has come to the surface. I can sing. By discussing how acting is to be done, I am discovering the actor within myself. This is a very big thing: that the potential of artists comes to life here.

When I am discussing the problems that people face with them, then I feel I have become one with the people. So, with that feeling of unity there comes a feeling of love. Those hundreds of us who do theatre create those relationships – between all of us artists. In Jana Sanskriti, what we have received through relationships is love. And lots of people are by my side. To love me. I think the relationship of love is the biggest relationship. Because people will come and go, but the relationship must have a certain calling. They will remember this love, and this will call them back.

Chitta

I have worked with TotO for a long time. TotO is done by the Oppressed, so we do the acting. We are the Oppressed. So, the problems we encounter are also the subject of our work. In the process of doing this work, a lot of good things have happened to me. For example, I could not act, and now I can. We have gone to a lot of places in the process of doing TotO and met a lot of people. We have been trained by a lot of trainers. We have proceeded in various ways. We have spread across villages to different countries.

I have progressed in the world of thought.

The relationship of love is the primary weapon in this work. Without this relationship, the work would not have been as good as it is. We are making theatre throughout the country and abroad. We have to widen our field of thought. People who are falling behind we desire to take to improved levels of thought. We want to make friends beyond our country in this work. I want this whole world in the future to become one so that we can sit together and talk. So that our sorrow will be the same as their sorrow. We will sit down and talk about each other's problems. This is our objective.

Satya

The first word that comes to me is trust.

Trust is key. And to have that, you have to have faith. If we don't have faith in the people, then we will not be successful in want we do.

In society, a certain section gives the orders; a certain section caries out the orders. One commands, the other obeys.

But there is power in the people.

There is self-confidence in the people.

There are values in the people.

If we go to the people with this belief, the people will befriend us. This is very important. The foundation is the belief. If this belief is there then we can establish this relationship with people. You can't relate to bricks and wood and stone. You have to relate to people.

Whatever I do in society stands on relationship.

You have to be genuine: 'Am I really loving the work that I am doing? The people I am working with: do I really believe in them?' Only then will a soul connect with another soul. Relationships can only be found when one trusts another. When you feel like giving your love to him. When you try to learn from that person and also to give your knowledge. To be by his side through thick and thin in his good and bad times; only then does a relationship get established between people. This is what we see in Jana Sanskriti. We are going to be by one another, live together, eat together, be together in difficult times.

If the child of a colleague of mine is performing well in class, then I feel genuinely happy for him. It's not just the parents who are feeling happy; we are feeling happy. This is a relationship. This is the logic of living together; otherwise, there is no point. If we put self-interest first, then relationships don't get formed.

In today's society, relationships are collapsing because of excessive self-interest. In Jana Sanskriti, the obsession with me is not there. The idea is to get from the obsessive 'me' to 'we'. To keep that position of 'we' is the goal.

There is always an opportunity to discuss. That is when there is dialogue. If I think they don't have anything (to teach me), then there is dogma. Then there is no space for people. This theatre gives a space. It says, 'Come together. You can talk about what is on your mind'. We try to talk about this to one another. We try to talk to one another about our happiness together when we are having our *mouri* (rice).

Kobita

I was a housewife, confined to the four walls of a house. I did not know anybody except the few people in my house. Now, I can recognize people in my village and around the villages of five neighbourhoods. In Jana Sanskriti, I have made a lot of friends.

I have got a lot of love.

The relationship is such that if something happens to somebody then I go and visit them. I know that person.

When there is a dialogue, when there is an argument regarding a subject, we create a space for people to voice. When the audience is saying something – when a person is talking – then the audience gives a space for them to talk, and the person feels lighter. They can talk in this space, but they can't talk inside the family. What they wanted to say was bottled up inside them.

Dipak

I am not a great speaker. I am not very good at talking.

I have been associated with Jana Sanskriti for twenty-five years. And my life has changed. Jana Sanskriti is organized not just in West Bengal but outside of India as well, spread all across the world.

Wherever we work, there is a team that takes care of the work. This is how we have various teams. Jana Sanskriti may not be able to solve all the problems, but they try to logically help the people, to help them think clearly.

Then there is acting; acting is a more effective way of helping people understand their family and society. The simplicity with which it is conveyed cannot be achieved by other means.

Renuka

I've now been twenty-eight years in Jana Sanskriti. Jana Sanskriti is a place of love. If there was not love, then people would not have stuck together for so long. We see that a certain class delivers the orders and a certain class obeys.

Jana Sanskriti is a place where human beings are made.

In TotO, we work with people who work in the fields. We work in factories. They lose hope in themselves. They don't believe they are capable of doing anything. We bring them together in the belief that they are the person who can do anything. Other places do not provide that opportunity. We tell them that book education is not the only education. That general common sense and awareness are the main thing.

Why are we together after thirty years? Money is not the main factor. This organisation will continue even if there is no money. People are joining every day. Here, there is a lot of love. Genuinely. People love staying together. We don't believe in class, inferiority or superiority. That is why we are together for thirty years. This could not have been done just with money. If there was no love, then this would not have happened.

We have come here since we were young girls. Lots of problems have come our way, but we have stayed together. We believe in one another, come what may; even if there is a severe economic crisis, we will stay together.

Nobody imposes decisions on us. What we learn here we don't go to the fields and impose. We listen.

The whole world is recognizing us today. I want our work to spread all over the world, in different countries. So, those connections are happening. Sometimes I think there must be some other force behind this work.

We are trying to create a second generation who will follow the way that we have lived. So that those people who are young will be empowered. That is why we are working with children and their mothers. If we train them from early childhood, then we are not teaching them so that they can sit on thrones but to be peaceful inside. So they don't suffer from an inferiority complex. You create your own power.

I think that theatre can unify people. That is how theatre is our weapon. Mostly we reach people with our theatre. We don't try to break them apart. That is what we have been doing for many years. We believe in what we have done.

I don't know how the young generation is going to carry this forward. But we will try to create a proper foundation for the second generation (of TotO). So that they will also turn out knowing that every human being has power in themselves.

That is our effort and our expectation.

Frame Two

It is the early 1990s, and at my partner David's house in King's Cross, London, we are having a celebration to mark the publication of my play *Anansi*. But the big attraction is Augusto! I know the place will be packed with all kinds of people wanting to meet a theatrical legend, and I have no doubt that our guests will inevitably be hungering for that extra taste – a story! – from Augusto, in person, of how TotO has grown into such a transformative movement for so many of us European practitioners and activists.

Hunger. How is it so many of my relatively well-off peers are always hungry? By that, I mean far more than physical hunger, but today that's what I'm going to address, on the more mundane level of a feast, featuring, among other dishes, the chicken recipe I learned a while back in Uganda. I've cooked all the previous day and night (Augusto's coming!), and a gigantic platter of chicken is the proud centrepiece of the resulting spread as everyone piles in, filling all four floors of the old town house with laughter and questions and...

...where's Augusto?

I find him on the top floor, neatly settled on an old chair, tucked away behind the door so you can't see him, his plate piled high, clearly seeking a moment of peace in which, simply, to eat. I've been run ragged (I haven't stopped for hours), but I'm so glad he has found a spot where, just for a moment, none of those hungry-eyed fans can find him until he's eaten. He looks up and for a split second I see that flash of 'What now?' we all feel when we just want a moment of peace, simply to rest and be fed.

'It's okay, Augusto', I say, turning to go. 'Finish your food in peace. It does me good to see you eating!'

He gives me a most seeing look. *I'm tired and so is he.*

'And you Ali. Have you eaten?'

I look down. He's caught me there. *He sees me.*

'Because you need to be fed too, Ali, before you feed all these others.'

(And this is my penultimate Frame.)

Theatre of the Oppressed NYC (TONYC): 'Radically Unsentimental'

I find the irrepressible Katy Rubin, executive director of TONYC, in a half-packed-up office in their current location in Dumbo. TONYC is an organization that partners with communities facing discrimination to spark transformative action through theatre. Katy has facilitated and directed Forum and Legislative Theatre workshops and performances in partnership with various communities including homeless adults and youth; LGBT homeless teens; people living with HIV/AIDS; recent immigrants; and court-involved youth and adults.

Katy trained with Augusto Boal at the Centre for Theatre of the Oppressed (CTO) in Rio de Janeiro and later with Jana Sanskriti in India, Mind the Gap in Yorkshire and Cardboard Citizens in London. With a keen-eyed strategic genius TONYC are moving right into the heart of Theatre-land in Manhattan, and have mobilized all of their networks, online presence and flair at grassroots fundraising to make this possible. I'm grateful for an hour of Katy's time at this juncture! Our conversation has the unique pace of NYC behind it.

I've spent the year since I attended TONYC's intensive Level Two Joker training in Queens reflecting on how their adroitness in relationship-building and their clarity of purpose are to be seen, felt and learned from, in every aspect of what they do and how they do it. The setting could not be more different than Badu but the ideology underpinning how TONYC engage with the myriad communities of New York, and how they create troupes with the capacity to work in genuine solidarity with them, is coming from the same place. Of that, as we begin to talk, I have absolutely no doubt. I first noticed the company's work during the riots triggered by police brutality in Ferguson, Missouri in 2014, when they were on the scene with rapid-response Forum Theatre pieces made right beside violence that was escalating night on night, but presenting to community leaders (and youth in particular) an alternative to that violence, channelling rage into an transformative opening up of what might be done about the underlying oppressions that had burst out into the open and onto the street. I knew their training in such rapid responsiveness must be fluidly paced and intensive. I went to New York that August, just as the Ferguson work was happening, tracking it online and meeting TONYC members for the first time. It was then that I realized that merely observing their Forums wasn't going to be enough to help understand the way their Jokers were trained and how they operated so deftly. I had to do the training!

I start my conversation with Katy by referring back to that intensive weekend at La Guardia Community College in Queens in 2016. I have worked out that there must be a formidable, multi-applicable efficacy in that training: the number and reach of TONYC troupes, working with all kinds of interest groups – from Black youth to mental health, from homeless groups to housing organizations, and encompassing many other diverse sections of New York's communities – must mean capacity-building with a really firm grip on quality. TONYC simply excel at creating troupes and the Jokers required don't just work with and for them but emerge from them. And underpinning it all, a constant rhythm: the lived ideology of TotO.

TONYC, to me, approaching that training in 2016, epitomized abundance (of groups, connections and effective networks) underpinned by rigour (in training and in artistic and pedagogic integrity). I knew I had to immerse myself in that training. It had had a breath-taking

Figure 7 Katy Rubin, executive director of Theatre of the Oppressed NYC (TONYC); New York.

momentum that from the first exercise in de-mechanization I could feel in my bones was no mere side effect of their (excellent) time-management over that crammed two days. I knew it came from a deeper place and I wanted to hear how that had an ideological connection, configured in the training itself, to the way TONYC's (and all good) Jokers operate.

AC *I got a sense of your abundance. I have a question about that, about the principles that you are imparting through that way of training. A phrase you used was radically unsentimental.*

KR At the very beginning we say, we ask you to take care of yourselves physically, emotionally and psychologically.

We've been trained to not think we have the power or capacity to make our own decisions or to take care of ourselves, and to expect that other people are going to be managing our emotional or psychological or physical life. We are asking people to take care of themselves. It doesn't mean that we absolve ourselves of responsibility to watch the group, because drama is real and I don't know what someone else has experienced. I don't know what another story will bring up in some person. What I do know is that they chose to come to whatever space we're creating, whatever rehearsal, whatever performance it is, whatever training it is – and we're doing rehearsals and performances much more than we're doing trainings. They chose to come there because they want to change something in their own lives and in the world. They are so often told that we should adapt to the things that are oppressing us, as opposed to try to change them actively. And so if someone says, 'I want to try to change something', my job is actually to step back and make sure that I'm allowing them to take care of themselves physically and emotionally and psychologically. So I'm checking myself not to assume what other people can do, because they chose to come here and they chose to tell whatever story they told and they chose to listen. I am also reminding people that what we believe here, is that you know best about yourself. Again, it doesn't mean that if somebody looks like they're having an overwhelming emotional experience that I'm ignoring that, but I'm not stopping them, I'm checking in with them.

I am compassionate because I have the same programming: that the teacher decides how much I can learn right now, … But it does come up a lot, because we are in social service spaces where the understanding is that the clinicians and the staff know best what a person can handle. And the same in school: a teacher knows best.

AC   *I also remember you telling me you sit with young Jokers reading, paragraph by paragraph,* Pedagogy of the Oppressed, *and it didn't take me long to realize that even in the spaces in between exercises, that the* Pedagogy of the Oppressed *was being enacted. It was being enacted: you were still on duty when we were on a break.*

KR   That's right. We're always on duty. And I would say about the *Pedagogy of the Oppressed* that we're still working to improve the way that we incorporate political education and Freirean pedagogy and the roots of this work into all of our shows and events and rehearsals, so that there's no trying to erase the idea that the Jokers, who've been trained, hold some information about why we're doing it this way: that we're not being transparent with the actors or the Spectactors. We're trying to erase this idea of the patriarchy of the Joker: the Joker being the one on stage who holds all the information. You know, the Joker becomes all-powerful and the Joker gets to control the conversation … the Joker's still running everything and holds more information or context than the people in the room. So how are we being transparent about how the Theatre of the Oppressed developed; why we're working like this? We start without a lot of mechanized processes, but we are transparent later about why we started that way.

AC   *There was a word that came to me (in the training) and that was* **momentum**. *And that is not a skimming kind of fastness: it's pace … I kept being re-set because about every five minutes it was either a new voice or a new direction: in a pair or a circle. I kept being re-set and required to move the next step forward. I wasn't being pushed, I was being invited, but with momentum. Does that sound like the right word to you? Would you own that about your style of pedagogy?*

KR   I would own that about my style, and I would say that we believe in that at Theatre of the Oppressed NYC, but I would say that we understand particularly how we are a part of the New York City energy and community, right?

I think that good facilitation has some momentum, but the way that we do it, I would say, is not prescriptive for every Joker in every community or every setting. And it's really important to us to be in the rhythm and in the style and the culture of our community. I believe it's really important to Theatre of the Oppressed work to be local and based in its community, which means to me not training in a university people who are going to go all over and be somewhere else: not going from city to city to do fancy workshops, but working in a place where people live, living there yourself and working on the issues that affect you and your neighbours. I think that's really important to Theatre of the Oppressed: that's what CTO Rio does, that's what Jana Sanskriti does. And so I think that the momentum that we feel matches the energy that people bring to New York City and get from New York City, right?

Here we have less time because everyone's running towards things they have to do in their life. We're always talking about time and fighting against time, and I think that's cultural. I think that's part of being in New York, and I think we value constantly trying to adapt and improve our style of work to be in the flow of the place that we're in. So, that's part of momentum. I think the other part of momentum is something that I took very seriously from Boal and from the Theatre of the Oppressed is the idea of de-mechanization. We try to think about de-mechanizing all the time. De-mechanizing the way we work in an office, de-mechanizing the way we have a staff meeting, de-mechanizing the way we have a check-in with our colleague. Constantly re-evaluating and looking from the outside and re-engaging. And part of – to me – part of momentum is a pace or a rhythm that keeps people from re-mechanizing.

On de-mechanizing as an organizational principle

With our board and our staff and our Jokers and our actors, we set agendas and we set plans and we think of what we need. We address our partnerships and our troupes and our shows. We're working on our new strategic plan right now, which is really zeroing in on how we're doing rapid-response Forum Theatre to address the advocacy needs of New York City and rapid response Legislative Theatre, really deeply in partnership with our advocacy partners. We're being really rigorous and equitable and anti-racist about our Joker development and our leadership development and thinking about who should be working in the office here and who should be running all our programmes in the next few years.

It has to be questioning and it has to involve everyone. It has to be my thinking about me: when I should step down, that's part of the story, to me.

I love being a Joker, but right now I'm the executive director, which means that when people want to know what Theatre of the Oppressed is doing – like you're doing – they come to me. And that is not necessarily accurate in terms of who really knows what we're doing and it's not the story that we want to tell in terms of the power shift that we want to see happen in New York City and in the country and in the world. So I have to be rigorous with the rest of the community about when it is that what I have to bring is valuable enough for me to sit in this position.

AC   *Can you give me an example of Katy practising her own de-mechanization?*

KR   I'll give you the day after the *(presidential)* election: we had a show with Concrete Justice, which is a troupe of actors with experience of homelessness, and it was supposed to be an event about civic engagement and it was supposed to be a celebratory event, but it was the next day. And we were all having a very bad day, you know, people didn't come in and we were up all night. And I got to the show, because I was supposed to be there helping, and the actors were all hanging out eating pizza, and they were like: 'What's your problem? The world has always been like this; it's not going to change for us. Now you are shocked because of White supremacy? This is how it is here.' So I would say that the first de-mechanization is that we are not shocked, and we should not be shocked, because being shocked means that we thought it was better before, or perfect, and it wasn't. It's just these kind of middle-of-the-line Democrats that can make you feel like there's some progress and change, but the people who are homeless or the people who are poor, or the people who are Black and Hispanic, people of colour in this country were experiencing a lot of oppression before and they're experiencing a lot of oppression now. That doesn't mean it hasn't gotten worse, but if you were really struggling before maybe it doesn't feel, all of a sudden, all that different, or like people had your back before, because they didn't. Or like the government had your back before, because in this country the government didn't really have your back. So maybe it's more shocking for the people who were living in a lot of privilege.

I think the main point that we need to pay attention to is: are people really starting to pay attention to racism and oppression in this country and to take it seriously now? This is a moment to make sure that they are going about it in a creative and community-centred way, using this kind of tool as well as all the other tools they're using. So we're trying to make ourselves available to the communities that are seizing on this moment. We are not saying that we are the beginning and end of a social change movement. We have all these partner organizations who are really good at mobilizing thousands of people; who are really good at going to City Council hearings every day; who are really good at handing out flyers at the subway station. And we are really good at generating stories from people who have lived experience of oppression and having creative, fun, challenging, rigorous Forums to generate new ideas, then coming up with proposals based on that. We need to work with them so that we know the issues: so that we are in the right place at the right time so that the right people are hearing those stories.

On being an Ally and when not to impose Forum

I'm not just an Ally, I'm also someone with a lot of privilege. I have class privilege, I have race privilege: there's a lot of White ladies running non-profit organizations.

And so I constantly need to step back and take the back seat. When do we say 'not Forum?' All the time. It's our conversation: because we're working in partnership we can never say definitely Forum, it's always: 'Would this be useful to you?' Sometimes they just want a little moment, and so an actor comes and does a poem from a play. Sometimes they just want us to show up and be there and so, we just show up. We're at a rally, we're at a march, we're bringing our energy that is creative to someone else's needs. Our staff go to campaign meetings for the Close Rikers campaign, the School to Prison Pipeline campaign, all these campaigns we're a part of and part of our work is to go be in their campaign meetings. We're not just evangelizing Forum.

On how to judge the timing of a Forum: the example discussed is the attempt to repatriate the 'Dreamers: or unregistered people born in the USA'

AC   *Just yesterday, I spoke to one young Latino woman whose girlfriend is Moroccan, Muslim and is about to be sent back. She will be sent back 'home' unless they hide her or unless something else happens with the Deferred Action for Childhood Arrivals (DACA) programme. And outside, a young guy whose best friend since they were five and at school together, is of Nigerian family, was born in Britain but his younger siblings were all born in the US. His family have a big business, they're good employers, they've all gone to college, but he's the one who might be sent back to Nigeria where he's never been. And this guy's telling me: 'It's my best friend, he's as American as me.' And they both cried. I'm standing there getting ready to come and see you for an hour and talk about when Forum (and when not Forum). How do you respond as opposed to react? Could you, right now, see some of your troupes making a piece about those?*

KR   Yeah, for sure, because there's so many questions. 'Where do I get a lawyer?' 'How do I get a lawyer that I can afford?' 'How do I get an ethical lawyer?' 'Who has the resources?' 'What kind of non-profits are safe and sanctuary spaces to go into?' 'How do I talk to my teachers so that they write letters to the Congress?'

There are so many action points and choice points within that problem …. But the question is, for that person: 'What do you need right now?'

Do you need to engage your community in solidarity building and creativity, because you have questions along the way to get you to hopefully closer to what you need? Then maybe Forum is what you want. Do you want to bring this question; do you have other questions? Not just 'Do you need a lawyer', but 'How do you get one?'. Why don't you do a Legislative Theatre event trying to get the City to provide free lawyers, which they're doing?

I think that Forum is about finding new alternatives when you're stuck. Something that privileged people – who are not faced with being ejected from a country – sometimes feel is that this problem is so big that I can't do anything. That's why we don't need Forum, we need just a lawyer. Again, I would turn back to the person. I wouldn't make the decision myself about what you need right now. I would turn to the person and say: 'What are the questions that you have, going forward? Do you want to engage with other people in trying to figure out those questions?'

New York State is passing the DREAM Act itself. New York State can choose to not allow ICE into different spaces. There's potential for New York City as a sanctuary city.

And also, the city just came out on a day that the president decided he wasn't going to renew DACA, and said they're providing free legal services. So they're doing a lot of things. So, what I'm saying is: not to be overwhelmed by somebody else's problem or to say, 'I can't help with that' or 'I'm too emotionally overwhelmed by how difficult that is'.

It's not about me. It's about 'What does this person need?' and 'What questions do they have?' and 'Can the things that we're doing be useful or not?'.

I think that's the key: all of us don't know enough, and to assume that any of us do know enough – especially if it's not directly our problem – is another way that privilege is exhibiting itself.

It's appropriate to state the seriousness of the problem and to be in relationship to the seriousness of the problem, but to become overwhelmed and then to make that overwhelmed-ness about us … is not what we're doing. So, to your question: there are many, many, many times when Forum is not appropriate. And there are many, many, many times when we don't know enough about what kinds of questions people have, until we ask them.

On Applied Performance and academia

A lot of the understanding of any kind of Applied Theatre or Applied Art is that it's about, you know, social and emotional, behavioural, 'wellbeing'. Like, it's about feeling better. It's about feeling better, about being … homeless or about being in prison. Or, if you're in prison, it's about feeling better, so that you'll get your degree, so that you'll stay out of jail. It's all what society wants. It's never about confronting structural racism or … not never, but not a lot. And with love I say that.

It's just not the only thing that's needed.

I think that all of us need things to make us feel better and the more privileged we are, the more access we have to massages and wine bars and those things that make us feel great. But that's not actually going to solve the problems. We are looking at structural change. Our Forums need to be looking at structural change. Structural change happens by changing the actions between two people. Then those people go back and change the actions in the institution and then those people go back and change the actions in their policies, or the structures that oversee those institutions. So that's what we're working on. *I don't care how you feel.* I don't want people to feel bad, but I believe that we will feel better when we are seeing concrete change happen between people, and between people and institutions, and between policies and institutions.

So we try to avoid the word 'feeling' and we try to avoid the focus on feelings. We see that that's the focus of a lot of (this kind of) work and that's what people think is going to happen when they come into our space.

AC *Feel, see, act, vote. That's the sequence that you talk about in the festival.*

KR Right. I want the audience to feel when they see a play, always.

I want them to feel and then act. But what happens on the stage, what we're trying to do, is not change somebody's feeling about a problem that exists.

What we're trying to do is create social change here in New York which is influenced by what we know and by the people. Conferences about Theatre of the Oppressed don't move me. Neither do academic settings about Theatre of the Oppressed. What I learned at CTO Rio was that it was about being in a community and about working with the institutions that exist and trying to change them. And so that's where we feel like we need to put our energy and that's where we get energy from.

The Lawnmowers Independent Theatre Company: 'Nurses Jump In. Teachers Don't'

The twenty-second of October 2017 finds me at Gosforth Racecourse near Gateshead, Tyneside, in one of those huge function suites usually reserved for corporate junkets but today hired out for a big conference, as many such places nowadays seem to be. One thing I am never surprised by is the range of settings that my twenty-five-year journey with Lawnmowers has brought me to and the adventures we have shared as we take the most pared-down, in-your-face variety of Forum directly to audiences of all kinds. The space we are in is set up so that NHS staff can share best practice and Lawnmowers have a slot to run a Forum: the fruit of many years' diligently pro-active brokering of relationships with universities, service providers, policymakers and all those whose choices and actions impact upon the lives of learning-disabled adults, who make up the largest section of the population with severely compromised human rights with regard to housing, access to financial independence and of course all matters concerning health.

I have written extensively elsewhere about the company's work and won't replicate that here, save to say that it is to Lawnmowers and Geraldine Ling that I owe a great debt as a writer out of this practice. Lawnmowers first gave me the creative space to write pieces such as a book chapter in Caoimhe McAvinchey's excellent collection *Performance and Community* in the way I did, shaping it so as to show the way we explore our questions about TotO through performance practice itself, and assuring me that the knowledge thus generated is of unique value in complementing the proliferation of theorizing about Forum: the claims and the demands made upon it. It is with Lawnmowers that I have learned the most about how we need physically to take Forum to where the most productive encounters with those who have power over our lives, and learning-disabled lives perhaps most of all, are to be found.

I reconnect with Lawnmowers as a company member at a time of transition from one artistic director to the next.

Since training with Geraldine Ling (Lawnmowers' founder and first artistic director), Claire Hills-Wilson (the new artistic director) has concentrated her efforts on training packages, using Forum as a way to educate and create awareness among professionals who have been and are potential Oppressors. This has raised crucial questions around the adaptation and customization of Forum and even departure from it. Our trip to the NHS event and the subsequent workshopping of new strategies gave rise to the three-way conversation in this section, edited to shed the light of practice and experiment on those questions as having relevance to all of TotO.

The training packages under development with Lawnmowers actors have been piloted with the NHS and social workers, looking at bullying and more recently hate crime issues. All the new work has been developed to incorporate both professionals and learning-disabled voices showing institutional oppressions from more than one point of view; for example, one Model shows the nurse not having time due to funding cuts and therefore rushing her explanation of how to take medication.

Figure 8 Claire Hills-Wilson (the new artistic director) with members of the Lawnmowers Independent Theatre Company; Gateshead, UK.

The current work has been developed in partnership with Northumbria University. It is now part of three university undergraduate and three master's degree courses in a variety of different fields of study. It has also been taken up with the regional hospital as a Continuing Professional Development (CPD) training Model. At the time of my visit, Claire's plan for this going forward is to create a variety of different packages that can be adapted to the pressures of working with the NHS, the police and social workers in different training settings such a conferences, CPD sessions and within universities. All this I gather at some considerable pace, in that think tank of Lawnmowers pedagogy: The Van.

In the case of NHS staff and service providers (on this particular day at Gosforth) it is clear there is nobody present who would not wholeheartedly agree that in the context of the creeping privatization of the NHS and the toxic consequences of the austerity ideology, there is a world of difference between just *showing* what actually is happening on a daily basis (to people who know perfectly well that they are fire-fighting with dwindling resources) and the business of using Forum and Legislative Theatre to bring about *palpable change.* We all know that the real Oppressors (those in management who are carrying out cuts and those in government who have ordered them) are not in this huge, bustling room. It is full of well-intentioned people from all quarters in health provision and although some look uneasy ('Will they make us do something?'), they are basically on our side, in principle, when it comes to agreeing we all need to manage to do *more, with less.* The only trouble is that even that very phrase was used some time back by the now prime minister when she was still home secretary, lecturing the police about how they might improve their own 'performance' under austerity measures, whilst diverting attention from any link between austerity and criminality itself. We internalize these vapid sound bites. That's why I use the word toxic.

So even though Lawnmowers resolutely turn up at gigs like this, bringing a signature capacity for improvisation and adaptation (at the heart of learning-disabled culture) to a conference format that potentially feels perilously close to the well-meaning infomertial we all rightly dread, I know I needn't worry.

Because Lawnmowers know how to hold a space and to what end.

Claire dives into a bright and bold introduction to the company's overall mission and is accompanied by an excellent short film that is packed with vox-pops and examples. Behind her, those ubiquitous conference chairs (why are the frames always gold plastic?) are being deftly assembled into a mock-up of a generic waiting room: the scene of many a trenchant Lawnmowers Forum Model of yore and as such the place a lot of the company's members' lives have been lived. This introduction has the audience of over 100 health workers smiling, chatting and engaged. But I can bet that most people still think they are just going to see a sketch about how the NHS could do better, if only …

But that's not a Lawnmowers Forum. The Model is economically delivered and an absolute classic, with Andy Stafford (with whom I've worked for twenty-five years) as 'Brian' showing a chain of events where one well-intentioned, hapless receptionist, case worker and doctor after another assess him for an operation, each in their own little box doing their best but none noticing his rising panic as he struggles to understand the process; fails to read his documentation correctly; gets rushed from one place to another; gets the date of the operation wrong and finally has a full-blown panic attack. It's nobody's 'fault': that is, no one person's. We do not see who has authored this compromised system but as he is passed along this line of quiet failures we can see as an audience where institutional breakdown intersects with the ten minutes (or less) each stressed-out worker has to process him and how in that very momentum are inscribed the consequences (to both health worker and Brian) of NHS cuts.

The person who makes those cuts is not in the room. But there is no-one in the audience who isn't caught up in their implementation.

There is no need to detail Interventions here. The presentation, although participatory, is more what Augusto would call a symbolic Forum: we are preaching to the converted. What is worth noting is that Lawnmowers show up with something that fits the overall bill of this taster day. You can absolutely see how Forum works in its fuller format by the end. More than this: almost nobody has expected the whole piece to be researched by learning-disabled actors in collaboration with university partners, trainee nurses and health professionals. That's the difference, together with the fact that for this short presentation on a busy day the space itself, the format and the nature of the participation is held by the company. We are not just filling a time-slot, but occupying a performance space, an intellectual space and training space, a political space.

After the Model has run, one of the company joins each of the large round tables (wedding receptions are another thing that happens at Gosforth) and holds that space too, much as they do in the simulations that Lawnmowers run in training sessions where it is the learning-disabled adult who takes the nurse through key techniques such appropriate touch and the explaining of equipment, not just as tweaks to the existing, unspoken power relationship normally governing transactions in clinics and waiting rooms but from the point of view – the *expertise* – of the person who is normally on the receiving end. Here, round the table or in the Forum accompanying the show, that relationship is exposed and replaced with one that models equity.

That's the most singular innovation at work in terms of TotO, apart from the relaxed and at the same time wonderfully focussed work around those tables. At no point are we invited to replace Brian. Sitting at my table, a very experienced practice nurse beside me, we are taken through what the presentation has meant to us by one of the newer Lawnmowers and all ten of us agree that given time we would need to intervene early in the chain of events that leads to Brian's meltdown. We need to replace *our own performative selves* with realistic, improved strategies. There will indeed be Forum (given time) but the groups the company have researched this training package with so far have all rejected the option of replacing a learning-disabled adult as tokenistic.

Given time! The practice nurse I'm bonding with has been deeply impressed by the running of the short session and has completely understood the power shift implicit in its structuring. I explain I am here for three short days and that we are going to create two or three different formats out of the longer structure. One is to be delivered as a rapid response Forum, in waiting rooms if necessary: we are going to use only one moment from the sequence in our 'Scene Bank' with maybe just one warm-up that can be done in chairs, plus one participatory technique designed to get all the staff in an NHS workplace (in their lunch hour) to make realistic Interventions in only 20 minutes. That's going to be my job: deconstructing the original show which runs as a very bleak chain of cumulative disasters ('A Day In The Life Of Brian') so that the short form still identifies one issue that matches a given NHS setting on any one day, zaps the workers there with a clear challenge, enables them to convert their good intentions into concrete, possible actions that will migrate through their existing practice ... and all in a space that needs to be safe enough while they do so. *Given time.*

I ask her whether (again, given time!) she reckons most nurses and other staff will embrace the risk of authentic participation rather than just giving good advice.

'Oh yes,' she says. 'Nurses jump in. It's teachers who don't, as a rule. I know. I'm married to one.'

As we clear up (again, that deft professionalism of the Lawnmowers' get-out in evidence and much admired), I take a moment to reflect on what she has just said.

Somehow all of this galvanizes the pacey sessions back at HQ that follow. That is how an iterative practice works. Once we've gone through each scene back at home base in the Old Gateshead Library home of Lawnmowers, we think about the spaces that company members will be most comfortable holding and we tip our metaphorical hats to the doctors and nurses who have said that rather than miss any training they will take out twenty minutes from their lunch hour if we can create something that goes to the heart of what they can genuinely explore and hopefully change, through some adaptation of Forum, in that time. All the time they've got.

And we do!

What I take forward, out of the work and into my subsequent conversation with Geraldine Ling and Claire Hills-Wilson, on the final day we have together, is completely shaped by the way the Gosforth session has been infused with questions Gerry (Geraldine Ling) and I have chewed back and forth ever since we met. Now Claire, in the artistic director role that is now taking on her own shape with our support, will carry forward into these new partnerships the fresh research imperatives we discuss below, working within all of the limits attendant upon them. What has been unanimous for all partners and audiences is that when it comes to deploying Brian's story – and some of the frankly un-improvable scenes have been in the Bank for a long time – there is no longer a tenable option of the 'classic' substitution through Intervention of the Protagonist. We need to find ways of enabling the NHS staff, whoever they are, to look clearly at their own specific behaviours, authored as those are by forces outwith immediate control. We have to expose those behaviours as oppressive to learning-disabled adults as they play out in that always-pressured real-time situation encapsulated in the Model. We have to show in microcosm how that oppression is unwittingly being passed on to Brian and compounded by haste and lack of awareness, no matter how intractable the undeniable limitations of time, resources and money might seem.

We have to go beyond Forum without letting the health worker who is an accomplice to oppressions they haven't authored (but are nonetheless enacting) off the hook. Not blaming, but exposing. Not telling people what to do, but offering a space for them to enact realistic and possible change.

Given time.

AC *There was at least one thing that happened today that is totally Lawnmowers. I walked over to the group who were really clear about not replacing Brian. The main Oppressor is not in the room.*

So when I say 'Beyond Forum' or 'When not Forum?', I'm talking about a moment like that. Are we in a place where we might create workshops that are in the spirit of Forum but are either going round it or beyond it? Or are we actually creating a hybrid that takes us into the future, because we must and because people are asking us to?

GL I've got quite a lot to say about that. We often take it into Legislative Theatre, which is for me much more interesting than just leaving it at 'Classic Forum'. There aren't many groups that take it that next step. I'm interested in that happening. I think that the dynamics just interest me a lot more.

Here's a story. And you kind of rehearse it through. I'm just broadening it out.

AC We *can go into a zone – 'not-Forum' – where the learning-disabled person's not a victim. You're framing it differently. The space in all these three workshops will be held completely by learning-disabled people for non-learning-disabled people. So maybe we're addressing it in the format of the whole thing and the learning-disabled space.*

I think you mentioned 'Classic Forum'?

CHW We haven't been able to do Classic Forum … with this training model, they don't want to get into their (learning-disabled) shoes because they feel like they're patronizing them: that just doesn't feel like an option. A learning-disabled group have come in and they are professionally running a room. The assumptions are even turned on their head a little bit there. That's why I'll say 'professional actors'. There are 35 core professional actors and there are 100 participation places a week. I try and make sure that even in the way I'm framing what Lawnmowers is, this isn't something to be patronized.

AC *So the framing makes it impossible to patronize.*

CHW Yeah. But I have struggled with the fact that they don't step into Brian's shoes. I was at Northumbria Uni and I was sitting there with 100 students and I thought, I am with potential Oppressors in the room. If they want to step into those shoes, I can't stop them.

GL What if you did a Forum with the practice nurses and a Forum with Lawnmowers. They watch these Forums and step in and Lawnmowers watch their Forums? I think you've done so much work with it now it's just brilliant to be able to start experimenting with it.

AC *There is Classic Forum. Today you made a really good analogy. You play a violin, you learn the skills, you tune it up. You use the resin on the strings. There is a classic way to play a violin. You learn some pieces; you do your scales every day. You've got to know what it is you're departing from.*

GL Forum's a great system. You learn it, you tell your stories, you create your Forum, which is just a little flowchart, and then you do your Forum. Maybe it doesn't go into Legislative Theatre, but it has to go back into social reality, one way or another. When I did the training, I did director's training with Boal: really straightforward. The more you do it and develop your own practice, it can become more complicated and more useful in the way that you're adapting and changing it, thirty years on. But that is what Forum is.

CHW Systematic …

GL A straightforward system and it's step by step …

AC *Originally described as a game played with the audience …*

GL Creating maybe a piece of legislation that involves all the voices involved …

CHW   And different contexts, different realities, different situations.

GL   Lawnmowers take on things, they make them their own. You learn all of that through them adapting and changing and things that work. I mean we used to have a joke at Lawnmowers in the early days that before TotO was ever printed in a book, those games and exercises that have been collected from all sorts of people and practitioners over the world, put in a cover with ownership on it …

AC   *Curated …*

GL   … created and curated, and developed and tested, were certainly games for non-disabled people for the most part!

AC   *You can line the walls with theatre game books, but it's not in learning-disabled culture, which is improvisatory, which allows for a much higher amount of adaptation and inclusion, as a practice rather than an aspiration.*
   There's something called Forum, but improvisational games-based work; the world of learning-disabled practices, is such a hugely non-copyrighted, non-systematized thing.

GL   It's a political theatre system: Forum Theatre. But if you look at games and exercises, that's like folklore, or folk songs: they've been handed down, people have sung them, they've changed them, they've adapted them, you've learnt them or not learnt them as children.

CHW   If you look at the games world, how many are actually learning-disabled, accessibly friendly.

AC   *I think 90 per cent are out the window before you start.*

On adaptation of Models

CHW   So we were talking about working with a group of health professionals or nurses to kind of create their own Forum, why would I want to create their Forum?

GL   They would then learn to create Forums with other groups, not just themselves.

CHW I would worry about giving that learning-disabled Forum to the potential Oppressors, the people in power, the people who do oppress us.

If we create it with the nurses, does it not become …

GL Something else.

CHW … something tokenistic?

GL I think you're right.

CHW I don't know if I'm bothered about changing their world.

GL It changes their world because they get to see a group of learning-disabled people saying: 'This is our world and you're watching it.'

CHW Yes.

GL And what they want is a Forum with learning-disabled people 'showing their issues'. So what do we need to do? You might, if you're working with a group of, for example, mental health survivors, invite health providers to come and look at that. So it is going to be critical of the health services, but there will also be other service users. People will be stepping in and saying: 'You need to phone someone', but there's no-one there and they end up in prison.

Then you unpack that and the health providers find it hard. They just want to look and see what it is, what is the 'issue', what are the 'problems'.

If they could answer the phone, that would have kept him out of prison. He's ended up having a five-year prison sentence and fucked his life and ruined everything, because he had an episode, but *no-one* was there at the other end of the phone. You're working towards, what should that change be.

On Constituency

CHW I think having learning-disabled voices within the audience of health professionals has forced us to look at different techniques, because we can't just use Classic Forum.

CHW It has really made us question whether or not we actually are creating a social change. It has really made us think: does it need to be legislative before it will make an ultimate change, or will we spend the next three years just going to conferences about health and will we actually be making a difference.

GL Forum Theatre does make a difference: social change rather than policy change. Legislative Theatre is about policy change, and we should also do that.

On unintended consequences

GL As you know, when D**** (one of the Lawnmowers) was in the hospital, he was having a terrible time. He was just up the walls with pain. I mean he was seriously ill: he nearly died. One of the nurses said: I've done some Lawnmowers training. And just came in and did a different thing …

CHW Three actors round the bed, around D**** … She said: 'You're the Lawnmowers, I did my training with you guys.'

GL And that made a big difference. And then D**** lit up.

AC *On his deathbed.*

GL I can tell you, that is social change at its very best.

CTO Rio: 'Given a Recipe, You Can Go and Do'

It's December 2017 and the year-wide frame of my enquiry has taken me where I knew it had to: to a conversation and an exchange of techniques with Geo Britto, one of the original members of Augusto Boal's CTO Rio group, whom I have known since my first trip to Rio in 1993. We are planning how best I can contribute to the summer school that Geo hosts as one arm of the work coming out of the company's HQ in Lapa.

Dominated by the famous Arcado, Lapa is the most exciting part of Old Rio and as with TONYC's new home in New York's Theatre-land it is a crossroads of a place where the company's position claims a centrality: the old town on one side; the *Cinelandia* entertainment district on the other; the glass towers of the business district only a short walk away. By day Lapa is an increasingly gentrified tourist district like London's Soho; by night, it returns to the streetwalking, partying, hustling and edginess that I remember as dangerous. Today in some ways Lapa now feels as if its edginess has been sanitized as part of Heritage Rio: the *Cidada Marvilhoso* where TotO was developed; where the world gathers for the biggest collective performance – Carnival – on the planet; where tourists can now safely take *favela* tours and there discover astonishing entrepreneurship only a short bus drive from the opulence of Ipanema and Leme; where at the time of writing (March 2018) the bold, brave politician Marielle Franco was assassinated in broad daylight, in the open street. It is the most beautiful and the most heart-breaking city I know. The city where Boal, my teacher, made his most lasting and influential work and in the 1990s, like Franco, was a *Vereador* (mayor).

In the studio at CTO where I will be working later this week, I will take the international students through a reflexive session, *Acts of Reflection*, first created at Badu, Kolkata in April. I've negotiated with Geo the best 'use of me' arising from the conversation about pedagogy that is to follow. But the real shape of the summer school and the thrust of its ethos will equally reveal itself in collaborative evening sharings with young people from *favelas* all across the city, where the international cohort will take the floor at Lapa, simply sharing their work as a group of temporary equals. Brought into ever-more effective collaborative contact with CTO's host of partner community groups, the students' Models and pilot workshops will be rigorously tested in an enactment of the pedagogy of TotO, going back into the constituencies they are intended for before the students go back to their universities and other settings. Back to social reality.

How is this emerging pedagogy to be articulated, accessed and systematized in a way that speaks equally to postgraduates and youth groups from the poorest parts of Brazil? How do we teach the underpinning principles (the Method) of TotO with one eye to maximum transferability, whilst maintaining this enactment of the fundamental ethos of the Movement? How do we ground our pedagogy through direct contact with the full range of groups across Rio that CTO was founded to work with? My conversation with Geo starts with those questions and requires much deployment of imagery as well as other kinds of translation (that between English and Portuguese being the easiest kind, as Geo's English puts my street Portuguese to shame).

GB   I have worked with Centre of the Theatre of the Oppressed – CTO – since 1990. I have co-ordinated and participated in many projects: in slums, prisons, mental health institutions, schools, cultural centres and universities and others. I co-ordinated from 2013 to 2016 the 'Theatre of Oppressed in Maré' with young people of the complex of *favelas* of the Maré. I am currently artistic director of the School of Popular Theater (ETP) project along with [Augusto Boal's son] Julian Boal: a mobile training space taking TotO to many kinds of groups.

AC   *From the first time we talked on Skype about how we partner universities (mine included) we've discussed the next generation of people who won't be just Jokers, but they'll be half and half: hybrid, academic Jokers, you know, thinking Jokers. All Jokers should think!*

What we are going to address is: 'Nothing about us, without us.' If these people are all going to come and learn from the source of CTO, we want a partnership that's going to work for CTO. There's a word there: sustainability. And there's a word that I've thought about since our conversation many times: capacity building. Can you tell me how that's gone?

What have you now learned? How is it working, making partnerships which are building a generation of the Theatre of the Oppressed, but which are also economically benefitting CTO here, doing what CTO always did?

GB   We call it the Popular Theatre School. We try to do the work with the social movements, the grassroots movements. We are connected directly with the landless movement, the housing movement and then others not so formal, like in *favelas*, for example. Our idea is to try to learn and to teach with these people: to give the means – no – the production of culture.

AC   *Classic Marxist pedagogy.*

GB   I still believe you need to get some important things from Marx, from the other Marxists. I think a dilemma is that we need to *become* a Joker, but all the time you need to ask: 'What is a Joker? What are you doing as a Joker?' Not: 'I'm the best guy; I know the best Joker; I know the best games, the best technique; like a teacher in university; like a PhD in the Theatre of the Oppressed. I think it's important, this connection with the university. But you have all the time to stay alert, to be careful with this relationship between the university and how you are doing with the Theatre of the Oppressed.

AC   *I always remember Augusto saying that the reality of power relationships is inscribed in small transactions. Behind the individual person you will see that same shape of top-down power. It just keeps changing shape.*

GB   In this school I'm making with Julian, we are using Theatre of the Oppressed techniques, political techniques, agitprop techniques. It's like a rehearsal. We are trying to make some research *through* these many different techniques, because today we have 3,000 kinds of Theatre of the Oppressed.

Why, for Forum Theatre, would you have only one kind of the scheme for the structure of dramaturgy? This is a problem when you go to make some work in the *favela*, in the prison, in the school: if I go there and no matter what the problem in the prison, no matter the problem in the *favela* or in the school, I go to use one tool. Like one key …

AC   *But lots of different locks.*

GB But the same doors and the same keys to open all those doors? No.

AC *That Image is beautiful. I've been looking! If there were all these different doors and one is a prison, one is a favela, one is a school, then it's more like: 'I don't have the keys!' It's more like being a burglar. I need to go with some soap: you push it into the keyhole and then you take it home and you've got a print, then go back. Then I go to the prison. I don't have the key, but I do have the Theatre of the Oppressed. I get an imprint of the prison key. I'm going to go home and make that key.*

GB Soap!

AC *Yes! Soap! A bar of soap in my pocket. It didn't cost anything, hardly cost anything. I just spent thirty years learning how to do it.*

GB But it's very difficult, because we don't have financial support: we are making this work with nothing. And we are working with the grassroots movements. We have the difficulty of time, because most of them are activists and they have their work. It's very difficult because we start with the group, then half of the group changes, then people need to go to do work to make money to survive. But you stay. You need to stay together with these people. All the time. You don't have the answer, You have this process. What is possible to do. At the same time you don't know which key is to open the different doors today.

You need to change the structure of the Theatre of the Oppressed. You need to change some things, you want to change, but what's the limit? Who decides the limit? Because before, we had 'God', no? Had Boal. Now God's dead.

AC *He's gone.*

GB And one point that is very important too today, special for me, is: I'm a White guy, heterosexual. Can I do Theatre of the Oppressed work or not? Because I think you have these beautiful and wonderful movements now: women, Black people, minorities. Sometimes I think you have two sides. Sometimes it's only the Black women can work with the Black women. Or only the Gay people who can work with the Gays. But what is the limit of this? Because if I'm going to think like this; if I go to try it [laughs], I won't work any more, because I'm a White guy. I'm a White guy, I'm heterosexual and middle class.

Of course, you can listen, you need to listen. I think it's important, this dialogue.

AC *Katy Rubin and I ended up in the old TONYC office in Brooklyn and I was looking over her shoulder. Behind her on the wall there's a big collar, a prop for the street theatre: a big tie. Remember you always used to have an 'Uncle Sam', back in the day, twenty-five years ago? Well, it was a collar with a great big tie, and it said:* White Guy. *I said, 'Katy, I'm sorry to be distracted, but I keep seeing* White Guy. *What am I supposed to do?' And she said, 'You must constantly check how you are behaving. If there is one of those important meetings, for example, where we're deciding what will we do for the next five days with the Black group, the Homeless group, the Trans group, the Mental Health group, I have to stand back, let one of the other Jokers lead the discussion, be there for them and listen, listen, listen.'*

GB I struggle all the time for which direction to go in the Theatre of the Oppressed. You have this technique, this wonderful methodology, but sometimes we see some people make 'wrong' work, no? I don't know how to guarantee this work. I think it's difficult to answer about the future.

AC *I believe that here in Rio, using the mechanism of a school, of pedagogy – for example, building the capacity of a new generation of Jokers and then immediately taking these people into lots of contexts – that's the way to grow the Theatre of the Oppressed. People will come to you and say: 'Geo, we did this thing, is this it?' Can you check, can you mentor us?'*

GB I don't know if I have all this power!

AC *You'll give your opinion.*

GB Opinion, yes, but not a decision. Of course you need to listen to the grassroots movements, to what they say, but another point is: they, not you, can decide everything. For example – a real example – a long time, ten, fifteen years ago, I was working in a *favela* that the army, the Brazilian army was occupying ... . And the people in the *favela* said: 'We want to make a play about this, about the army inside our *favela*.'

And I said, 'You can do this, but you know, this is very dangerous, because if you go to do this, you're going to have a risk, a real risk to your life.' That is my responsibility: to come here and to say: 'For me, this is not a good idea.'

Another time, in the prison, the prisoners said they would do a play about torture in the prison. In the audience would be the director, the guards. With one hour to do the play, the prisoners said, 'Oh, it's very nice you are here, you're going to protect us, to make this play.' I said, 'No, no, no, no. I can't. You need to decide if you want to do this play or not, because tomorrow I'm not here. You need to decide if you can do this, but you need to see this is a real risk. You're going to make something that's not good for the director or the guards.' This is a very complex situation. I think this is a big political problem, not only for the Theatre of the Oppressed.

AC   *I think it's really interesting that you should say you and Julian are going to research what is the Theatre of the Oppressed now? I hear you use a word there. That's the first time I've heard it: Responsibility. And I've suggested maybe Mentoring. There is a relationship where you're not pretending that you are the most experienced person in the room. You have got other examples that might be relevant to this decision that you sincerely want to help people to make, including: Is it safe? Is it ethical? Is it necessary? Has it got a future, or is it just 'cathartic', right?*

Do you think we need to make a decision-making methodology that comes from the research you're doing with Julian? You're watching these people using the techniques and making new soap, right? New soap and new keys and new groups. Do you think we need to find out from the grassroots and extrapolate that decision-making methodology, so that people can respond in an informed way to 'bad ideas', you know, unsafe ideas, possible ideas?

GB   I think one thing is to make the practical parallel. You need to study too. You need to create this study with groups to look at the principles. A lot of people never read the book: *Theatre of the Oppressed*. For me it is a most important book. And I think what is equally important is the connection with the world, where you are. And in consequence, you go to look in both the practical way and in the theoretical way. I think there are some things you need to see together, to study together. I think this is one way,

AC *Geraldine [Ling] said a thing to me last month: she said I think there is a 'Classic' Theatre of the Oppressed, but that does not mean fixed. She said, you could be a fantastic jazz violinist like Stéphane Grappelli or jazz pianist like Oscar Peterson, but still you must learn the classics. You do your scales, you do your exercises, you learn Bach, you learn Beethoven. And then, when you improvise you know where you came from, you know what you're departing from.*

On TotO practice-as-research

*You've been talking about how you and Julian doing the school **is research** and then, you go out and **respond.** That was another thing you said several times, the word respond. I know you chose it carefully. To all these new people saying: 'Is it this? Is it this? Can we do this?' To be able to respond. Then you said another thing: 'I'll go alongside, not in front, you lead. I will go alongside, I will research, I will respond, and then after you've found out what you need to find out with the group in the favela, we'll come back and say: "Now, what have we learnt through the making of the Theatre of the Oppressed?" I've got to make TotO as flexible as I can, because I know if we give that time to research and response, then they will show us the Theatre of the Oppressed and tell us what the Theatre of the Oppressed is going to be.'*

GB Exactly. You need to go and to do the work. You have responsibility. You need to respect, to listen, to work together, where you don't have the maximum authority. You need to exchange. The people want a *receita* (recipe) like a cake. You will go to make a cake …

AC *A recipe?*

GB A recipe. Given a recipe, you can go and do.

PART THREE

Conversations

Introduction: About the People You Will Hear from in This Section

Applied Performance is a conversation. And whether the people I have met within the frame of 2017 reach all the way back to the original CTO Rio line-up with Augusto himself (as with Bárbara Santos and Osmar Araujo) or whether (like Alegna Dezlein and Jennifer Little) I have connected with them more recently, if not less strongly, there have been conversations on my journey that have simply shone: with the passion we share for the work, however different its contexts and manifestations; with the joyful energy of discourse that is the core of Forum and so surges through the way we talk about it; with the urgency that comes from knowing we must address questions around legacy, development, capacity building and training if a new generation is to take the work forwards in appropriate and sustainable ways wherever it is needed.

None of the conversations here offer 'answers'. I have refused to be prescriptive: in my own work, in my many meetings and makings with others and, now, in the way I bring our dialogues to the printed page.

What follows then, after careful consideration, is as unmediated as I have been able to make it. The conversations are arranged (after my discarding several fancy thematic structures) quite simply in the order they happened. And yet as they were transcribed and distilled into what you are going to read, I began to hear, after many re-readings, a voice that I do indeed recognize as my own, responding in deeper ways to that person who set out, on that year-wide set of intense meetings. The understandings I am helped to by my friends in the Theatre of the Oppressed are cumulative ones. I have noticed, for example, how often I refer one conversation back to a previous one, just as we have always done in the work, as we migrate around the globe to try things out with one another, each meeting and every making informed by the one that went before. The chronological shape has revealed over the editing process a deeper structure that honours circularity and iteration, and furthermore refuses "answers" in one final way, by having, as it were, a double ending.

Alegna Dezlein

... on running of one of the newest Forum companies in the UK; their research-intensive work with vulnerable men and how the TotO system has been adapted through the group's innovative approach.

We are in my house in Seaford, Sussex, discussing the latest piece of Forum I have seen from Speak Up! Act Out!, Alegna's (Angela's) small and close-knit group of Forum actors. Like all the company's work, *Contact Order* has been developed through an intense research period, in this case with men who have been refused contact with their children. The Forum has happened in a small pub theatre space in Brighton and has been intimate and intense. Some of the key research points are projected behind the tiny stage before the scenes unfold and one has stuck in my mind: that 98 per cent of separated fathers have compromised contact with their children, or none at all. The Forum is a sequence of scenes that at points are almost Verbatim Theatre. The audience is a mix of professionals who work with separated fathers and some of the men who have contributed to the development of the piece. One striking thing about Angela's Jokering is that we are not necessarily invited to replace the father. This the new play shares with previous pieces I have seen from the company, woven from the testimonies of adult survivors of sexual abuse. The way Angela operates as Joker has been adapted accordingly. All the company's pieces are frequently brought into spaces where those directly affected by the issues meet for complementary types of support.

AC *You're the newest company that I've made a really good connection with.*

I can see you absolutely inhabiting 'Joker', right? And I've noticed a lot of the traffic going between, going through you. What is 'Jokering' to you at this moment? You've been Jokering a very meticulously researched piece and people have had a lot to say before they feel like coming out. When you're doing that Jokering, which seems to me to involve more summing up and talking, it's discursive: quite often using the phrase, 'How do you feel?'

Angela the Joker, what does she do?

AD   There are so many different levels to that question. So many different pathways. I think the first thing is that Jokering is a bit like being a bridge. It's a bridge between two sorts of worlds, two spaces, two areas. I think people don't talk enough, people don't ask enough questions, people don't explore, because we're kind of stuck in this notion of getting something wrong. You know when you're in a group and you use the talking stick? It's almost like that. I feel like sometimes I'm a bit of a talking stick.

AC   *So you're a conduit?*

AD   I don't say anything new. I'm reflecting back what's being said.

AC   *I've heard you do that. I've heard you being very precise: it's almost a therapy skill, which is another of the bits of thin ice in the Theatre of the Oppressed, because is it therapy? Accurately reflecting, summing up and then speaking back to a person is quite a counselling skill, quite a therapeutic skill. Without an audience member necessarily needing to stand up and do anything, because they're hearing, they're seeing the story that triggers their desire to speak to you and they hear you reflecting back. And you very often reflect back almost exactly word for word what they've said. So there's that in Jokering for you, that's quite company-specific isn't it?*

AD   I think for me it's about listening. It's about listening and people feeling that they're listened to. Often when people state their opinion or their thoughts, it is laced with emotion: it's laced with their own experiences, so when you take away that, their own personal connection to it, and it's said in a neutral way, then other audience members can absorb it better to a certain degree. They can absorb it to a level that they can connect with.

AC   *It sounds to me like summing back and reflecting. The second thing you seem to be doing is universalizing: that's a term that Augusto definitely used.*
There are certain people with really raw personal experience in the audience and those with expertise – I mean the people who are from agencies – who directly deal with those people, mixed up together.

You're universalizing, so more people might feel they've something to say, or maybe do. Have I got that right? That is your policy as a Joker, is it?

AD 'Who are we for and why are we for them?' If we're going to use terms like Protagonist and Antagonist, when you've got people in the audience who might be present when something similar is happening, or they know someone who's experiencing it, it's about giving support and knowledge:

'I know what you're talking about, I haven't experienced it, but I know.'

AC *So they're a witness? So people are getting more than information, because they're seeing something live, they're witnessing. But they're also part of this thing we call an audience, which is always an animal that's more than the sum of its constituent parts, right?*

AD Because they're the people that will make …

AC *The Constituency. People who wouldn't normally meet.*

AD They're the people that will make a change. And it's people that wouldn't normally meet. Put them together, give this to them and let them discuss it. That's why it's more. I feel that sometimes I'm that channel between them.

AC *So you're a channel, but you're also a catalyst. You're also deliberately triggering.*

AD Everyone we've met, everyone I've met in the last two, three years that we've been doing *Contact Order*, always says: 'Oh, I know someone who's experiencing this, but people aren't talking about it enough.' Each of our scenes has got bits in it which could lead into an Intervention which could reveal a wealth of information regarding people's rights, regarding the law.

We know about family law, through research, through speaking with solicitors.

You come and you watch and you can take, as an audience member, as much away from the performance as you want. We've had audience members who've said to us: 'We had no intention of going up on stage, but it was so strong, this reaction that we had to what was going on, that we were compelled: we couldn't not go on.' I've had people saying to me: 'I decided from the beginning I wasn't going to go on stage.' But then they come and find me afterwards and they say: 'Well, you know, I couldn't help myself.'

At this particular show, I mean with *Contact Order*, we've had fathers go on stage and say things to the partner, or to the other characters, that they haven't said in life. They've said to me: 'That was so relieving, because I was able to say the things that I've not been able to say in life, on a stage, with strangers.'

We work a lot on characters. We don't work so much on script

AC *This comes from an improvised, researched staging of what you are doing. The plays that I've seen are a string of quite short Models. They've got to be character-based, because the basic improvisational reality of Forum; however it is that you're reconfiguring it, is coming from a place of detailed research, but the bedrock is character-based work.*

AD Character and objectives.

AC *So the characters have got a **line**. The culture of it is from the world of improvisational character-based comedy.*

AD This is my other thing, comedy improvisation. I'm in a comedy improvisation troupe. A lot of my work is comedy improvisation and how improvisation can be applied, the principles of it.

AC *That's why you've given yourself and the group permission to play around with the configurations and not get hung up on the terminology as if there were laws or some sort of orthodoxy, because there isn't. It comes from an improvisational culture that existed long before Forum. Viola Spolin, who's very unspoken of because she didn't spend ages in the university systematizing her work; Dorothy Heathcote, who trained Geraldine [Ling]; then Prosper Kompaore, whose big company is based in Ouagadougou in Burkina Faso. I've worked at the Centre of the Theatre of the Oppressed there – it's rather like Jana Sanskriti's. He said: 'Listen – all over West Africa there were improvisational methods of community problem-solving where everybody met under a tree. There are many, many examples of improvisational cultures.' And another* *one is learning-disabled culture itself. That too is non-alphabetized. It is about improvising. So there was no need, really, for the insistence in* Theatre of the Oppressed, *the classic book, to claim this direct, unique lineage from Aristotle.*

I ask people: 'What's your Image of the Theatre of the Oppressed?', and from Bárbara Santos through Jana Sanskriti they say again and again: 'A tree, a tree, a tree.' Lots of different roots growing, constant nourishment, many, many branchings and different kinds of fruits and flowerings and different seasons, depending on where you are. The need to systematize and create an orthodoxy has come from Western academic or funding structures, or Western theatrical expectations.

AD   I have an issue with orthodox things, especially when it comes to expression, especially when it comes to people and to this kind of work. If you keep with the spirit and if you have the objective and the goal clear, you can get to it in any way you want.

AC   *It's having a star that you navigate by.*

AD   It's always useful to have certain knowledge, but then if you wish to apply it or not, that's a different matter. It's what you want to do and what moves you: the motivation. This is why, when we do public performances, I want it to be in a small, intimate space. Not many props, not much set, because that's just intimidating: that becomes 'theatre'. It's not: 'This is a theatre performance.' The energy and the feeling I get when I'm Jokering is electrifying. You're there with a group of people who want to be there and you see they want to make a change. There's no other energy and atmosphere like that. It's right there. People are talking, they're raising awareness about it, they're going to go home, they're going to think about it, it's going to be triggering. It's there: there are seeds. In the hour and a half that we do something, we're planting seeds, whether or not they're going to grow right away or later. The seeds are there.

AC   *So the principle in this role we're still calling the Joker, is that you are opening that space. The space is opened in a building and it's opened in an area of society where the attention has not been previously directed, with the aim or with the intention of change or transformation. And the space has been opened up in individual folk and between* *individual people and what you described as the kind of traffic between those people and the stage. You make that happen. You are being a bridge and somebody who provokes people. Triggering things in people who are not necessarily required to substitute for the Protagonist, because we're not actually saying that's either necessary, essential or even appropriate to the subject matter. However, what you've been describing as that galvanizing feeling is the witnessing going on. The people who maybe don't act a thing out but they say a thing, witness a thing, suggest a thing. That feeling that is not possible to arrive at in any other way: of heightened meaning. Suddenly the audience, who are this collective, more than the sum of their parts, this think tank, realize that they can put together this jigsaw of everybody's impartial experience. It's felt and experienced as expertise, as empowerment, as agency, right? It's about the aim, and all the other things that you're choosing to do with the company and as a Joker are to that aim.*

AD Exactly. We work backwards. What do we want the audience to walk away thinking and feeling? What do we want the audience to walk away talking about? It wasn't about what the Protagonist can do to be empowered, it was: What can the people around him do to feel empowered, in order to support him, that will then empower him?

Jennifer Little

The NYC-based director of Strength out of Shadows, Jennifer Little, speaks about using Forum with young people in a wide range of settings and challenging the mythologizing of Boal.

We meet in a café in New York's Theatre District. Jennifer's company, **Strength out of Shadows**, work throughout the education system and she also trains and collaborates with higher education institutions internationally. On the day we meet I have a specific purpose: to recreate in our conversation a milestone moment that she first reported to me a year or so ago while I was in New York doing Level Two Joker training with TONYC. We have a friend in common, Sudip Chakroborthy, with whom as chair of theatre in Dhaka University's prestigious Theatre School we enjoy a shared connection as colleagues and work partners. Both Jennifer and Sudip have separately told me a story about a most revealing moment in the always interesting and often fraught saga of how the TotO sits in academia, as a methodology for which many

Figure 9 Jennifer Little devising work with young people; Strength out of Shadows project; New York. Photograph courtesy of CREDIT ZE' CASTLE PHOTOGRAPHY.

claims have been made and to which sometimes alarmingly heightened expectations have been brought that seem to have little to do with TotO as it operates in social reality. A short walk away, on Columbus Circle, a demo is scheduled right outside the Presidential candidate's flashy hotel HQ. Jennifer is heading there, right after this.

JL There is a national conference that happens in this country, called The Pedagogy of Oppressed Theatre; I think that's what it's called, The Pedagogy of Oppressed Theatre. This was the first and only year I attended and led a workshop. I would not go again. It, to me, was very self-indulgent exploration of the work. It felt to me like a group of practitioners who were looking at Augusto Boal's work as pure and almost like a Bible: something that had to be revered as the word of God, versus a technique or a practice that could be adapted, refined, adjusted, utilized: pieces pulled from it, tools taken from it.

The work I've done with TotO has always been what I laughingly call a bastardized version of TotO suited to the communities with whom I've worked. But this group was very committed to this idea: that Augusto Boal is this almost mythic, not just charismatic, leader. Almost divine touched. It was a very interesting energy in the space. They had a large group event where everybody at the conference came. Julian Boal was there, and spoke, which was the main reason I went to this large group event.

The anointed. The son. The Son of God, basically: that was the energy in the room.

He was there with a colleague, and they had just come from Europe. They had been doing some work: some resistance work. They were not doing TotO work: they were doing resistance. And he started to speak, because there had been a huge debate before he came into the room about the actual TotO work and whether or not it was making a difference on a macro level. That there was room for it to make a difference on micro levels and in small communities (and you could certainly work with these smaller communities), but given the shifts in the country and everything else that was going on, what difference were we making on a macro level? There was also dialogue starting to happen about the fact that corporations and the Oppressors themselves had taken the techniques of Augusto Boal and were using them themselves. So how do you come back to that if you are a practitioner for social justice?

Julian started to speak. He had been part of a resistance movement – he had not been practising Theatre of the Oppressed – and what he said was, that with all due respect to his father, he was not sure the Theatre of the Oppressed wasn't now becoming obsolete, as a form of resistance. For a couple of reasons. One, he wasn't sure that it was having a big enough impact in terms of pushing back against Oppressors. It did have a micro-community impact, but it wasn't necessarily having a bigger community impact. Two: given the level of oppression that was happening around the world, he wasn't clear that it was as effective as it had been during his father's lifetime.

The other thing he said was that because it had been stolen by the Oppressors themselves, the technique itself had been sort of bastardized: that Forum Theatre and TotO had been bastardized by corporations, by governments, to train their own workers and then had turned back on marginalized communities so that as activists and resistors and people who wanted to practise social justice, we needed to rethink our approaches. We needed to have a broader lens. We needed to start examining new approaches, new techniques, new styles. This caused a great deal of pain in the room. People were in tears, people were very upset, people were very angry. There was a lot of talk about how it had changed their lives and that they couldn't imagine doing any other kind of work: that it was that powerful. There was a lot of pushback, there was a lot of argument. People started arguing amongst themselves, people started arguing with the presenters. Julian was very laid back and cool.

I actually thought, personally, it was a wonderful sort of perspective and one that made me stop and think about how we use TotO, where we use TotO. Is it truly effective, are there other techniques we need to be thinking about? For me, it gave me a lot to think about and to ponder on. But I watched people in front of me get into these heated arguments. They weren't listening to one another any more. Then they got defensive. People were saying: 'My voice isn't being heard and nobody's listening to what I have to say', and there were people in tears: both men and women, in tears. The meeting broke up. People left.

What was really interesting was the second day of the conference. We showed up the next morning and the leader of the conference did an *ad hoc* gathering of people in the lobby. Julian again was there, but this time merely as a participant. He wasn't speaking *per se*.

A couple of members from the conference showed up and they were very distraught and very upset and wanted to make sure their voices were heard. They felt that they had been dismissed and that the whole premise of the conference had somehow been endangered. So it was a really fascinating dynamic to watch play out.

Some people were so upset that they just spent the rest of the conference talking about how they had been invalidated and their voices hadn't been heard.

For me it had this feeling – and again, this is a personal bias and a personal lens – of somebody coming into a church and saying that Christ isn't the Son of God. It had that same level of pain and intensity because it came from the Son of God. It was somehow such a great betrayal.

AC *Truly iconoclastic?*

JL Yeah. So really, it couldn't be looked at from a theoretical point of view. It was looked at as a betrayal of a fundamental belief system. He didn't say it was dead; he merely said that he wasn't sure it was an effective means of resistance any more and that it might be obsolete.

AC *There's nothing wrong with saying that's obsolete or maybe you need to see the end of it: know that there is an end, there is a limit, there's a time you don't do it. And if you have to say the word obsolete, then that right-sizes it back into a compartment of the Toolbox that is your responsibility, knowing the people that you are from, to choose or not to choose it. People want it to be fixed. They want to be led, they want to be healed. They want to feel that it will work with everything.*

JL Yes. It definitely felt that way.

AC *That's what you witnessed?*

JL Yeah. And it felt like it had happened in the church, which I think gave it that extra resonance. I think if it had happened somewhere else it might have had a different ... it felt like it happened literally in the church.

Bárbara Santos

One of the co-founders of TotO and an international exponent of Forum, now Berlin-based and here focussing on work with Black women and her discoveries through Kuringa (Joker) training.

We are in the offices of CTO Rio in Lapa and downstairs the International Summer School are getting ready to make their Forum: part of a community sharing later this evening that will include many youth groups from all across Rio, including a number of Black groups and those from *favelas* who I haven't seen here before. The international group, as I have learned from Geo (Britto) and from my own workshop with them today, will be on a level playing field with the others as they share and get feedback about what they have been making. Among them is a now rather elderly group of housemaids about whom Augusto often shared.

Bárbara is one of my *s/heroes*. Her intrepid furthering of the work and her restless curiosity have brought about many changes in the core

Figure 10 Bárbara Santos, artistic director of the Kuringa qualification programme and the Madalena Laboratory; Berlin. Photograph courtesy of Noelia Albuquerque.

CTO group, as I have seen today for myself. She has moved where both the work and political necessity have taken her and now operates internationally from her Berlin base. From the first time I met her 25 years ago until now she has become a poetic and fluent English speaker, where to my shame my Brazilian Portuguese is what one might term 'street'. So we talk in English. I will try here to honour the rhythms of Bárbara's speech, that in their underlying Carioca music remind me more of Augusto's own style than anyone else I have spoken to on my journey.

AC *How has the timing of your book come about?*

BS I started by writing some articles, because you know we do a lot of training for people? I work in several areas where the people have no formal education. Areas with a lot of people who are really dedicated, really engaged, with strong commitment, but they don't have formal education. And that for me was like a challenge, because I wanted so much that these people had the same opportunity to get the theory of the Theatre of the Oppressed. It's not just practice. I wanted so much to talk about these topics and then I wrote articles, but in a really accessible way, in a sense that everybody can understand.

Let's talk about, for instance, feminism. You don't need to go to the university to understand feminism. Every woman in the community: they don't know, but they are feminists, because they are in everyday life fighting for their rights. They are real feminists. They just don't know that this is feminism. Or, what is patriarchy? Of course, each single woman can understand what *machismo* is about, or sexism is about, but maybe they don't know exactly what each concept means. How do you write about things in the way that doesn't look impossible to understand, doesn't look so difficult, doesn't look so far away from the reality of the people with whom you want to communicate? In our trainings we do a lot of exercises, but also we have moments to read, to make seminars inside of the workshops: not just to learn exercises and games, or to learn how to do a Forum piece, but to understand: 'Why I am doing this?' The result was so interesting: everybody can see how we all are intellectual. We are all intelligent. We all can talk about theory, is not something mysterious, like just inside of the academy.

AC   *And it's not outside the body.*

BS   Exactly.

AC   *So the articles pointed to a book? Did the book say, write me? That's what I want to know, because that's the same with me. I had to be convinced.*

BS   I had several articles. I saw how this was working in the seminars: it was helpful for the process. Then I started to write others, about solidarity, ethics or dramaturgy, or the aesthetics of the Oppressed. I started to organize it: the Jokers, what [it] is to be a Kuringa in the Theatre of the Oppressed. Just put together in the simple way, using stories as examples.

I think this is my heritage from Boal. I tell stories, because, you know, Boal was great at telling stories. And you could understand everything because he always used stories to give examples. The whole thing is about how I take the theoretical part but not as theory: as a piece of a story that you can *see*.

Then the book was born, from a process of necessity, because I wanted so much not just White privileged people (who have more chance to go to university) to have the chance to understand the philosophy, the political base of the method. I had a lot of these articles and I thought: 'Now is the time to put this together as a book.'

AC   *My friend, Caoimhe McAvinchey, is now the head of my department. Caoimhe was asked by Bloomsbury to publish a collection of articles from different points of view about applied performance. And she said to them it must be lots of articles by different people, because it's a chorus, and she asked me to do one. And I said: 'Look, I can only tell stories about me and what I did.' So she said: 'Could you write about Lawnmowers?' So I wrote – it took me a long time – I wrote examples from June's story, Andy's story, Paul who died, Paul's story. The article was dedicated to Paul. Then the publisher came to me and said: 'We want a book with more of your work with the techniques of the Theatre of the Oppressed. We want you to do it that way.'*

I still sometimes struggle with convincing an academic colleague that a story has – what's the word – the same status, pedagogically. But Augusto's pedagogy had storytelling in the centre.

BS It's much more, actually. The answer that I have from everybody that read the book is that it's so easy to understand. I think the academies sometimes say: 'No, we don't want it this way, because this is so easy for people. It's too easy.'

AC *And they depend on things being not easy.*

BS 'This is secret.'
I wanted the Kuringas not only to be people that are middle class and well-informed, well-qualified. I wanted the person in the *favela* or the person in the community or the person in the countryside, who is a Kuringa by action. They could get the knowledge as well.

AC *Where's the word Kuringa from, Bárbara?*

BS In Portuguese Curinga is a card, like a Joker. Internationally I started to use Kuringa with a 'K' to keep the Brazilian pronunciation.
As a Black woman from the South of the world and at the same time as a leader – as a Kuringa, as a person organizing – I was like a complete exception, because I didn't find many people like me in the leadership of the Theatre of the Oppressed. I didn't see them. And then I saw – I found for myself – that I was more similar to the Oppressed people, but I was a real exception among the Kuringas: the experts. And one of my tasks that I took on was to change this.
If you see the CTO now, you see far more Black people. And if you go round the Theatre of the Oppressed world, especially in the South of the world, you're going to find more women. At this moment, we are a really big network. Our network as women in the Theatre of the Oppressed is internationally organized. We are in discussion and communication and exchange. We are saying that we want more women in the leadership places *as Kuringa*. Sometimes I saw a lot of Jokers, Kuringa males, directing women's groups and the perspective of the oppression was super-influenced by this male direction.
I work a lot in Africa and I really put a lot of energy in the qualification of Black people in an African context. In our conference here in 2009, we worked hard to bring African people because I was tired of international meetings of Theatre of the Oppressed that didn't have Black people. No Africans: Africans that live in Europe or Africans from African countries.

AC   *You want lateral exchange: why should it go through Europe?*

BS   Exactly. We brought here for the conference five representatives from five different countries: Angola, Mozambique, Senegal, Sudan and Guinea-Bissau who are internationally well known, right now. But you'll not find me saying: 'This is missing something.' I'm trying to do what I think is necessary to do. I'm seeing the method and if I see something missing there I am going there and *I am trying ways of doing it*. My commitment with this method is to do what I think I have to do, because I am not satisfied.

I will not make a list of what Boal didn't make. He made what was possible for him. In his context; his *possibility*. I make a list of tasks for myself: things I can see it is necessary to develop.

For instance, over the last years, part of my work is investigating the aesthetics of the Oppressed. I made a lot with sound and rhythm. I do a lot of Forum Theatre without words. I took out the words, because sometimes words are not helping us to understand. When we are going to understand, for instance, topics like capitalism or work exploitation, if I'm going to make a scene, do I have to write like Brecht? I'd have to write a lot! This is my research: how to represent the complexity of topics through Images and sounds so that the audience can best understand the content.

My criticism (of Boal) is about *doing* what I think is *missing*. I have transformed that into concrete actions and proposals. I wrote a book because I want to make the essential concepts of the method easier to understand.

AC   *My students and the groups I work with kept asking me again and again: 'Can you give us an example of the Joker? What is a time that it didn't work? What is a time that you maybe tried an exercise but it wasn't okay?'*

I told them stories, and especially I told them stories of when I made a mistake and when the group showed me: 'We need it this way.' The disabled group showed me. The mental health group showed me. The old people showed me.

How I identify with you is this: there was a gap, there was a confused place, and I moved towards it, because that's all I know. It's not a criticism.

BS Some people say I'm a disciple of Boal. How can somebody be a disciple of someone who was not religious?

AC *Of a Humanist.*

BS Exactly. There's no sense. But you see, in this field, you still have people that they want [to] say they are the disciples of Augusto Boal. He was not Jesus: he has no disciples. Boal was insistent that the multiplication (of TotO) has to be creative. This, you cannot just reproduce.

AC *Replicate. Like photocopying.*

BS You have to look to what you have and what the people need. What's the necessity of this moment: how do you embrace the necessity that the people bring to you and how do you invent work together. We have the basics. We don't go with nothing. We have a method. We have to embrace necessity and say: 'What have I here, how could I work, how could **we** work together?' And this is a creative multiplication that has open space: open space for creativity and flexibility. This is, I think, the mission of the people that work with this method. My book was my answer to the necessity I identified. I received e-mails from the people that read it, and people were so happy to say: 'Wow, finally, something that I need.'

AC *I've got some intellectual questions, but most of all there's a group of people in front of me and they're saying to me: 'Listen – we need this, but we're not understanding this.' I respond to them. I send myself towards them, I go towards them, I move towards them. And with you, from your starting point, where are the women?*

BS Theatre of the Oppressed when I came in, was everywhere: male, White, hetero-normative, upper class. Internationally, we had a few exceptions in Sanjoy Ganguly and Prosper Campaoré (Burkina Faso). In 2010 we created Madalena Laboratory, a theatre laboratory just for women. This is a special space where women can openly talk about abuse, the violence that we face and that is so hard to talk about in a mixed group. From this place we have started increasing the number of female Kuringas.

I made one of these labs in India, in Calcutta in 2010. Thirty women. I didn't allow the participation of White women, especially women from the UK: it's so deep, the colonial relation; [it's] still like that.

I worked with 30 local women. I have amazing stories from this time. One of the amazing stories was from one woman who told me: 'I have to leave tomorrow.'

I thought: why?

'Because my husband called me and told me to come back home. It's so hard, I have to leave.'

The next day she was there. And I asked her: 'You thought that you had to leave, but you are here – what happened?'

And she told me: 'You know, this laboratory, this space is so nice, I feel so good, this is so great. And I thought, if I leave today for home, my husband is going to hit me, for sure. If I go at the end of the workshop, he will go to hit me too. But until then I'm going to enjoy the workshop. Because I cannot avoid being hit but I'm going to take the workshop for myself.'

This woman looked so Oppressed, so like a victim. But she was a survivor. She was saying: 'I will take what is better for me.' And she was there.

AC   *'And then I'll take the consequences.'*

BS   The consequences, she cannot avoid anywhere.

AC   *'It's going to happen anyway.'*

BS   In Jana Sanskriti, a woman never uses trousers: always they have a sari. And when they want to play a man, they put a jacket over the sari. We played one story in the laboratory: the story of a young woman that wanted to study, she didn't want to marry. And she escaped from the wedding ceremony. She wanted to study. And the family followed her and really beat her. She was at the hospital. They broke I don't know how many bones. And we told this story. Her desire was she wanted to be a doctor. She was a young woman who wanted to be a doctor but with no possibility. And they didn't want her to study, because she is dark-skinned. And they said how difficult it is to find a husband for a woman, because they have to pay. Especially for dark-skinned woman, it's more difficult. If you study it will be more difficult, because no-one wants this kind of woman.

AC   *Dark-skinned and educated.*

BS   Educated, no chance. And then, to play the man, I asked them to wear trousers. And they said: 'We cannot use trousers.' And I said: 'But I think it's correct, it needs trousers, you know, because I want one character as a male character. And then they told me that when a woman is married that she cannot, she has to perform in a sari, especially in the countryside, because our presentation would be in the countryside. I insisted, insisted, insisted, but then I was convinced. Okay: it's reality.

AC   *Trousers, gone.*

BS   Yeah, gone. And then, one minute before we came on stage, one actress was with trousers. The first time a woman in Jana Sanskriti would use trousers in the performance. They told me that after the presentation. The audience was 5,000 people.

That was incredible, because it was so powerful.

AC   *But with Boal: if the next generation come along and TotO has now become fixed, it's an orthodoxy. No matter how wonderful the original growing and developing – the mistakes, the discoveries – there is the danger of it being frozen.*

And if you've frozen it or if you've written it in a book, then somebody might say 'this is what we do' and impose it.

I've got one more question: what happens after we're gone? Is it a book, is it a group of Kuringa, what is it?

BS   For me, there's two things. One, I think when people say that Boal was fixed, I don't agree. What I can understand is *some people fixed Boal.*

Boal passed away at 78, writing a new book, and dedicated ten years of the 2000 until 2009 decade creating something new. He was really dedicated to discovering the aesthetics of the Oppressed: to go in deep, with something new. A re-foundation of the Theatre of the Oppressed; a re-questioning of Theatre of the Oppressed; a criticism of the 'only way'; researching Theatre of the Oppressed. Boal did it by himself with us and with other people too. If you see the life of Boal, his whole life, he constantly re-created things. He's definitely not fixed.

When I go to France and I hear people say that they are disciples of Boal, I just get sad. Because *they* fixed Boal, in a place. But reality's not like that. In Latin America, every two years we make a meeting of the Theatre of the Oppressed with a hundred people. We have a big network of people, creating something new. I don't know if the North of the world is aware of it. They just don't know what's going in Latin America. It's so strong. And I am not afraid at all about the future, because my whole work is about sharing with other people. It's about creating a network of autonomous people, not [getting people] to do the same as me. The whole process of my work is qualifying people. I don't believe that just this leader knows something. A strong leader for me is the one that's able to empower new leaders. I am surrounded by leaders.

For instance, in my group, Madalena Berlin, when we are going to make a presentation, I don't need to be a Joker, I don't need to be a Kuringa, I don't even need to be present, because I qualify people and then there are several Kuringa. Any one of the group members can be Kuringa of the group.

I don't follow the White tradition of Verticalism. It's like you have a god, you have a king, you have a queen, you have a …

AC   *Expert.*

BS   You have an expert. You know, somebody that is up. And the others are down.

Of course I have much more experience than the people in my group – of course. No-one is questioning that. It's not about that. Of course I worked with Augusto Boal [for] 20 years. I worked with Theatre of the Oppressed [for] almost 30 years. Of course I have more experiences – it's not about that. It's about how can we come with our different levels of experience and produce something together. Or even if somebody comes, like you do: sometimes you know a lot about something, but you don't know about this place. This person knows much more than you. Okay, now we are going to exchange our knowledge and from this exchange we are going to do something. But what I really want, when I work with a group, is that the people from the group, they appropriate the Method in their own way. They appropriate and then what I want is that I am no longer necessary. In India, in one of Jana Sanskriti's meetings or festivals, we had a discussion – I think it was 2010 – and one woman was telling her story: that she was working in an African country for 14 years. She's from the UK too. I don't remember her name, but every year she goes and makes something there now. And I asked, how many Kuringas has she been training there, to be autonomous?

She answered me: 'No, no, I have to go there.'

If you have to go somewhere for 14 years continually, something is wrong. Something is really wrong.

If you work with people and the people are not able to appropriate and understand the method by themselves, it's a big failure for you. It's like you didn't do your job. Your job is to help them to be autonomous from you. And you have to lose this job, or you have to revamp your job. This is a process of really training people: believing in and accepting them too. You have to accept that the other person has another way, not the reproduction of your way.

Osmar Araujo

A prominent Brazilian practitioner on the processes of customization and adaptation beyond his origins in CTO, Osmar Araujo now works independently with his wife Yara Toscana in settings markedly different from his many years as one of the core team of Boal's original CTO Rio group.

We meet in a little street bar in Lapa and our conversation about how he separated from the group is very personal and emotional at first, and of a wider significance later. We detach with love from those intense relationships of the past, before honouring them in our conversation, falling silent for a while, and then looking forward.

AC *I have found myself writing about the pedagogy of the Theatre of the Oppressed. What do we need to be doing about capacity building? For example, Jana Sanskriti are putting more and more energy into training more troupes. How do I make sure the legacy is the same, when in New York, Kolkata, Newcastle, Rio, all of these different ways of doing the work are diverging?*

OA I think this capacity building is essential. To go forward so that we can *see* the methodology. I think Boal's intention was not just to give everything to the groups. He kept the main part of the energy for making plays with Jokers and practitioners and so on. Capacity building is a journey that every Joker has to do in their life. That's my view about it.

This is very similar to what Paolo Freire said: 'The Pedagogy of the Oppressed is not only a Methodology.' It is a way of life as well. If you don't agree with that, then for me – Osmar – it is not possible to get to the Methodology. If you don't understand the life of TotO.

AC *I think I believe that too. I know that truly because I've just done a workshop (at CTO Rio in Lapa). There were things I had to do. I haven't just done a TED Talk. 'Why don't we just download Ali's 30 years as a Joker?', no. I have to do a workshop with you and run the same risk of making mistakes, meeting new people, trying some things that work and some things that don't. Today there was a lady from Iran,* *a guy from Germany, young people from North America, a woman from the Philippines who does AIDS/HIV Education, a guy training doctors. I'm not going to tell them: 'Here's how you do Jokering.' I'm going to ask them.*

OA One big difference (for me) between Augusto Boal and Paolo Freire is that Freire said: 'Everybody can do the Pedagogy of the Oppressed.'

Augusto Boal said: 'Just Jokers can do the Theatre of the Oppressed.'

For me, that's a mistake. For me, truly, everybody can do TotO, as well as the Jokers. Just as Boal said everybody can do Theatre, not just actors.

AC *So there's a contradiction there, if you follow Freire. I think there has been a struggle, as if there is a copyright – a brand of Jokers.*

OA I think there is a reason that the six original Jokers from Boal said: 'This is how we do TotO.' If you read all the papers Boal wrote, and one or two magazines that interviewed him, he said that the Jokers of TotO were the original Jokers. This was a big mistake. Boal said everybody can do TotO, but he never said everybody can be a Joker.

AC *I think he mystified the role. I just went and did it. I never stopped. I didn't need to come back to Augusto and ask: 'Am I doing it right?' he said to me: 'Ali, you are already a good Joker. Go to Africa. Go and do what you do.'*

I was just lucky. I had my own theatre company. I knew how to do participation. I needed new ideas and new vision, but at some point (in Kolkata in 2004, for example) I noticed that the French groups were saying: 'This is the real TotO.'

'No: this is.'

You need to be doing it live. It's not in a book. But the contradiction is in saying that there is a unique brand. It should take different forms. It should always keep the DNA of Forum.

OA A new generation of TotO can say: 'I can mix everything.' It's quite automatic. But I still keep contact with everyone because it is the way to keep TotO alive.

AC   *It is time to agree to differ. As long as you keep doing it, as long as you stay open, the same principles keep coming up again and again. We just work together. The principles are still there: Create as much participation as possible. Give the audience as many chances as you can to influence the question.*

I don't feel a contradiction. I don't need to do Forum Theatre all the time. But when I do it, I hope it's the right thing to do.

There is a template. It kicks in. I write the terminology on the wall:

- *Spectactor*
- *Intervention*
- *Model*
- *Joker*

OA   I think the best way to teach TotO is to go through it like a recipe. And afterwards you can say: try it.

AC   *I think it takes about five days, but if by then people are saying to me 'I need to do it this way', it is not going to break any 'rules'.*

OA   When we worked in prisons in Sao Paolo, there are moments I always remember. CTO were running workshops with teachers who teach prisoners, in prisons. It was about human rights in prisons. I had researched a lot about prison in Brazil and I knew that one thing that was necessary was to give a voice to prisoners, and to make a dialogue between them. To understand why prisons violate human rights in 2000.

Bárbara [Santos] and I nearly fought each other. I said: 'You need to respect the knowledge of the people in the workshop. Because they know that we don't know.' I know about human rights. I might be wrong, but I saw some workshops where the Jokers tried to *manage* the stories.

AC   *In order to fit the system?*

OA   Yes.

AC   *Sometimes there has been a danger of imposing the template.*
'We will do two games, two exercises, one technique and then we will do the Forum. Because that's what we do.'

There is a danger of it becoming an orthodoxy. To love Augusto so much that we fear being disloyal to his memory. But it is not.

OA   The danger is that the template becomes a way to *manage the subject* as well. It is necessary to create dialogues between these persons: prisoners, guards, women prisoners, educators, those who run the system. Because the dialogue between them has broken down. We have to find a solution for the conflicts inside the prison. Because TotO is a way to understand groups, relations. And to find the oppressions, to understand them, not necessarily to 'solve' them. This is the way to do it. But to TotO there are limits. And that is another reason we hear people saying: 'You are doing TotO/You are not doing TotO.'

That's why I said it is a kind of way of life. When you keep TotO as a way of life, it is quite difficult to know that there are limits to this way of life. Can TotO change the world? I think yes, but working with other things.

Julian Boal

Augusto's son Julian Boal here explains how he redirects his energy into new collaborative initiatives and talks about the continuing need for reinvention of the TotO in response to changing circumstances and emergent learning.

Julian and I meet in the lovely Secret Café, off the Largo do Machado where I first saw CTO one lunchtime in the early 1990s doing Forum on the street, as his father Augusto campaigned for Vereador. Julian was a teenager then. He is a father himself now, working internationally on many new branchings out from that original work.

As he has often reminded me: 'Augusto Boal is in fact the father of Julian Boal.'

We don't pull any punches when it comes to a touch of iconoclasm!

JB I co-run with Geo Britto one of the projects inside CTO which is the Popular Theatre School.

AC *How is it that this is the right project for you to be doing with Geo?*

JB Right now I think this is the right thing because the members of the school are all people who come from social movements. There is not a single person who is not a member of a social movement. And there are many reasons that this is right, regarding Brazil, regarding Rio. It is not so common to have a union of the militants of the Left that is more at the grassroots level.

Most of the time you have a platform where the activists do come together, because we have a strike or we have a march and the people are going to march together, but the people from the movement are separate.

The idea was to have many people from many different social movements and we are creating a space where this union of the Left is not happening from above but *from a practice* that unifies social movements.

We did an activity two weeks ago. It was beautiful to see so many people from so many different organizations working together. Other reasons may be specific to Brazil. We talk about going to the *favelas*. We talk about community work. But at this time the most common cultural thing among groups on the Left in Brazil is linked with what we would call agitprop or propaganda. You go in front of the house of a very bad politician, make a performance, record it and send it to Facebook. It works with the delusion that every time you get a click you get a new activist.

The idea is to work with theatre. To have a space in which people are going to meet on a regular basis – who will *have* to work together on a certain issue. This implies a lot of process that moves you away from the immediacy that social media have implied is their way of 'doing'. So there is no deeper reflection on *what is done.*

Now we are happy because we got funded and they are going to receive a scholarship of maybe 150 Reals (£30).

AC *Where did you get the funding from ?*

JB From Petrobras.

AC *How many people got the scholarship?*

JB Between 15 and 20.

AC *So they are already self-identifying.*

JB Now we have a big rise in identity politics in Brazil: LGBTQ, Black issues. We are the country that kills the most LGBTQ people every year. Women: we are in the top ten. Black people: we are the same. So these issues are real issues in Brazil, but identity politics portrays them in a very abstract manner:

'The' LGBTQ

'The' Blacks

'The' Women

I'm not seeing how the materiality of society itself constrains those identities.

Let me give you a precise example. Most of the time here in Brazil when people talk about 'Black issues' they are going to show the resistance of Zumbi.[1] They are going to show that 'Blacks are amazing'. But they don't show what is happening right now. I've been to work with a social movement yesterday – 'The Movement Without a Roof' of Bahia – and I've been asked precisely to bring **contradiction.** One of the things that I've asked them is to use a scene of Brecht, from St. John of the Slaughterhouse. St. John goes to the slaughterhouse. And he gets to see it's not about bad poor people, but about poor people who are bad.

AC   *He's continuing a Victorian distinction that there were the Deserving Poor and the Undeserving Poor, which was to moralize as if their morals were something to do with their being poor as opposed to standing back and looking at the structural causes of poverty.*

JB   The scene shows that yes: poor people are constrained into badness by the social situation.

I asked them to make new scenes and in one they showed us how the poor mothers of Bahia exploit their own children. And they showed the children playing with paper planes.

> *The mother is cooking something.*
> *They ask the mother: 'Is it ready?'*
> *The mother says: 'Yes it's ready.'*
> *They turn their planes into the paper cones that they fill with peanuts to go out begging.*
> *Then they fold the paper again like it was money and they give it to the mother, and the mother takes it and she yells at them – she's a very good actress – that it is not enough money for them to eat.*

This was showing concrete complication. Contradiction. Not: 'We are good. We are nice, really, really.' I think that most of the time we don't confront the facts. That we are not good. That there can be a

---

[1] Led the first Brazilian Slave revolt.

contradiction and a conflict within the groups of the Oppressed. And these things are not *complexified.*

AC *What this says to me is that you are choosing places: spaces where people agree to keep coming. That whatever else you are doing ideologically because you are from different trade union groups, different left-wing groups, different activist groups, you are making that messy, risky, complicated work, through meeting, through making, and these relationships aren't automatic.*

It sounds as if you are looking from a place where these relationships are complicated, are consolidated, are nurtured through the making of theatre together. Can you make this as complicated as anybody else's theatre? As rich, as annoying, as provocative as anyone else's theatre? You've got multiple points of view. You've got your collaborators' points of view. You don't pre-decide. You were invited.

JB I just offer Models or scenes.

AC *As middle class White men we have to stand back and know that, as only one lens, the loudest narrative in the political North, we've heard that we should now say: 'I'm just a catalyst. I'm only a facilitator. I'm a White guy. I'm not really here.'*

I only want to go somewhere I'm invited. But we're allowed to make the things we want to make.

JB For me, as a White guy in Brazil, I am only 100 metres away from where there is shooting. Imagine how it is to live in a society where you fear how you are going to get your kid home from school. Ten days ago there was a huge gunfight in Copacabana. It lasted for an hour and a half. There is a WhatsApp group of parents at that school, where my kid is at school. They were putting our kids in the basement. The whole city was like this. So privilege in Brazil is to be able to afford things that shouldn't even be afforded. They should be rights.

The facilitator is not someone that does not suffer from problems. I suffer in a different manner. I've been to the School for the Landless (*Sem Terra*) many times, when my kid was 20 metres away from where there are guns. There is the school where the landless are and the police come in, shooting. That close.

AC   *You're a father. That's it.*

JB   Friends of mine were there the day of the invasion. And my kid could have been there. You are not in a place that is 'neutral'.

The games, exercises and techniques do have an ideology. And that is not to pass through the games and exercises and *then* do something.

The exercises are not neutral. There is an embedded ideology, that sometimes is very problematic.

AC   *They enact an ideology.*

JB   And that is my biggest reflection. My reflection is: 'What is the ideology that is embedded in TotO and how can it work – or not – today?'

AC   *What is it **now**?*

JB   We know that the political situation we are living in today is completely different.

AC   *Bárbara [Santos] said there is a danger of there becoming an orthodoxy or a one-size-fits-all-template and then all you will do, when it comes to the next generation of people who you hope will take some of the good things and use them in their way and in their context, you will be replicating, but you won't be multiplying.*

*The word I have used with Sanjoy [Ganguly] is **propagating**. There is a moment where we are in the middle of something, in the middle of a field, this field, something really messy, like gardening, like digging. What is TotO here? Which TotO is going to bear fruit here? You and I are physically present to one another, our hands are dirty, and it's got to be remade. Then you go back out into the field again, with the people you are working with, and again you ask the question: What is it here? What are the aesthetics of it going to be, here and now?*

Everything that anybody has said to me that has mattered, has been about Now. I'm not going to say something about the Future.
   I thought I was going to write about it, but no.

JB   I've a sentence: I think it was said of Brecht:

'To use him without criticizing him is to betray him.'

I think we have a problem in TotO that we think that there are techniques that are written in stone forever. That they were laws written by God in those epiphanies that my father had.

AC   *When you've been invited to Bahia, one of the tools you're going to use is Forum Theatre. How are we going to do this Forum so as not to reduce the lived experience to an individualistic identity politics, just so that we can do Forum Theatre? Have you found out yet?*

JB   Lets talk more about the Popular Theatre School, which we've been doing for a year now. How do we make a dramatic Protagonist who is not a 'hero'? We use scenes from Brecht as Models, *to move away from*.
   So we need to figure out: how are we going to create Forum Theatre knowing that the form is the problem?

AC   *Would it be that you still have a Joker, or two Jokers, that you still have somebody calling out Stop! and replacing someone, whether or not you called them the Protagonist? Would that still be the idea?*

JB   We look at how he goes against certain expectations: rubs you up the wrong way. I think the core thing is how you write the play.
   As a friend of mine says: Dramaturgy *is* Ideology.
   So we need to figure out how dramaturgy can live with ideology in a positive sense.
   I was in this Latin American meeting of TotO in Guatemala. There was a play where not one guy but four guys raped a woman. And there was one woman, a very clever woman, who entered the Forum and made self-defence moves.
   I said to her: 'Is that the only answer?'

And she said: 'Yes, if that's the only question. If you ask me what to do at this precise moment of the rape, and not about how rape culture is embedded in society as a whole and where we can fight it; if you ask me what to do at this very moment, then that is the answer.'

So basically: lets change the question!

How do we create a society in which rape is seen in a very different manner?

AC *So maybe we show a Model of a group of only boys to an audience of only boys and we work with, say, 14–15-year-olds, and make a Model where some of the boys are watching porn and one of them says: 'Wait a minute. I've got a mother. I've got a sister.'*

I say to an assembly of High School boys: 'What are the things that you might now do?'

It's about the Dramaturgy asking the right question.

JB I think we are maybe talking too much about Forum Theatre as a problem-solving methodology. If we are into problem-solving.

Brecht was showing *Mother Courage* to the German Communist Party and they were saying: 'But you are showing a character who enters the play blind, leaves the play blind and doesn't learn anything.'

They were very disappointed at that. And then Brecht answered back: 'Yes! She doesn't understand a thing. But maybe the audience will.'

I think we are too much into the idea of seeing on stage a process of learning, a process of winning.

Why do we have to identify ourselves positively with the Protagonist? With the main character who is to be replaced? For ourselves to have a sense of emancipation?

I'm saying this because my favourite network of TotO, in Portugal, called *Opprimo*, is now getting dismantled because they've got no money: none of them is a theatre professional. We had a meeting – a very good meeting – and the most exciting thing in the performances was an unsolvable one.

Every night they performed a play. None of the people liked the plays. They were saying: 'You're watering down Oppression. You're making it too easy. Just do this and do that. If we vote for the "right" trade unionist there will be no more machismo, and if you stand up in front of the perpetrator there is going to be no more sexual aggression on the subway. Just do this and that.'

And the play that made them less frustrated was a long play, but based on Forum, by a group of teenagers from Capo Verde (their parents are from Capo Verde; they were born and raised in Portugal) they were making a play about their mothers and the fact that they were ageing and that it is more difficult for them to work. It was about an undocumented mother who can no longer work and wants to retire, wants to have benefits, but it is impossible for her.

I'm not going to tell more about the play. It was very beautiful. But it was completely unsolvable. We tried it as if from the position of a very active social worker (the only position from which we could deal) because there was no collective organization. And everything failed.

But in this failure there was really a sense of changing things that was much more complex than just standing in front of the Oppressor, putting your finger in the nose of the White boss and saying: 'I've worked fifty years for you, now you do this and that for me.' There was no such thing. And this play was the one that got people the most excited because the situation was such that the attempts from the Spectactors were not just a display of bravery. There was something else.

And even though it had failed, I felt that it was the most activating play, because it was a real question that was asked of us and not just: 'Be brave and then things are going to get better.'

AC *It's almost as if we go back to one of our original sources. As if you are saying that one of the sources of our work remains Brecht. Mother Courage: she is benefiting from ignorance; she is benefitting from war; she's being completely pragmatic.*

JC And being destroyed by it at the same time.

It's a contradictory process. A friend of mine from Sao Paolo saw a picture of a native guy defending the tractor that was destroying the trees, defending this machine, sent by agents of the government, defending it to the point where he was getting pepper gassed in the eyes, because the object that was destroying nature was also his way of living, of surviving.

It's the same thing with Mother Courage. War is destroying her but at the same time she is surviving on it. And it seems to me that if we leave out this relationship with the thing that is destroying us, then we are not playing it right.

In Brazil we have a Fascist country. The worst possible president, who was helped in the election by an Australian newspaperman. But what is worse is the fact that people like him. That they think (like him) that it is a solution to kill all the bandits and then Brazil is going to be better.

What is that mind-set?

To which reality does this correspond?

AC   *That's the right question.*

Epilogue: 'From Damascus'

The Recreation of a Journey, with Mojisola Adebayo and Ali Campbell

In 2005, I was invited by the British Council to run a Forum Theatre training for two weeks in Damascus, based at the prestigious theatre school. I said yes to this. What does it mean, this saying yes to a group who have self-identified as being ready to add the Toolbox of Forum Theatre to their existing skill-sets and resources? Under their formidable teacher, Professor Maria Elias, this group of students had already formed themselves into a small NGO (FIRDOS); were working in rural communities including those on the Golan Heights within UN peacekeeping boundaries and had read *Theatre of the Oppressed*, translated from the single French dog-eared copy that Professor Elias owned. They were already constituted in this way and had self-identified as being ready to extend and adapt their range of strategies. They knew their Constituency well, although as ever there was that timeless gap between the privileged urban students and what appeared to be the relatively uneducated rural population, situated in traditional villages only a couple of hours away but still living very traditional lifestyles.

Tradition! Damascus, the oldest continually inhabited city in the world, is a palimpsest of living, layered traditions. The Umayyad Mosque alone tells the whole Mediterranean story: first a pagan temple (whatever that might mean) then a Phoenician one, then a Christian site and finally the awe inspiring Islamic space it is today, with Saluddin's Tomb in the central court; some of the first minarets ever built and yet, still there; and, high in the opposite wall, the window where Paul and Barnabas were lowered to safety in a basket.

There is no linear narrative if you walk your own history, rather than read about it.

The central open space of the Mosque is a dazzling, white, shining expanse of marble floor, so polished by millions of devout feet over the millennia that you see everyone's reflection, suspended upside-down beneath them: families gathering to look at the tombs, groups of men (always separate from women) chatting. People, and their Images, only touching where the two worlds meet. Travellers like myself.

Every day I went there to learn about Islam by chatting with people and trying to copy the patterns from the tiled walls into my notebook, waiting for Mojisola Adebayo to come and co-facilitate the Forum training with me.

Final Frame

Late at night one of our delightful students takes me through the astounding labyrinth of the Old Town. Damascene houses are so old that what once were the first floor windows are now the main doors: the street of compacted earth has risen, constantly beaten down by daily use over the centuries, so that now we walk through what was a first floor window, down the cool stone steps into the cool interiors. There are no street signs. It is bewildering by day, but by night …

I am silenced by it as we walk.

We are looking for a different kind of tomb: a Sufi one, half-hidden, said to move around and elude the seeker who isn't ready. The saint is buried beneath a wooden ceremonial floor on which the Dervishes sometimes spin. The gate of iron bars is festooned with hundreds of padlocks, some very old, all keeping

tight a secret, or a promise, or perhaps a hidden gift. We find
it after getting quite lost. It is the middle of the night and I have
no idea where we are. I only met this young man a few hours
ago. We find the tomb after winding, winding our way and as if
he senses my mounting impatience, just before we turn the last
corner, he says:

> I didn't know the way here exactly sir, but we are soon
> here. They say of Damascus that until you have been lost
> here first, you will never find your own way.

We say yes not only because certain things have been set up well (the
self-selecting cohort; the NGO; the ongoing work in the Golan villages)
but because we have been invited in a good way: an honest way.
Professor Elias is the real deal. She is exiled from Palestine: a place Moj
(Mojisola) has made Forum a lot (in Ramallah). They connected very
quickly. Her eyes widened a little when we explained how the two of us
would be imparting Forum in tandem.

We decided to model Sparky and Moley: Moj leading the training
as a Kuringa, me moving around the edges and popping up in groups
(only on request from them) and using various visual documentation
techniques to create the bespoke template-cum-diary that will
gradually fill the wall for transparency, for memory and most of all for
customization.

The groups made three Forums: a men's, a women's and a
children's one. Syrian villages, as I say, are traditional! Now, in 2018,
in my office at Queen Mary, University of London, after a long day
teaching our own students, Moj and I do some re-creation: of how
that decision to operate as a Queer Black woman and a Gay White
man played out, enacting the cumulative sum of our own learnings in
TotO, not only in what we do but, crucially, in how we do it in reality
and especially in our sharing of focus and power. That modelling was a
vital part of our pedagogy and the way we worked was intrinsic to the
ethos of the TotO our Damascus group experienced in collaboration
with us.

We are looking at photographs.

Figure 11 Mojisola Adebayo at the Umayyad Mosque; Damascus, Syria.

AC *That's you at the Umayyad Mosque.*

MA You've got an astonishing memory, Ali.

AC *Anyway, you and I went. I've got some ideas. One is Constituency. We were invited, they were really, really nice students, 90 per cent of them. They had an NGO called FIRDOS and they were already consistently going out and working with communities. I'm not really interested in hearing about the Theatre of the Oppressed unless* *somebody has managed to forge those relationships. They don't need to be long, but they're authentic.*

Do you remember this place? You and I had done a couple of really strategic things. First, you walked through the gates of Damascus airport: it's so vivid! My memories of you are particularly vivid. And you were wearing a man's suit and a couple of security guards came up, because they were frisking almost everybody, and you shouted out, 'I'm a woman' ...

MA   Did I?

AC   *I hadn't seen you for a bit and you were wearing a really, really beautiful suit and your hair was dead short and I couldn't work out where you were, and I'd some flowers that were kind of wilting in the heat.*

MA   Yes, I remember that.

AC   *And I heard your voice shouting, 'I'm a woman!' and I thought, I know that voice, and then I realized they thought you were a bloke and they were coming to do the blokey frisking and you needed to be frisked by the lady who did the lady frisking.*

What I am bringing to life now, is: we were going to model being not just the Jokers, but the imparters of the whole system. Very quickly we agreed you were going to be in the middle of the room and I was going to do the things I love: the documentation, the storyboard that gradually filled the walls every day, and they were going to look at you and listen to you, because we knew they were a real conservatoire bunch. But good-hearted folk with their own little NGO. We didn't particularly go Queer, but they knew we were modelling Man, Woman, Black, White and that you were foregrounded and I was the support. And we decided that before day one.

This is a village in the Golan Heights – can you remember from your point of view, anything about that?

MA   I remember it was a school playground. In a village in Golan, not too far from Occupied Territory. And they were quite amazing, that young theatre company. There was a class difference. They were kind

Figure 12 Forum on the Golan heights. A trainee Joker conducts a village Forum; Syrian Golan Heights.

of middle class educated Syrians, and so one thing that really struck me was this whole idea of working with a particular community, especially when you're an outsider, because we were training trainers, as it were, or training a theatre company. But there was a class difference. And they were city young people, middle class.

AC *Yeah, like this guy, he made this beautiful Joker. We started incredibly early in the morning and we went through the UN checkpoint. They really did intend to do the real thing, they had read the whole* *of* Theatre of the Oppressed, *they had read Freire, they were trying to model and follow* Pedagogy of the Oppressed, *they were not parachuting.*

MA   And they wanted feedback, didn't they?

AC   *They wanted feedback. They could still be doing that thing of inadvertently looking like parachuters. I remember this day, this incredibly important day.*

MA   Yeah. I mean he was remarkable in that he was combining both his knowledge, his sort of theoretical knowledge of Theatre of the Oppressed with this Hakawati Arabic storytelling form, and I remember that, I remember really enjoying it: the Hakawati being that sort of traditional form that they were able to blend and make into their own kind of Forum.

AC   *But they knew who the ones who were dead good at being Joker were and they knew the ones who wanted to act, but they all did hang together. Would you agree with that? Is that what you remember?*

MA   I remember them being a really strong, good company. I remember them hanging together, I remember them being full of heart. What I also remember is that there was a slight air at times of 'we are the artists and you are the community', and I remember being quite critical, saying: 'Come down off a level, engage with that community as your equals.' I don't think it was anything conscious, it was educated city, young, people versus rural country people.

AC   *Almost like looking at those eighteenth-century plays where they talk about the Town and the Country.*

MA   And they were fantastic actors as well and they were great dividers. What I remember from the Forum is – what I learnt there I still carry with me today – is that in the Forum the men all spoke first and they spoke and they intervened and it was a good hour of male-only interventions. And I remember sitting there with my training hat on, thinking, come on guys, you've got to bring out the women. Bring out the women! And then eventually, after some time, the women started. The women started talking and the women started intervening. And that taught me a lot about patience with Forum, having a level of acceptance of a cultural mode. Because the women's Interventions were fantastic and they were really astute. I remember one woman. I can see her in my mind's eye now, really, really strong. I think she was a teacher herself. But I struggled, and I remember in some of the feedback saying to them: 'Would it be an idea, as one does in a mosque, to have women and have men separate their Forums out so the women don't have to wait; don't have to feel they have to wait for the men to talk?' But they disagreed with that because they felt like it would just reinforce a mode of being that they're trying to break, which I thought was kind of interesting. But I really remember that: patience, patience with the Forum.

AC *I know she was a teacher. I know that lady was a teacher because, look!*

This lady waited. I can't quite remember the way we showed them, but there was a men's one and a women's one. This particular lady waited and waited and waited, and then this scene happened and it was in a Hamam. It was blokes arguing about land and land inheritance and it went on and on and on and on.

She went: Stop! And the blokes who had remained in this kind of like wall of blokes, (perfectly nice blokes, no jeering or catcalling when women had ideas, nothing like that) just were The Blokes. And she came out and her Intervention meant that she was walking into a Hamam. She stood and addressed the scene from the outside, but because the acting was really good, you thought, basically, that she barged into the Hamam and goes, 'You lot!' and then she gave them this piece of her mind. And she said: 'If you sit in the male-only space, doing the things that men have always done in the most male-only space that there is, the Hamam, you're only going to get male solutions of where we're going to.' And got a big round of applause from the women. She didn't come in and replace anybody. She just went, 'You lot!' and it was kind of meta. And afterwards, you were saying goodbye to lots of people and I walked down through the village. Do you remember, those houses were made out of great big stones? They were one-storey, traditional, made out of huge stones. She was sitting in her doorway and she said, 'Come over here', and she spoke to me in English. She said: 'Half the women in this village have got degrees. I'm a qualified teacher.' She said: 'You go back and tell your fancy friends' – not quite that, but, – 'tell them that'.

And the idea of Constituency went, 'pfff!'. And one time bomb under Syria was that a highly educated population were nevertheless being kept down.

MA   You're right, yeah. Yeah. Well remembered.

AC   *I needed to check it with you, Moj. In terms of the end of the book, I'm not wanting to say you need to find somebody who looks different from you and be a double act. But how do you think we did? You and I made really good decisions and we sat in that hotel every night, having the same dinner again and again, with a big flash TV. Condoleezza Rice kept appearing, talking about the Axis of Evil. How did we do when it comes to pointing away from this Joker, this fetishized person who has in 95 per cent of my experience been a man?*

MA   I think in terms of training it was modelling something that a lot of people wouldn't have seen before and for a man, as you did, to voluntarily step back with all of your experience, wasn't about stepping back, it was stepping *sideways*. I think that was really positive. I look back at all these projects and think we should have evaluated in some way, should have tried to keep a record in some way.

AC   *I wonder how they all are now?*

MA   Where?

AC   *And where, yeah.*
How did we do with our two weeks modelling what we Modelled with that positioning, in terms of leaving behind something? If they're still there, those people, if they're still alive, would they have got enough to be able to layer it into their very strong existing practice, the good set-up they had, their good intentions? Do you think the answer was in our honest attempt to model and make it all transparent on the wall

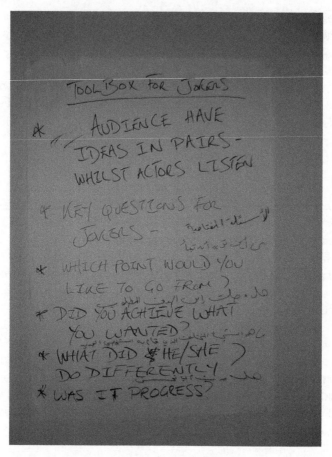

Figure 13 Damascus recipe. Part of a template for Joker techniques developed with theatre students; Damascus, Syria.

and be led by them, told by them, 'we're going to the Golan Heights, it's what we're doing'? Do you think that other people aspiring to impart Forum, as well as they can, in someone else's country and someone else's culture, do you think those are pointers? That we did quite well at hitting on a few?

MA   I definitely think that the idea of training people rather than trying to make a piece of Forum Theatre with a community group and then leaving them behind – actually working with people who are already at a certain level or are already working with people who have got a long-term relationship, working with people who are professionals, handing over those kinds of skills – I think that's a really positive kind of way of doing it. I don't do anything any more unless I'm training local people. I don't want to work with 20 young people in a school in Uganda and leave them: that's crazy. So I think that model was great. And I think you are absolutely right in the power of deciding that a woman of colour in an African top, even though I'm in Syria, even that is not my cultural heritage.

I think in those situations where there are fewer women in leadership positions – fewer Arabic women or Indian women or African women in leadership positions – I think to read that from an outside perspective is a very, very powerful thing. I think the quality of the training would have been very, very different if it had been the other way round. If I had been writing things up on flipchart paper.

And its amazing that this is still how so much Theatre of the Oppressed work is done, despite the extraordinary content and tools that Boal shared with us and developed with his comrades like Bárbara. Still, the power relationships are completely stuck in 1970s Patriarchy. It's not acceptable any more. It can't be that way. It's not just about what one's doing with Theatre of the Oppressed, it's *how*, how that work is happening.

If those people are still in those power positions and don't let go, then the work has not succeeded.

What came out of that Syria project, as I reflect on it with you is: what we were modelling there goes to the heart of some of the issues of Theatre of the Oppressed as a movement, globally. What I was saying before is that if the structures of theatre companies, of groups, don't reflect or don't look like what we aspire society to become like; if the leaders are still all city-educated middle-class men; if the structure's still exactly the same, then the work hasn't succeeded.

We have to model other ways, even at the very basic level of facilitating. And that decision for you to step sideways and to be by my side, rather than for me to be behind you supporting: that decision for the dynamic was very powerful.

Figure 14 The author in Syria. The author with boys from the village Forum audience; Syrian Golan Heights.

Why do I leave this Image to last and draw no conclusions? Because my beloved teacher Augusto told us that the Theatre of the Oppressed is never finished. The boys on the Golan Heights in this happy picture would now be in their thirties. How many are refugees? How many have survived? What use is my practice when we are dealing with despots and dictators, North, South, East and West?

My journey began with questions that cannot be answered. What I will continue to do – as long as I am invited, as long as I am able – is to follow those questions back to the theatre I call home.

The path is made by walking.

Ali Campbell
London
May 2018

Glossary

The Theatre of the Oppressed is remarkable for its coinage of a number of technical terms specific to its methodology. The interrogation of these through examples drawn from my own practice and that of many others is one of the main themes of this study and as such many of them – such as **Forum** and **Model** – appear on nearly every page. Throughout this study I am interested in unpicking and interrogating such terms and this being so would suggest readers familiarize themselves with the brief definitions below. In the body of the text they will frequently be capitalized to signal their particular significance.

Antagonist: The character in a Model or Forum scene who holds oppressive power. Originally a term used by Aristotle in his analysis of the workings of tragedy.

Conscientisation: After the Portuguese *conscientização*. A term central to the theory and practice of the Brazilian educator Paolo Freire. The process of making others aware of political and social conditions (as a precursor to challenging oppression) while becoming increasingly aware of one's agency in so doing.

De-mechanization: The aim of many of the games and exercises in the Theatre of the Oppressed 'arsenal': to free up through radical, improvisational play the performing body of the Spectator from internalized habits of obedience and complicity in external structures of oppression.

Forum Theatre: An experiential, educative system of theatre-making designed to expose and confront oppression as it is encountered by the Spectators in their own lives, through Interventions enacted by Spectactors and facilitated by a Joker.

Great Game of Power: One of the key exercises of Image Theatre, using both objects and the Spectactors' own bodies to recreate, inhabit and deconstruct oppressive power structures, in the process of dynamizing these as Models.

Handshake Forum: A simple template for a Model, played like a game, whereby Spectactors seek to elicit a handshake from one 'player' who represents the Antagonist. The aim is to free up the Spectactors' innate, collective repertoire of strategies to make imaginative and effective Interventions in the Forum.

Image Theatre: A set of developmental exercises, using freezes or tableaux as building blocks to explore and embody the Spectactors' shared experience of oppression. A freestanding method of performance-making in its own right as well as serving as capacity-building towards the creation of Models for Forum.

Intervention: The action by the Spectactor of interrupting the original staging of an oppression (the Model) by not talking about but acting out realistic ways that oppression might be resisted. A rehearsal for the Revolution!

Joker: The pivotal role of the facilitator of both the Interventions during a Forum Theatre session and the exercises whereby Models are devised by Spectactors.

Legislative Theatre: A development in the application and intention of Forum Theatre, bringing Models enacting specific oppressions directly into participatory contact with relevant policy makers: those with the actual power to take up Interventions as the starting point for real social change.

Model: A short scene or sequence, created by Spectactors from lived experience of oppression and replayed in a Forum Theatre session to challenge all participants to make Interventions.

Prospective Techniques: Games and exercises (such as those that make up Image Theatre) designed to dig beneath the surface of lived experience so as to expose the hidden power structures underpinning everyday life.

Protagonist: As with Antagonist, a term originally used of Greek tragedy to denote the character the story is principally 'about' and (specifically in Forum) who faces the challenge of confronting a given oppression.

Spectactor: The active participant in Forum, from the exercises that generate Models to the Interventions in a Forum session conducted by the Joker, collectively rehearsing realistic ways to confront oppression.

Theatre of the Oppressed: The term used interchangeably to encompass both Augusto Boal's methods (Forum, Image and Legislative Theatre, etc.) and the worldwide movement of activist networks who deploy them in a wide range of contexts.

Lexicon

In addition to the terms above directly attributable to Augusto Boal, I have over the years either coined or customized my own, often with groups such as school-age children, with the aim of making them clearer: accessibility to the best practice of the Theatre of the Oppressed is my chief aim. As with the Glossary, I list and briefly define these here, so as to equip the reader with the terminology necessary to an unimpeded reading of the book as a whole.

Constituency: A group within the wider community who might not as yet identify as Spectactors (through shared oppression) but who understand themselves as having interests in common. I often associate this with a physical space where exchange and participation already take place in some form, such as a school assembly hall or the central open area in a village.

Conveyor Belt: An adaptation of Boal's 'Lightning Forum' designed to give the maximum number of participants a chance to try in swift succession a single word, phrase or action within a Model. The Joker creates a queue on stage and these mini-Interventions are enacted in swift succession, using a collective momentum as part of the resistance to the oppression. Good for shy groups!

Crystal Ball: An adaptation of Image Theatre, held in silence, whereby anyone in a circle is free to sculpt an Image. As with the Conveyor Belt this uses flow and momentum to build a sense of collectively looking more deeply and critically into a theme or issue without the interruption of verbal discussion or interpretation.

Granny's Footsteps: A much-loved game, played all over the world in many forms, whereby a powerful figure is crept up on and can spin round at any time to send anyone who moves back to the beginning. The aim is to replace 'Granny' (anticipating the dynamic of Interventions) and the necessary skill of freezing is an effective training for the holding of tableaux and freezes required for Image Theatre.

Hotseating: A well-established improvisational technique, used to enable actors to inhabit a character and 'discover' their backstory. I have customized this over the years to give first-time or shy Spectactors a chance to 'warm up': questioning from their seats the characters in a Model and challenging the Antagonist or advising the Protagonist as a bridge into active Intervention.

Identification: I use this term in this book and in workshops to mark the point where mere sympathy or passive empathy becomes a more visceral connection with the Protagonist, as a precursor to Intervention.

Ludic: Serious playfulness: the energy (and attitude) that lead from an active engagement in games and exercises to the deployment of that agency in Forum.

Oracy: Non-scripted, experiential pedagogy (including storytelling).

Praxis: Embodied knowledge, generated and disseminated by creative participation (in this case in TotO).

Rainbow: My simplification for large groups of an exercise from Boal's *Rainbow of Desire* methodology, whereby through Identification, participants can create a spectrum of responses to a person or situation, each making a single Image around the original character.

Recipe: The term I use to encourage participants to document the games and exercises from a TotO training that they feel most able to take forward in their own words and into their own diverse Constituencies.

Sparky and Moley: A performative split in the Joker function, designed to free up one facilitator (Sparky) to hold the space and conduct the 'traffic' of Interventions while another (Moley) moves through the Spectactors, side-coaching and encouraging quieter participants to come forward.

Storyboard: A group cartooning technique designed to put both the means and responsibility for the documentation, editing and sequencing of games, exercises, techniques and complete Forum sessions into the hands of participants.

Toolbox: The bespoke, customized set of games and exercises, including strategies for independent facilitation of Forum, negotiated by each group I work with and Storyboarded by them as Recipes for autonomous TotO work.

Wheel: A dynamization of Image Theatre pairs work whereby two concentric circles of participants sculpt Images and then physically rotate them, creating an animated, collective meaning from these moving friezes of individual Images.

Suggested Reading

The Theatre of the Oppressed is emphatically *not* a reading programme! Here instead is a selection of Augusto Boal's most relevant texts about his work, followed by some useful case studies and critiques. Below these are links to the companies I have referenced or explored in the book, and finally I have included the URLs of films documenting some of my own, more recent practice.

My only guiding rule in compiling this modest list is that I have either met, worked with or in significant ways connected with every cited author or practitioner. That has been the simple selective device I have used and so what follows does not pretend to be comprehensive. I apologize for any exclusions.

Books by Augusto Boal

Boal, Augusto. *Theatre of the Oppressed*, trans. by A. Charles and Maria-Odilia Leal McBride (London: Pluto 1979).
Boal, Augusto. *Legislative Theatre: Using Performance to Make Politic*s (New York and London: Routledge 1998).
Boal, Augusto. *Games for Actors and Non-Actors*, trans. by Adrian Jackson (London and New York: Taylor & Francis 2002).
Boal, Augusto. *The Aesthetics of the Oppressed* (London and New York: Taylor & Francis 2006).

Adaptations and Critiques

Babbage, Frances. *Augusto Boal* (New York: Columbia University Press, 2004).
Da Costa, Dia. 'Tensions of neo-liberal development: State discourse and
    dramatic oppositions in West Bengal', *Contributions to Indian Sociology*
    (n.s.), 41, 3: 287–320 (2009).
Da Costa, Dia, ed. *Scripting Power: Jana Sanskriti On and Offstage* (Kolkata:
    Camp, 2010).
Da Costa, Dia. 'Subjects of struggle: Theatre as a space of political economy',
    Third World Quarterly, 31, 4: 617–35 (2010).
Drain, Richard, ed. *Twentieth-Century Theatre: A Sourcebook* (London and
    New York: Routledge, 1995).
Duff, P. and Vettraino, E., eds. *Youth and Theatre of the Oppressed,* (London
    and New York: Palgrave Macmillan, 2010).
Fritz, Birgit. *The Courage to Become: Augusto Boal's Revolutionary Politics
    of the Body*, trans by. Lana Sendzimir and Ralph Yarrow (Vienna: Danzig &
    Unfried, 2017).
Fritz, Birgit. *InExActArt: The Autopoietic Theatre of Augusto Boal: A Handbook
    of the Theatre of the Oppressed* (London and New York: Ibidem, 2012).
Ganguly, Sanjoy. *Where We Stand: Five Plays from the Repertoire of Jana
    Sanskriti*, trans. by Dia Da Costa (Kolkata: Camp, 2009).
Ganguly, Sanjoy. *Jana Sanskriti, Forum Theatre and Democracy in India*
    (London: Routledge, 2010).
Ganguly, Sanjoy. *From Boal to Jana Sanskriti,* ed. by Ralph Yarrow (London
    and New York: Routledge, 2016).
Kuppers, Rita and Gwen Robertson, eds. *The Community Performance Reader*
    (London and New York: Routledge, 2007).
McAvinchey, Caoimhe, ed. *Performance and Community* (London and New
    York: Bloomsbury Methuen Drama, 2013).
Nicholson, Helen. *Applied Drama: The Gift of Theatre* (London and New York:
    Palgrave Macmillan, 2005).
Santos, Bárbara. *Theatre of the Oppressed, Roots and Wings: A Theory of the
    Praxis* (Rio de Janeiro: Ibis Libris, 2016).
Schutzmann, Mady and Jan Cohen-Cruz, eds. *Playing Boal: Theatre, Therapy,
    Activism.* (London and New York: Taylor & Francis, 1993).
Thompson, James. *Applied Theatre: Bewilderment and Beyond* (Oxford: Peter
    Lang Publishers, 2003).
Thompson, James., *Digging Up Stories: Applied Theatre, Performance and
    War* (Manchester: Manchester University Press, 2005).
Yarrow, Ralph. 'From performers to spectactivists: Jana Sanskriti's training for
    agency in and beyond theatre', *Indian Theatre Journal*, 1, 1: 29–37 (2013).
Yarrow, Ralph. 'Performing agency: Body learning, Forum theatre assnd
    interactivity as democratic strategy', *Journal of South Asian Film and
    Media*, 4, 2, Body special issue: 211–26 (2013).

Links to Companies and Practitioners

Bárbara Santos and Kuringa
http://www.kuringa.org/en/kuringa/team/barbara.html

Cardboard Citizens
https://www.cardboardcitizens.org.uk

CTO Rio
http://www.ctorio.org.br

GRAEAE
http://graeae.org

Jana Sanskriti
http://janasanskriti.org

Mind The Gap
http://www.mind-the-gap.org.uk

The Lawnmowers Independent Theatre Company
http://www.thelawnmowers.co.uk

Theatre of the Oppressed NYC (TONYC)
https://www.tonyc.nyc

Documentaries Featuring Ali Campbell's Own Adaptations of Forum and Image Theatre

Respect and Dignity facilitated by Ali Campbell, Mile End Films, 2011
https://youtu.be/673zL_Ltywc

This is a documentary tracking the devising and development of a consultation into NHS initiatives around the treatment of Elders, using Forum and Image Theatre. It follows a collaboration led by Ali Campbell with QM Applied Performance Students and the Black and Ethnic Minority Community Care Forum (BEMCCF)

The Backstory, facilitated by Ali Campbell with MovingSounds, 2007

http://youtu.be/A0hswYPYy0U

This features a national education conference event hosted by Anne Fenton (W. Sussex Education Authority) and the Moving Sounds Collective piloting a template devised by young people for young people exploring the life issues of an imaginary young person as they grow up and move through school.

Embodied Emotions: a child-led research project led by Ali Campbell with children from Osmani Primary School. Film by Bhavash Hindcha/ Loud Minority Films (see also below).

https://youtu.be/Ct5r5s5_ypl

Do I Have To Go?: a child-led project with PhD Dentistry students led by Prof. Ferranti Wong from the QMUL School of Dentistry and pupils from Osmani Primary School. Film by Bhavesh Hindocha.

http://loudminority.co.uk/wordpress/?portfolio-type=research

Index